Praise for *The End of College*

"Building on prodigious research, Robert Wilson-Black takes readers under the hood to examine the intramural skirmish between teaching religion and teaching *about* religion on college and university campuses, a conflict exemplified by the divergent missions between chaplaincies and departments of religion. *The End of College*, however, is much more than an insider's approach to the topic. Readers with interests ranging from secularization, neoorthodoxy, and the eclipse of Protestant hegemony to the separation of church and state, multiculturalism, and the spiritual crisis brought on by World War II will find Wilson-Black's analysis riveting."

—Randall Balmer, John Phillips Professor in Religion,
Dartmouth College

"This is a highly readable book on a highly significant subject. The story of the decline of religious colleges and the rise of religion departments is not just a story about college and religion—although those are big subjects indeed. It is also very much the story of a nation transforming, debating with itself what constitutes knowledge and character, and what it means to be an educated person."

—Eboo Patel, founder and president, Interfaith Youth Core, and author of
Out of Many Faiths: Religious Diversity and the American Promise

"Wilson-Black helpfully illustrates the competing and contradictory purposes behind the emergence of religious studies departments and the fragmented and confusing consequences. For those of us who have endured this chaotic field as undergraduates or graduate students, Wilson-Black provides a helpful genealogy to understanding the shards of the wreckage left after the former queen of the sciences fell."

—Perry L. Glanzer, professor of educational foundations;
Editor-in-Chief, *Christian Scholar's Review*; and resident scholar,
Baylor Institute for Studies of Religion, Baylor University

The End of College

The End of College

Religion and the Transformation of Higher Education in the 20th Century

Robert Wilson-Black

Fortress Press
Minneapolis

THE END OF COLLEGE
Religion and the Transformation of Higher Education in the 20th Century

Cover image: Photo by Noah Negishi on Unsplash
Cover design: Landerholm

Print ISBN: 978-1-5064-7146-4
eBook ISBN: 978-1-5064-7147-1

For

Martin Marty, my Doktorvater
Kenneth Black, my Father
Juli Wilson-Black, who made me a Father

Contents

Robert Wilson-Black, PhD, has served as CEO of Sojourners in Washington, DC since 2013 and is cofounder of the newly established National Museum of American Religion. He was the penultimate student of Martin E. Marty at the University of Chicago, where he later spent nearly a decade as an administrator before serving elsewhere as a seminary, college, and university vice president for another decade. Rob is a liaison to the World Economic Forum.

Acknowledgments

I am grateful to have been surrounded by scholars, friends, critics, family, and colleagues while writing this book, and certainly thanking them here should not implicate them should I have fallen short in my research and phrasing, or the broader implications of it.

Thanks to . . .

The Archives and Special Collections staff at Chicago, Harvard, University of Pennsylvania, Princeton, Columbia, Iowa, Stanford, University of North Carolina, and Yale Universities.

Kerri Allen, Abdullah Antepli, Margaret Atwood, Judy and David Bailey, Randall Balmer, Dennis Barden, Trish Beckman, Thomas Berg, Fred Beuttler, Joan Bisset, Leslie Black, Bob Boisture, Thomas Bonfiglio, Mike and Amy Bonnette, Carson and Laura Bonnette, Catherine Brekus, Luke Bretherton, Frankie Brown, the David Burhans family, Diana Butler Bass, David Carlson, Kevin Carnahan, Tim Child, Michael and Melissa Compton, Kris Culp, David and Kira Dault, Julian DeShazier, E. J. Dionne, Raymond Dominey and Emma Goldman, Chris Dorsey, June and David Dorsey, Greg and Diane Downs, Mark and Lynn Barger Elliott, John Elwood, Kathleen Flake, Peggy Flanagan, Monica Cawvey Gallagher, Steven Garber, Bryan Garman, Kenneth and Sheila Garren, W. Clark Gilpin, Nelson Gonzalez and Jeffrey Alan Baron, Douglas Gragg, Angela Graham, Wes Granberg-Michaelson, Kilen Gray, Anne and David Grizzle, Mamadou Gueye, R. Scott Hanson, Pamela Harlem,

Phil Harrold, Van Harvey, Christina Self Hatherly, Patricia Harwood, Stanley Hauerwas, the Haw family, Joyce Hinnefield, Jim Hauser, John Holt, Scott Hudgins and Mary Foskett, Jon Huertas and Nicole Bordges, Kevin Hughes and Bridget Bedard Hughes, Tisha and Michael Hyter, Marci Jacobsen, Rob James, Socrates Kakoulides, Shiv and Urvashi Khemka, Min Kim, Grace Ji-Sun Kim, David K. Kim, Hana Kim, Tim and Hannah King, Clifton Kirkpatrick, Heather Krajewski and Robb Moore, Andy and Anji Lacatell, David Larsen, Karen Lattea, Diana Lazarus, Jonathan Lever, Laura Lieber, Brie Loskota, Darin Lowder, the Jim Luck family, Brad Lyons and Courtney Richards, Kevin Madigan and Stephanie Paulsell, Tim and Trisha Manarin, Chuck Mathewes, Dan McKanan, Brian McLaren, Mohammed Mohammed, R. Jonathan Moore, Richard Morrill, Alison Morrison-Shetlar, Anne and Brett Nelson, Carey Newman, David Nirenberg, Jill Ottman, Jill Otto, Teresa Hord Owens, Cindy Paces, David Painter, James Perkinson, Larry Perry, Robin Petersen, Sam Portaro, Craig Prentiss, Paul Pribenow, Julie and Watt Price Hamlett, Stephen Prothero, Paul Rauschenbush, Laura Reak, Nate Reak, Kate Reak, Dana Rohde, Clare K. Rothschild, John Roush, Richard Saller, Carol Saller, David Saperstein, David Sawyer, Tammi Schneider, Bill Schulz, Klaus Schwab, William Schweiker, Raj and Shivam Shah, Robert Shepard, Kevin Shilbrack, Jonathan Z. Smith, Robert Spivey, Chris Stevenson, John Stonestreet, Sophia Swire, Adam Taylor, Matt TerMolen, David Tracy, John Treadway, Laura Truax, Beau and Casey Underwood, Peter Vassilatos and Julie Crutchfield Vassilatos, Dale Walker, Jim and Joy Carroll Wallis, Kathi Webb, Tyler and Natalie Wigg-Stevenson, Dan and Paige Wilson, Theo and Miles Wilson, John and Nancy Wilson, John F. Wilson, Hannah Wilson-Black, Claire Wilson-Black, and Owen Wilson-Black, among many others I may have forgotten.

Preface

I had not been living on campus at the University of Richmond very long as a freshman in the fall of 1987 before three dynamics struck me. First, the religion department was not on speaking terms with the chaplain-campus ministry office. I now understand it seemed odd to my fundamentalist Baptist self because I had yet to discover the difference between the practice of and study of religion. I also did not yet know about the fraught crisis my college's religion department had recently survived. An outspoken religion department professor had lectured to a church gathering and indicated Jesus was not God. Courtesy of the still culturally Baptist leadership of the school, that lecture bought the professor a new department of one—called the "humanities department," no less. Various disagreements among the remaining religion department professors and no doubt the chaplain's office ensured detritus from the affair. As a new student, I came to smell the smoldering embers from that explosion. Later I would learn about departmental and university politics and the difference between ministers and professors quietly practicing their religion nonliterally—and sometimes revealing how their literal thoughts about divinity and other matters translated publicly (often not well). A decade or so later, the department found itself facing a second crisis when part of the religion department resisted hiring a young Jewish scholar from Princeton University to teach the New Testament.

Second, it became clear to me that professors and administrators had differing ideas about what college primarily meant: some had our future careers on their minds, others wanted to welcome us into the ancient and universal company of scholars, still others were creating a community of hearts and minds who would be lifelong friends and perhaps lifemates who could support the school's heritage and endowment. The religion department itself became an engine of much of this collegiate impulse for many of us academically and socially. It was not only where we made friends among a small community but also where we figured out what mattered most to us and others. The work the religion department engaged in felt like what college was supposed to be about.

Third, I became fascinated with how the college ideal, religion departments, community, and vocational formation had their own histories, both at my school and around the country. I was learning how each of my professors came to be members of the religion department, variously through ministry, theology, politics, scholarship, and the Baptist faith.

University of Chicago professor Martin Marty lectured on my campus senior year, and I asked him about such observations, shared my questions regarding these collegiate dynamics, and eventually became his penultimate PhD student eighteen months later, in 1992. During my two decades of research for this book, as I dove into the archives of Princeton religion department founder, George Thomas, I discovered he had corresponded with the college religion professor who was booted from Richmond's religion department, Robert Alley. Thomas had also been in correspondence with Chicago professor Frank Reynolds, who became a dissertation reader of mine, corresponding with Thomas decades before I met him as a student. I felt like a kindred spirit of both Alley and Reynolds because of our curiosity regarding Thomas's 1940s founding of the Princeton department of religion. Their questions posed to Thomas were focused on curriculum, while mine on how the department came to be in the first place as I deciphered his handwriting, living in his personal files in the Princeton University archives.

Years ago, one mentor, W. Clark Gilpin, asked me what I thought best defined "modern" and I blurted out, "When we discovered that history itself had a history." Whether that comes close to a good definition historiographically, it was driving my questions as I came to realize entities like colleges and religions and disciplines like history were themselves very much in motion, were viewed from distinct perspectives, and were contested within and outside of the academy. Later that year, Professor Harvey Cox came to campus, and in addition to his informally inviting my now-wife, Juli, to Harvard Divinity School during a panel they shared, my conversation with him sent me on a quest. I asked him about whether you needed to "be one to study one," religiously (years later, I would learn this was known as the "Iowa zoo model"—the 1930s attempt to hire a Lutheran to teach Lutheran history and theology, a Jewish scholar to teach Judaism, a Buddhist practitioner to teach Buddhism, and so forth). He asked me in return if a newly endowed Catholic chair at Harvard would need to be filled by a Catholic. The answer was more complicated than I had imagined, and it encouraged me to discover why any subject is studied in the first place, then structured in a department, chair, or institute. What I learned over the years was to follow the money, follow the schools' interests and the professors who were hired to establish programs, follow the leaders who structured or taught subjects that were organizing knowledge and teaching in such a way, and finally, follow what was happening in the wider culture and its relationship to campus and the country as knowledge was organized in schools as a response to such.

I began to wonder why colleges would create a separate department of religion, and when that happened in American higher education at each school. Weren't the beliefs, behaviors, movements, documents, and religious communities able to be or already being studied and taught in linguistics, anthropology, history, English, sociology, and other developing disciplines by the early twentieth century? The impulse to study religion within higher education was much older, and the subject itself was taught across the curriculum before such departments existed.[1] Why was the subject (and later, departments) often named "religion" and not Christianity, Christian theology, Protestant theology, Christian ethics, or biblical studies? Finally, how did the college ideal morph into the university ideal?[2] And were the two related in their development, the college ideal and teaching religion in a department?

I wanted to understand how the college ideal might have been taken up by the religion departments as they formed in the crucible of the college-become-university: namely, the idea that here, in this new religion department, we hold Western civilization, Christian theology, moral community, collegiate ideals even as we are part of the larger university, which is changing and moving away from such ideals. There were many explicit arguments for creating departments of religion, which I detail here, but did the implicit arguments for their formation have an important relationship with the end or ends of college, or at least the ways in which the college ideal was shifting in higher education? The early religion department founders wanted their curricula and programs to provide something akin to the college ideal, and yet their larger context, that of growing universities, was moving away from that ideal. These shifts were also happening alongside debates regarding the importance of the humanities, the topic of religion balancing itself somewhere between the social sciences (history) and the humanities (literature).

As I read through the histories of the university's development in the late nineteenth century, I wondered, To where did the collegiate impulse retire (student life, athletics, religion, vocationalism), or did it merely disappear slowly? The history of how campus ministry and chaplaincy related to the impulse to recenter "religion" (Protestant Christian theology, ethics, and Scriptures) has been chronicled, but how was it related to the formation of the founding departments themselves? Recalling the familiar names of public intellectuals and popularizers of the Christian faith at midcentury, I was curious how they had driven the overarching story such that the formation of religion departments became an answer to their religious impulse. If Paul Tillich was one of the underacknowledged intellectual founders of many religion departments,[3] then Reinhold Niebuhr was a corollary, as he sometimes generated intellectual credibility among nonreligious faculty. Neoorthodoxy and its twin, liberal Protestantism, were the waters in which many educators were swimming on a daily basis in that era, while those administrators and public intellectuals who espoused either logical positivism / rational nonreligious thought or Christian fundamentalism were on the outside of these mainstream twins and were acknowledged as the contrarians of their time.[4]

I went into the archives of the leading schools of that time to find out who these department founders were, who populated the first departments, who fought against the rationale for creating the departments, why Chicago and Harvard didn't join Princeton, Yale, Stanford, Penn, and Columbia in creating departments, and how that might have related to their having particular kinds of divinity schools and university presidents like Hutchins and Conant. I wanted to determine and highlight the main forces, accidents, national trends, and leadership that eventuated in the creation of these departments. As my professional life led me to several university, college, and seminary vice presidencies around the country, I also gained perspective on how official documents, commissioned reports, and institutional founding moments differ from how things actually transpired in academe. My straightforward reading of official documents gave way to archival nuance, then personal experience with professors and public intellectuals, and finally a new perspective on how one speaks to one audience in an official college administration report, another in an academic analysis of religion, yet another when trying to secure funds from philanthropists to found departments, and finally, private correspondence, where all manner of frank analysis occurs.

This practical perspective provided me a much richer sense of how the college ideal migrated as religion departments formed, and how these departments became the early model (based on the old divinity school model, the research universities' specialized research model, and the collegiate ideal) for what would become a more widespread religious studies movement from the 1960s to the present. That would come to include the development of significant full-fledged departments in state universities (the largest eventually at the University of Virginia), then Catholic, and other more conservative Protestant schools, before such departments came to include religions other than the primary faith traditions of the school itself. There are other important stories to tell about historically Black colleges and universities and Jewish studies[5]; these were often, though not exclusively, born from the exclusionary nature of White Anglo-Saxon Protestant men of a certain social class in the twentieth century; today, Buddhist studies is likely more established than Protestant theology at Stanford, where once, youth evangelist Lex Miller was a founding figure before his untimely death.[6]

The story of religion departments and religious studies itself from 1963 to the present contains intriguing twists and turns that would require a second volume. To understand that period to the present requires a closer look at how the formation of religion departments occurred during this founding period before 1963, with their appreciation of the collegiate ideal and search for a way to unify a seemingly fragmented university curriculum and moral identity.[7]

Stanford provost Condoleezza Rice, later President George W. Bush's adviser, once asked the religion department chair in the 1990s, "Where's your theologian?"[8] It's a fair question for many reasons, and yet it rang odd then in a way that it would not have in the 1950s had one asked Stanford's Alexander Miller. A lack of clarity about the shifts from theological education to religious studies often left administrators either confused or convinced the former did not have a place in a research university. Northwestern University's president in 1949 wanted to eliminate the religion department,[9] and the University of Pennsylvania's senior administration wondered about making that same move decades later. Yale University's report on the study of religion in the early 1990s was equally devastating, though it focused more on the divinity school than the undergraduate curriculum.

As I write this, the University of Vermont is eliminating its religion department because there aren't enough majors, though enrollment in religion classes is healthy enough there. Also, in December 2020, the University of Chicago announced the establishment, with funding, of a new collegiate program (or at least its configuration among the majors) for the study of religion by undergraduates, in part administered with or by the divinity school. That announcement reminded me of my attendance at Princeton professor Joan Wallach Scott's lecture in honor of the founding of the Center for Gender Studies at Chicago (currently the Center for the Study of Gender and Sexuality) in 1996, when I was a graduate student. She said something along the lines of "in inaugurating this program at Chicago, I'm not sure if it's the final legitimation of the discipline, given Chicago is slow to acknowledge such, or perhaps it's the death knell of it, given Chicago has entered the fray so late." Was it legitimating a discipline or acknowledging it in a late stage of a discipline's development? Possibly both at Chicago; earlier for gender studies, currently for undergraduate study of religion. It has become ever more difficult to argue that studying religion is frivolous or professionally useless.[10] How it was originally conceived of as important enough to found departments in the mid-twentieth century at elite institutions is worth understanding wherever one stands regarding its current efficacy for college students.

Why is it so difficult to make meaningful and clear statements about the subject at hand, the formation of religion departments and the study of religion in colleges? First, the word *religion* is understood by many different people as many different things, both today and in the United States in the early twentieth century by the department founders. It can be synonymous in the user's or listener's mind with Christianity (the majority religion); or as one might note today, white American Christianity, as that group drives so much of our public discourse; or as previously denoted, Protestant American Christianity. Therefore, if a college professor in 1928 claimed, "Religion is no longer intellectually viable in our modern age," we might ask, (1) What college? (What was the regional or denominational context?), (2) Were they a full professor or adjunct? (What was their professional or social context?), (3) What time period do they mean? (Was this in reference to the nineteenth century or the 1920s?), (4) Is the statement intellectually viable? (Is it fundable or honest?), (5) Can they define *modern*, please? and so forth.

Religion can be a subject matter, as in the data to be analyzed that are considered by the student to be religious. Some religion professors may define *religion* quite broadly, and others quite narrowly. The subject itself has individual adherents; therefore much of the data and therefore the subject can speak back to the scholar personally, and in some cases, the religious individual is the scholar talking back to their own interpretations of religion. The human mind initiating a psychological study of the mind has similar complex problems associated with it. One can be performing religion as a nonreligious person who used to be religious but a different religious self, studying one's own origins religiously in a religion department at a school whose commitments religiously are complicated, teaching students who themselves are part of religious stories with religious selves. Adding to this complexity is that Catholic institutions were heading down similar but certainly not identical paths in their own development of theological studies and religious studies, often a few decades after Protestant Christian institutions faced a version of their secularization or shift from center stage or power centers.[11]

I began to observe patterns when reviewing how religion departments were founded. I started to notice that there were skeptics, pious true believers, and those who functioned primarily as reconcilers between them for each college or discipline. Each can appear to be technically winning (gaining influence, power, centrality in structures, and broader appeal) at different points along the time line or trajectory of each school's or department's development. It became clearer that each of these three may be necessary for forward motion, or at least motion. My personal interest is often focused on the reconcilers, perhaps because I was mentored by them or am preternaturally one myself when at my best. Skeptics are sometimes my favorite actors, and their attempt to seek the truth as they find it, often at all costs, is admirable. True believers, the pious advocates of the moral importance of studying the ultimate concerns or religions and improving upon them, can be noble and unflappable and often admirable as they seek to strengthen institutional structures. Sometimes, and for years at a time, the Walter Kauffmans, Sidney Hooks, Stephen Pinkers, John Deweys, Donald Wiebes, Bruce Lincolns, Russell McCutcheons, and often J. Z. Smiths seem ascendant in their skepticism, to one's delight or horror. Then other times, the Martin Martys, Diana Ecks, Reinhold Niebuhrs, Benjamin Elijah Mays, Georgia Harknesses, Van Harveys,[12] and Smiths (Huston, Seymour, Wilfred, and often J. Z.) appear to have won the day with their reconciling stance between the skeptics and the singularly pious true believers (far too many to list). To confuse matters, depending on who is observing and when, individuals play different roles and the categories themselves appear to move across the semipermeable membranes of institutions and time periods.

Which of these three is more responsible for the founding of the early religion departments or the sustaining work of those departments? I believe institutional structures have come to be and remain because of the interaction among these three rather than as a result of, say, the pious' energies, or the loyal reconciler's work, or even the creative contrarian energies of the skeptics. Perhaps there are more categories than these three, as there are certainly more names than one can list here, but understanding the roles they played in the formation of religion departments originally and on your campuses in particular is useful, as we have come to see the results of these foundational fault lines since 1963. Without a doubt, who gets labeled as one or another of these categories has much to do with which of them is doing the labeling and where the departments are in their forming with their institutions.

In recent years I have come to notice ways in which religion departments are formed, transformed, disbanded, and reconfigured over the
decades as relates to the ostensible needs of the "nation." The religion
department founders I examine in this volume were highly attuned to
the way in which their work to create a college religion department was
tied to what the country needed from the college ideal, the teaching
of religion, and its student citizens. Wartime campus developments
(during World War II and the Cold War) were directly related to how
professors and administrators thought about and wrote about the formation of religion departments and the teaching of the subject within
the college curriculum.

Just after the period covered here, the early to mid-twentieth century, similar shifts occurred in the formation of religion departments
(especially at state universities) as a response to the country's need to
address its new citizenry and their non-Christian religions. After the
attacks of September 11 on America, interest increased in the teaching
of Islam and a need arose for students to understand it to become good
citizens, or at least informed graduates.

The almost six decades (1964–2021) after the four covered in this
book (1924–64) have generated both interesting dynamics and names
that could be placed in each of my categories—skeptic, pious true
believer, and loyal reconciler. I look forward to seeing these figures and
dynamics in religious studies categorized, chronicled, and problema-
tized in a future volume. However, first, it is important to dig down
to see how cracks in the foundations have had so many consequences
for the roofs we see misaligned today across religion departments, religious studies, the college ideal, higher education more generally, and
the notion that each of these serves the country.[13]

Introduction

Wither College, Wither Country?

College in the United States changed dramatically during the twentieth century, ushering in what we know today as the American university in all its diversity. Religion departments first made their way into institutions in the years from the 1930s to 1960s, just as these significant shifts from college to university occurred. These departments of religion were created in part to address the demise of the college ideal.

The college ideal was primarily aimed at shaping the few to enter the Protestant management class through the inculcation of values associated with a Western civilization that relied upon this training, done residentially and primarily for young men. Protestant Christian leaders created religion departments as the college model was shifting to the university ideal, where a more democratized population, including women and non-Protestants, were beginning to study under professors trained in specialized disciplines to achieve professional careers in a more internationally connected and postindustrial class.

Religion departments at midcentury were addressing the lack of an agreed-upon curricular center while still in the wake of changes such as the elective system, the Carnegie credit-hour formulation, and numerous other shifts in disciplines that were spelling the end of the college ideal, though certainly also continuing many of its traditions and structures. Religion departments formed as an attempt to provide a cultural and religious center that might hold, enhance existential and moral meaning for students, and strengthen an argument against the

German research-university ideals of naturalistic science, whose so-called objectivity proved at best problematic and at worse inept, given the political crisis in Europe.

Elite colleges found they were losing sight of the college ideal and hoped religion as a taught subject could bring back much of what college had meant, from moral formation and curricular focus to personal piety and national unity. That hope was never realized, and what remained in its wake helped fuel the university model, with its specialized religion departments seeking entirely different ends. In the shift from college to university, religion professors attempted to become creators of a legitimate academic subject often quite apart from the chapel programs, attempts at moralizing, and centrality in the curriculum of Western Christian thought and history championed in the college model. They experienced therefore the dual role of the newly formed college religion departments: both to distinguish themselves from the practice of Protestant piety while utilizing that theoretical and ideological structure to legitimate the study and teaching of "religion" as a viable college subject by professors trained in the graduate disciplines of a seminary structure.

Today the way a university approaches the teaching of religion can reveal what is at the heart of its mission and intention toward students and where it fits along the college-to-university ideal spectrum. Where a university falls along the prescriptive-to-descriptive range in teaching religion can reveal the place of the humanities in the curriculum. As the college ideal began to fade, new religion department professors at midcentury began teaching toward a cultural, national, or moral end; as the university model prevailed, religion professors began to teach about religions as a social science like history or anthropology. Religion teaching and writing began to match the new university model of research, specialization, democratization, and the teaching of the subject by trained professionals who may not have had a particular interest in the health of the religions but rather in understanding how they functioned within broader society or cultures.

The historical path the university took in getting to that way of teaching religion helps place religion in its cultural place in higher education and the country. The year 1963 included so many watershed moments in the life of the country and the state of the teaching of religion in college that it can provide one bookend for this story. Prominent among them is that in this year, the National Association of Biblical Instructors (NABI) released a study that recommended that it change its name to the American Academy of Religion (AAR), signaling its professionalization.[1]

The country began to descend into an era of political violence and suspicion of government and leading institutions: within six years (1963 to 1969), two Kennedys were killed, there were 2,500 acts of public political violence, Dr. Martin Luther King Jr. was murdered, the Vietnam War escalated, and President Richard M. Nixon's political troubles began. The Supreme Court cases that were encompassed by *Abington v. Schempp* regarding religious instruction in public schools were decided 8-1 in favor of teaching "about" religion, not teaching it as practice (at least not in a college or university setting, private or public).[2] What happened at Yale the summer of 1962 was that religion department faculty returned from summer break and learned they were to reside either with the divinity school up the hill or down the hill in the graduate faculty, and that college was emblematic, if not well known outside of the faculty. Lastly, the Higher Education Facilities Act[3] and other government-funding decisions helped transform colleges and universities and, finally, gave way to a new understanding of how religion should become a studied subject, without Protestant Christianity as the driving force behind the teaching of that subject.[4]

One could easily assume that across campuses (and American society and communities), there was a slow and consistent march toward greater secularization from the early 1900s to the present day, but this would be incorrect. Whether one considers it a failure of nerve and a temporary moving backward or a heartening return to religious faith and a unifying of the campus ethos toward human development, there was an ebb and flow over the decades between moving poles, from college to university, from teaching religion as moral inculcation to its study as a subject like any other.

Educated Americans in the mid-twentieth century trusted that undergraduate education involved the encouragement or inculcation of scholarly, civic, cultural, and moral virtues. Underlying that trust, however, was a tension between those educators who advocated a primarily prescriptive education and those who encouraged studies that would attempt to primarily "describe" religion. Moreover, at midcentury in

America, many colleges were becoming more like the universities that their names and futures would suggest. This change brought about confusion and reflection regarding the nature and purpose of colleges.

Wartime needs, government funding, and the massive proliferation of disciplines and research areas contributed to the development of universities with identity crises, centered on the college's evaporating moral mission. At the same time, religion departments were forming in response to this identity crisis, and to the travails of Western civilization more generally. Many of these religion programs at elite universities were created with the expectation that they might bridge the gap between the character-forming college and research-driven university models.

Today, religious studies is a generally accepted discipline within the humanities or social sciences divisions of tax-supported and private universities and colleges in North America. It was not, however, always a part of the curricula of these institutions, and there is no consensus about what the teaching of religion is and should be.

Administrators, alumni, parents, and Protestant educators expected both that religion courses would create more moral or religious students and that such classes would advance understanding of religion in general. Some department founders experienced the tension resulting from this dual role, others ignored it, several used it to their advantage, and a few lamented the situation of having to serve two masters (the subject and constituents).

Both administrators and those called upon to create departments were hopeful that teaching religion to college students could provide help in finding a way out of the crises of the times. Some of these crises were clear: European institutions and governments were being threatened by fascism and communism, students seemed nihilistic beyond their years, and overnight, colleges were becoming universities filled with military-training programs. In addition, research and writing in religion were expanding under new stimuli ranging from neoorthodox theology to the widening definitions of religion provided by sociology and anthropology.

There were five stages of this shift from faith to religion during the corresponding move from college to university. First, Christian belief was so integral to the school that it didn't need special mention, and *religion* was understood to be "Christianity." Then Christianity was so central that it took the lead on campus but enforced its centrality among other priorities. Then Protestantism was important enough to be included throughout curricula, but staff and faculty didn't need to be steeped in it or hired based on it. Later, Christianity needed particular emphasis in chaplaincy programs and required courses, but some faculty need not be religious, and the word *religion*, which was used interchangeably with Christianity, began to mean not merely Protestant Christianity but other religions too. Lastly, faith was appreciated generally, and there were courses to take, and those faculty needed to be religious, or appreciate faith, but not Christian per se.

What could not be avoided, however, was the dual role of the religion department or program. Such programs had to survive in the college's academic environment, whose sine qua non was becoming discipline-based research and teaching while serving both college administrators and church leaders. The latter believed that teaching religion could offer either personal character formation or the basis of a renewal of the Christian West. Midcentury educators in various disciplines were committed to the battle for democracy against atheism and communism, though most had no desire to bring what they considered to be sectarian religious belief into the curriculum. They viewed religion as a nonconfessional category, another realm of study with which to combat these troubled times.

Midcentury founders of religion programs were called upon to create departments characterized by an inherent tension, if not an outright contradiction. College administrators and many faculty and alumni leaders wanted religion courses to inculcate Western moral and civic values. At the same time, in such a department, a student would hopefully come to identify religion as a viable academic subject outside of or in addition to advocacy for one particular religious perspective.

Establishing their programs from the 1930s to 1950s, many founders dealt with these contradictory demands by attempting to distinguish religion from other academic subjects like philosophy, from "the church," from "sectarian theology," from "Christianity," or from campus chapel programs. Their rhetoric, curricular reforms, and arguments for the uses of teaching religion encouraged the fragmented identity of religion departments, the residue of which remains to this day.

The story of how the college ideal transformed into the American university is inextricably tied to how the teaching of Christian faith shifted to the teaching of religion in these institutions of higher learning. How it happened, who and what drove the change, and what it portends for the future of higher education, religion, and our nation is the story told here.

CHAPTER ONE

Pious College Religion Meets New Humanism Skeptics

A Father of College Religion Departments: Charles Foster Kent

The basic argument for teaching religion to college students was repeated in publications, private letters, journal articles, campus memoranda, and campus lectures delivered by Protestant faculty, administrators, and ministers until the early 1960s. The primary themes of the argument remained constant: renewing democracy, civilization, and morality and offsetting the negative effects of naturalism and materialism. It relied on a strikingly pragmatic rationale, with less emphasis on the truth of Protestant thought, belief, or practice and greater emphasis on its practical benefits.

In 1924, the newly formed Council of Schools of Religion[1]—composed of leading religious educators, Protestant academics, ministers, lay business leaders, and theologians—surveyed the landscape of undergraduate education and declared it to be dangerously "utilitarian and materialistic." The cause, the council argued, was that the sciences and the scientific method had become "regnant" in American colleges. Although the group acknowledged that the sciences had brought "manifold blessings to mankind and [had] infinitely more to contribute," it nevertheless held that "they cannot fill the gap left when the study of religion was either quietly dropped from the college curriculum or relegated to a secondary place."[2] The educators on the council pointed out that because of the damages to the college curriculum wrought by the elective system and because of the advancement of science and the shift from classical education to research, religion had lost its place of influence: "This silent but fatal transfer of emphasis in modern education has been due primarily to three causes: dogmatism, sectarianism and materialism. Unfortunately, the teachers of religion at first refused to adopt the tested methods and to accept the positive results of scientific investigation. In clinging to its old dogmatic methods . . . they committed a fatal crime against reason and the youth of America."[3]

Charles Foster Kent, spokesman for the Council of Schools of Religion and professor of religious education at Yale University's Divinity School, laid much of the blame at the feet of his fellow religionists. It had been their useless if not damaging "irregular voluntary work" in the colleges that had failed to supply the "deeper need for the systematic, thorough study of religion under trained instructors." Kent saw their work as "irregular" and "voluntary" because courses in Bible or theology were offered sporadically, without systematic rationale. When courses were arranged, they were taught by local ministers, whose quality and regularity of teaching were guided not by any professional preparation or standards but by their own personal interests and schedules.

The council's critique of both higher education and previous attempts to teach religion to undergraduates provided the basis for the arguments made by Protestant educators over the next thirty years as to why college religion departments needed to be created or renewed. The basic line of reasoning was an exercise in self-critique. When religion was taught in colleges, it was done poorly, especially in comparison with courses in the naturalistic and materialistic fields, which had a negative impact on the perceived value of studying religious thought.[4] As a result, college graduates acquired an insufficient knowledge of "religion." This led to a crisis that "carries us, therefore, to the very foundations of our modern civilization."[5] Training in religious topics (primarily understood as Christian thought, ethics, and values) was needed because the modern world and educational institutions were emphasizing "the pursuit of beauty and happiness . . . storing away treasures . . . and social and industrial efficiency." Such an emphasis left students and modern civilization empty, so the argument went, thereby explaining "why so many thoughtful men are proclaiming that crime and corruption are rampant, thousands of homes wrecked by selfishness." Proper study and teaching of religion could serve civilization, the nation, democracy, the churches, and colleges because it would encourage "disciplines that mold character and shape moral ideals and determine conduct. . . . Able teachers must be trained and given every encouragement to interpret the religious and moral heritages of the race." Finally, Kent proclaimed that there was a "rising tide of public opinion that is demanding popular instruction in religion."[6]

In its publications, the council argued against competing perspectives without naming its opponents, acknowledging both that "a new humanism has arisen, in conflict with the scholasticism of our day" and that "there has been gathering a revolt against the incredible and inhuman assumption of theologians who can affirm the infallibility of the Bible and condemn the human race to hell without winking." Kent and his colleagues believed they were offering colleges and, indeed, Western civilization "a better, saner, truer conception of life and history, of human nature, of religion itself . . . to take the place of cruel creeds that have dominated and bullied our intelligence already too long."[7] They were equally opposed to Fundamentalism and scientific naturalism, hoping to offer a moderate cultural Christianity that would find its proper place within the college curriculum.

These educators, ministers, and laymen were not the only parties within American culture concerned about the state of democracy, civilization, morality, and religious heritage and about the dangerous overemphasis on science within college curricula and culture. The council's basic criticisms of higher education were echoed in the writings of leading educators of the day such as Bertrand Russell, John Dewey, and Sidney Hook. But these educators, less concerned with the health of Protestantism, had altogether different answers to the problems they agreed higher education was facing. There was no shortage of new plans, curricular ideas, and experiments for how higher education could renew itself.

Against Kent and the Council: Oberlin's Harvey Wooster

Presenting a proposal that was structurally different from the council's recommendation was Oberlin professor Harvey Wooster, who arrived at a rationale that turned out to be as ideological as those he criticized. He argued against a turn toward religion or theology or toward science as a subject that might bring focus or meaning to an integrated curriculum: "Education long ago gave up the theocentrism of the medieval Church. It is time to divest it of the too exclusively cosmogonistic slant which natural science introduced as its substitute."[8] Thus Wooster wanted to avoid a return to college curricula dominated by theological perspectives but also to move beyond the scientific replacements for those theological ideas. That the scientific outlook had all but taken over the role formerly played by the "old guard" of theology, Wooster had no doubts: "The older learning revered and paid homage to the past. Science not only gave it no homage, but manifested little reverence as well, questioning its conclusions at every possible point. The older learning was essentially authoritarian in spirit; science was pragmatic. . . . The older learning gave way until the liberal arts college became no longer dominantly classical in spirit or in outlook, but primarily scientific and modern. . . . This generation is witnessing the final surrender of the old guard."[9]

If the curricular role of religion and theology had been eclipsed by a too exclusively scientific outlook, Wooster's search was for some other principle or fundamental outlook that could unify the goals and approaches to education: "We need, and need desperately, some controlling, articulating concept or principle upon which our modern disjointed, more or less haphazard, over-departmentalized higher education can be again organized into an orderly process with more semblance of unity and continuity than it now displays. Is there such a principle?"[10]

His proposed solution was that the college replace both religion and cosmogony with "man": "Man and the universe are both important to man, but the greater of these in modern education is man; not man as a special creation, as the Church saw him, not man as the essence of creation, but man as one of Nature's children, the arbiter of his own destiny under her laws."[11] Instead of the old college culture, the newer cosmogony of the natural sciences, or the hopes that religion would somehow unify the curriculum, Wooster offered a "frankly anthropocentric" curriculum based on the "principle of continuous, if not always progressive, evolution." Writing in 1932, seven years after the Scopes Trial in Dayton, Tennessee, he noted that "no other product of the mind of man has ever taken such hold upon his thinking." From zoology to social ethics and religion, Wooster saw evolution as the primary unifying feature of modern education.[12]

His proposal that evolution become the organizing principle for college education was presented to the Oberlin faculty and accepted by them with only several minor changes. He recommended that eight departments be created to tell the "story of mankind" through the concept of evolution. Astronomy and geology would convey the sense of Earth as a "tiny planet in a universe of suns, where the ceaseless and unvarying forces of nature produce an unending process of continuous change." Botany, zoology, and ecology would show how humans evolved from lower life-forms. Anthropology, ethnology, sociology, history, economics, political science, and social ethics would portray man as living in society while trying to "understand group life, to adapt himself to it, and to mold it to his needs." Philosophy and religion, which would constitute one of the eight departments listed previously, would explain how "he strives to integrate his knowledge, and to see beyond the forces of nature, to ask the question, 'Why?'"[13]

Although Wooster's organizing principle for college education was diametrically opposed to Kent and his colleagues' plea for religion's curricular centrality, Wooster did agree with the Protestant educators that "there seems to be no agreement among the students of liberal arts education as to the fundamental principle or principles upon which a college curriculum ought to be built." He also detailed the history of how such a lack of unity in college education came to exist. The liberal arts college, he argued, had been based on "the older idea of culture." Because it was assumed that most college students would become professionals who would enjoy "a certain degree of leisure and a favored cultural status," colleges encouraged the absorption of culture that became the unifying feature of education. This culture of the colleges, for Wooster, was defined as "philosophy, the classics, and the humanities in general, the spirit of detachment from affairs of the present and of contemplation of the values of the past."[14] According to his analysis, when colleges left behind this idea of culture and the accompanying curricular power of such an educational ethos, disunity was the result.

The Council of Schools of Religion also encouraged the formation of religion departments, but the ostensible purpose of such departments was not to study the ways in which humans answered the question "Why?" but to provide a specific answer. Students, the council members believed, "craved a faith that will explain all these experiences and embody the highest visions of truth and reality, vouchsafed to the noble prophets of the race, whether it be Confucius, Budda [*sic*] or Plato or Isaiah or Jesus." It was left to professors to teach students that "in the Hebrew prophets and Jesus that vision became the fullest and simplest and most satisfying."[15]

So while Wooster and the council's members agreed that students needed to encounter a unified and coherent educational philosophy at college, the council proposed the "religion" of Jesus as the paradigm for leading the good life and helping create a good society: "Give them this sublimate of all that is richest in the religious and scientific heritage of the race, show them that faith and love and cooperation and service are the impelling forces in the religion of the prophets and of Jesus, and they will carry that religion into education, into the family, into the church, into business and into life. . . . Dramatize the needs of society and of the world . . . to give mankind that education which alone will save it from ruin and enable it to attain its divine goal." Wooster's own goal, shared by many educators dissatisfied with the emergence of the modern research university, was, as already noted, the unity of knowledge through the organizing principle of evolution. Such a principle was less "divine" in his eyes, though he did want his student to experience a complete conversion under its unifying power: "The student who has really grasped this concept carries it with him everywhere, no matter what his course. . . . Is it not plain that this is the unifying, organizing, articulating concept for which we have been groping? . . . It makes the past live in the present. It challenges the present to control the future."[16]

These two attempts—by the Council of Schools of Religion and by Oberlin professor Wooster—to retrieve a unifying principle for the liberal arts college represent two perspectives among the various plans to give colleges a renewed sense of purpose. Following the proposals of the council, many elite colleges and universities expended much energy, money, and faculty research time during the 1930s and 1940s investigating whether religion as a subject of study could provide a central renewing force for the campus curriculum and student life. The most visible sign that colleges were preparing together for such a large-scale investigation was the Religion in the Colleges conference, which provided the impetus for many Protestant activists on campus to launch their initiatives.

Defining Religion: "Man's Most Wholesome Response to His Environment"

Seven years before Princeton University commissioned their much-touted report regarding religion in the curriculum in 1935, the campus was host to the Religion in the Colleges conference sponsored by a committee working under the auspices of the YMCA. This gathering of three hundred presidents of eastern colleges (from Maine to West Virginia) and other leading Protestant educators took place February 17–19, 1928.[17] The conference presentations centered on educators' hopes to teach religion in colleges and universities with greater zeal and effectiveness: "In the discussions, strong convictions were expressed to the effect that it is not only fully possible, but quite desirable, that all teaching be viewed as an essentially religious function. The religious implications of biology, psychology, sociology, philosophy and literature, etc. need to be brought to the students in those courses."[18]

The participants at the conference took an expansive view of religion in the curriculum.[19] Religion was defined by the curriculum group of the conference as "a man's most wholesome response to his total environment. It includes . . . ethical fellowship of man with man, and a reverent, worshipful fellowship of man with God." The goal of religion courses, it was determined, should be "that the student may have the opportunity of tracing the religious development of the race as well as interpreting his own life in its highest meanings." The curriculum committee also acknowledged that "too often in the past, piety and good intentions have counted more heavily with college presidents than has the real teaching ability of the men in question." The efforts to recruit religion professors and generally to encourage religious education made

by the National Council on Religion in Higher Education (formerly the
Council on Schools of Religion), only four years old at the time, were
cited as "encouraging signs of the day."[20]

Echoing numerous educators, the committee complained that
"teachers of courses in religious study too often allow their courses to
be considered sinecures for students with lame minds and lazy intel-
lects." Although these observations about the lack of quality in teaching
became a clarion call throughout the community of Protestant educators, it was not synonymous with a call to remove advocacy from
the classroom: "Courses in the study of religion must be more than the
objective and scientific presentation of bodies of historical materials.
In their ultimate impact upon the student they must challenge him to
venturesome and heroically constructive living in his own situation."[21]
Several participants connected the coursework with extracurricular
activities that could serve "as a laboratory" for the religion classes. The
question on which the group meditated toward the end of the session
was, "Can the courses in religion—can religion itself—be the synthesis
which will make of life a unity of purpose and not a chaos of chance?"
There were few dissenting voices at the conference. This was due in part
to the intentional homogeneity of the group[22] and because the differences among them were considered less important than unity in the
face of campus opposition to the conferees' cherished spiritual values.
College faculty generally, as well as many students, were opposed in diffuse ways against the conference attendees' plans to reorder the college
religiously. However, the two issues about which there was mild dispute pointed to perennial problems. First, there was disagreement over
whether students' own points of view should be considered in devising
the course of study, perhaps even taking precedence over the content to
be conveyed in religion courses.[23]

Another underlying theme of the conference was that religion was
less a subject to be taught than an attitude that should be present in
teaching any subject. The attitude was that of "Jesus, and that is the
way we need to put it,"[24] but this was not a dogmatic theological notion
about Jesus as much as it was his general example of humility. This
intended faculty-wide expression of "humility" meant that the importance of the subject matter of theology or Christian history could be
taught in religion courses without being undermined by the chemist,

historian, or sociologist. It was this mixing of religious course content and religious attitude that appealed to the future founders of college and university religion departments, who discovered they became as much a Christian witness to the faculty as to the students. Reaching out to the students in a religion course was a beginning, but it was the participation of the whole faculty, regardless of their religious backgrounds, that would be needed if students were to receive an excellent spiritual education.[25]

Harvard's Willard Sperry Charts a Different Course

Harvard Divinity School dean Willard Sperry alerted the conference to the dramatically different purposes of a religion course in a denominational college, which should be "propagandist" in nature, and a religion course given in a secular or state university, which should attend to nonsectarian issues. Sperry, who also taught undergraduates at Harvard, asserted that the denominationally related colleges would inevitably "perpetuate" a certain brand of religion. The state or secular private universities had to seek "a broad interpretation of life" while striving to place religion generally toward the center of the school curriculum.[26] Thus the critical decision for each conference attendee was whether to teach propaganda, a legitimate option for the church-affiliated colleges, or present religion more objectively. The latter option at most would allow the professor to "lay dry kindling wood" under the student, so to speak, so that when a religious spark came outside the classroom, there would be something to ignite.

Sperry also distanced himself somewhat from the general outlook of the conference participants when he asserted that they were focusing far too much on the impact and import of "college religion." He argued that religion's most significant role in the lives of people—for example, helping them face career disappointment, death, family difficulties, or personal sorrow—could not have been experienced by most students. If religion is the business of "transmuting an agonizing sorrow," as Wordsworth put it, then, Sperry claimed, "this darker side of life which calls out much of the best in a religion is not felt in a cheerful college community. We may not measure what religion gives the world by the needs of the college student."[27]

While recognizing these two areas of disagreement among conference participants and the fact that no concrete plans were decided on, the conference proceedings nevertheless asserted its value: "There is, after all, a place for gatherings of serious educators who may or may not be agreed in their beliefs on religion and the cosmos, but who agree for the moment to ignore ultimate concepts in order to compare notes on the ways and means of meeting immediate problems." This observation summed up the heart of the problem for many Protestant educators. Their dilemma was that they were focused on the resulting "problems of religion on campus" rather than the philosophical and theological divide that was on the horizon, if not before them already.

This tectonic plate shift occurring beneath them was moving mainline Protestantism slowly off the center of the public stage of college life, if not modern life. They did not yet ask many questions about changing student demographics, shifts within congregational life away from denominational loyalty, or whether scientific naturalism or pragmatism might become the new religious movement. Fundamentalist ministers on their right and naturalist scientists on their left both challenged the continued broadly Protestant cultural, if not ecclesiastical, influence within higher education in America. The former wanted a Protestant formulation to assume that role, while the latter questioned the value of any religious talk about transcendence, though not of morality and social values.[28] Protestant educators' plans for renewing liberal arts colleges stood apart from those of other leading educators by the emphasis placed on religion's principal place in the curriculum. They differed from each based on their varying appreciation for what Sperry called "propagandist" or "missionary" teaching in college classrooms.[29]

One major theme arising from the Religion in the Colleges conference was the way in which students often confronted irreverent professors whose lack of interest in religion somehow damaged students' spiritual and intellectual development. The educators attending the conference believed Christianity and the philosophical foundations of its expression were integral to Western civilization and higher education. Their concern was that "the flippant or uninformed dealing with these great truths and the sly innuendoes of irreverent men, more often than not, do damage to the religious life of students."[30]

Conference participants did not argue for the separation of chapel programs from curricular offerings (as the later Princeton report would), nor did they bemoan the low quality of college religion teachers (as the earlier Council of Schools of Religion had complained). Rather, they proposed that the trends away from compulsory chapel and toward a general hostility or indifference regarding "religion" (often understood as all things "spiritual"), the latter a primary concern of the group, represented a new opportunity to institute a voluntary model of presenting religion to students in every area of college life.[31]

It was not coincidental that Yale in 1924, Princeton in 1928, and the University of Chicago in 1931 were host to conferences seeking to develop the rationale and camaraderie needed to launch a renewal of academically acceptable Christianity as worthy of departmental respect. Each of these institutions was known for either leadership or innovation in educational matters and, along with Harvard University, was closely watched by educators across the country. These four institutions (along with Columbia, the University of Pennsylvania, and Stanford) and their presidents or leading professors pioneered the proposals for the renewal of higher education during the middle third of the twentieth century. Though religion was certainly not the only proposed savior of the liberal arts college model, especially in view of the then burgeoning research university, it was central to the discussion and arguments of educational leaders. The college ideal had already given way to the university ideal for most leading schools in the country, and the formation of religion departments from the 1930s to 1950s became one way the college ideal could live on in the curriculum. There were certain religious or humanistic values that could be expressed, investigated, and propagated in the departments and in courses under the watchful eye of department founders that became an important repository for those collegiate ideals that could no longer survive in an institution as a whole. These religion departments became something of a literal seminary (a greenhouse for new plants), and their curricular structure along with the training of most of the early professors in these departments owed a great to the theological seminary curriculum: Old Testament (becoming Hebrew Bible), New Testament (often Christian Scriptures), theology or philosophy as theology, church history (Christian history), and some form of practical theology (though the smallest of the pillars in these new collegiate religion departments).

Spiritual Lives of Students: Charles Gilkey and Shailer Mathews at Chicago and Edwin Aubrey at Penn

During the winter of 1931, a national conference of college religion and religious education professors and church and denominational officials was held in Chicago, supported by the Edward W. Hazen Foundation.[32] This conference, like the one before it in 1928 at Princeton, brought together many of the key figures in Protestant education to discuss the latest ideas and issues in religious education.[33] The conference and its proceedings were to be widely cited by many of the educational leaders at midcentury who faced the need to make decisions about religion programs. According to the published proceedings of the gathering, its task was "To State Clearly the Reality of the Spiritual and to Open Our Eyes to the Real Trends in Scientific and Social Thought."[34] Minimally the conference attendees shared the goal of wanting their religious convictions placed more prominently in college curricula throughout the country. Shailer Mathews, dean of the divinity school at the University of Chicago and leading proponent of theological modernism, proclaimed,

> Religion in a college or university must be given the same recognition in the curriculum as is any other object of human interest. While it is true that Bible classes have always been more or less a feature of the curriculum, the tendency has been on the part of the larger institutions. . . . Too often these courses have not had the educational standards of those of other departments, and have not been touched by the spirit of investigation and reconstruction which characterize other teaching in the institutions. Until the curriculum in the field of religion is given educational standing comparable with the work in the various departments, it will not be regarded as an integral part of the life of the institution. So long as the curriculum of an institution belittles or ignores this type of courses, religion will not be regarded as genetically a part of the education in idealism.[35]

Mathews here touched upon the twofold nature of the formation of religion programs for undergraduate teaching. They were to be based on rigorous scholarly investigation but also to be part of the idealism and intentions of the institution. This was a difficult, though fruitful, crucible for the formation of college religion programs, forcing agents of such programs to walk a line between the humanities and social sciences that few other departments were and are expected to walk.[36]

Mathews noted that teachers must be moral guides full of inspiration, whether they are theologians or not. He recommended that college courses be taught by individuals who were themselves religiously inspired; Mathews had no hesitancy in suggesting that one needed "to be one to teach one." However, although the tension between the academic rigors and practical spiritual needs of students in the religion classroom today may not seem surprising to contemporary observers, during the period from the 1930s to the early 1960s, the tension was first articulated and dealt with in a systematic fashion by founders of college religion programs, only to become exacerbated during World War II and its Cold War aftermath. In the times of crises, the call to practical teaching grew ever louder. Academic integrity would become less important than teaching all soldiers "the basics" as quickly as possible. Such expediency disturbed many educators, as we will note in subsequent chapters.

Examining the rationale given by founders of religion programs created at midcentury reveals a particular inherent tension. At the 1931 conference in Chicago, future University of Pennsylvania religion program founder Edwin Aubrey[37] characterized the role of religion teachers as one of being both religious counselor and scientist of religion. The curious thing about Aubrey's characterization is that many, though not all religion teachers, assumed that they could become both scientist and counselor to their students. In any event, his comments were to become the blueprint for the creation of new religion programs at Penn, Stanford, Yale, Columbia, Princeton, and even Harvard and Chicago, though they were never implemented in precisely the way in which Aubrey had originally intended. Aubrey emphasized that "religion must be presented . . . as a respectable concern for a college man. One sure way to do this is to develop respect for the study of religion as a thoroughly scientific academic enterprise."[38] Any piety resulting from an unintelligent faith, he believed, would be rejected by students and other faculty alike.

Aubrey went on, however, to recommend that religion professors offer to help each student turn his or her own occupation into a religious vocation. Religion professors were given two roles to embody, personal minister and teacher. These two roles were ones that the dean of the University of Chicago's chapel, Charles W. Gilkey, and others also acknowledged. The latter role, however, when it involved "over-intellectualizing" religion, ran counter to the practical need to put religion to good use.[39] Leading Protestant educators acknowledged that keeping a balance between the two roles of a religion professor was difficult but necessary.

Dean Gilkey observed during the conference why it was that teaching religion would be difficult if one were not practicing that religion.[40] Professors would be unable to give religion its due, he argued, because "intellectualization and discussion are the outer-courts of religion." Christianity could only be understood truly by those who knew also its "inner-courts." This assertion pointed directly to the task given to religion professors: while they were to delve deeply into religion to study and teach it, they would never get to its source unless they practiced it.[41] This assertion was in fact part of the rationale for creating religion programs at schools such as Princeton University, where faculty were already researching and writing about religious texts, communities, and individuals, but not necessarily as part of an effort to provide religious inspiration to students.[42]

This dual role for college teachers of religion was felt by some to be too ambitious and formed the background for the primary point of contention during the Chicago conference: whether the "secularized" college was the ideal. To what extent could a college that did not place religion at the center of the educational enterprise effectively include religion as merely part of its curriculum?[43]

Charles Gilkey, in his summary remarks, also emphasized how damaging the disdain of science professors toward religious concepts in a university could be. This was especially the case in the university, where, according to Gilkey, "there is responsibility in plenty on both sides for this unhappy lack of mutual confidence and good will."[44] He accused "anti-religionists" in the universities of being "the real dogmatists," not religionists such as himself. Gilkey believed that unlike them, he was open to seeing the "science versus religion" divide as an unnecessary opposition. Metaphorically, science and religion were two different mountaintop vistas, and the valley below, reality, could be viewed from either peak.[45]

Gilkey's assessment of the way religious ideas were treated in the university went to the heart of the conference's purpose:

> Those of us who have heard distinguished biologists ridicule in pub-
> lic and in private the value and validity of religion from the point of
> view of a mechanistic metaphysics, which they have taken over with-
> out critical examination from the physical sciences where their own
> colleagues have already abandoned it; those of us who deal frequently
> with students who have swallowed whole in scientific classrooms an
> anti-religious dogmatism and closed-mindedness whose counterpart
> they would rightly reject, continue to hope that the modern mind will
> learn to wander widely enough over all the valleys and hills of human
> experience to learn at long last that the final word has not yet been
> spoken from any field—nor is likely soon to be.[46]

Two things become clear to one who examines the conference proceedings. The first is that these educators were not yet imagining religion departments that had the sole responsibility for conveying the
message that religious concepts and faith are important.[47] They still
believed there was a chance to refocus the entire university and student population on the Christian gospel. For them, the religion department would still be just a specific manifestation of the general ethos of a
Christian college—whether state, private, or denominational. Separating chapel from the classroom study of religion would have seemed to
the conference participants to be a movement in the wrong direction.
Second, the educators expressed distress over the loss of a religious focus
on the part of colleges while arguing that educational freedom would
not allow religious or denominational domination. What was needed
was a way clearly to present their case for the teaching of undergraduate religion courses that would avoid denominational particularism yet
restore the focus of religiosity to a liberal arts education. Thus while a
rationale for the teaching of religion to undergraduates continued to be

developed, it was still being sought in isolation from science faculty and continued to be mired in the humanities-versus-science debate of the mid-twentieth century. The focus remained on enriching the student's spiritual life rather than advancing scholarship.

The New Humanists Dissent: John Dewey, Bertrand Russell, and Sidney Hook

The debate over the ideal liberal arts college education was by no means limited to advocates for religion departments at Protestant, Catholic, and Jewish institutions. There was generally more agreement than dis-agreement among those who represented varying religious perspectives regarding the ideal education. However, when the conversation included the new humanists or those in the "secular" camp, such as philosophers John Dewey, Bertrand Russell, and Sidney Hook, the scope of the debate widened dramatically.

Sidney Hook, professor of philosophy at New York University and an embodiment of the philosophical naturalism against which founders of college religion departments in the mid-twentieth century railed, was throughout his career a vocal education reformer.[48] In response to what he considered significant changes in the social order, Hook called for the liberal arts curriculum to be oriented around the social sciences: "There is not a single value claimed for the traditional liberal-arts cur-riculum which cannot be more widely, adequately, and interestingly realized by a curriculum integrated around the basic social problems of our times. . . . Officially, however, the college must not identify itself with one partisan group rather than another."[49] Hook proposed that an integral part of such a curriculum become a study of the various faiths of different civilizations, the "partisan commitments justified only by the emotional security they give to believers." These must be studied not for their potential benefit to students seeking a "way of life," as described by the Princeton committee, but because of their potential danger: "They spread by contagion, unchecked by critical safeguards; yet the future of civilization depends upon the character of these faiths."[50] Thus the small common ground shared by Hook and the mainly Protestant educators of the three conferences was this conviction that the belief systems of citizens did matter greatly to civilization. Which particular "faiths" were chosen by students—socialism for Hook or Protestant Christianity for the founders of the early departments of religion—was understood to make all the difference as to whether fascism would find a foothold in Western democracies.

Systematic study by "competent teachers" was intended to help students understand the critical distinctions between each of the "great maps of life—the ways to heaven or hell—which are being unrolled in the world today." And though they may have disagreed about how best to go about the scientific study of faith, Hook also shared with the leading Protestant educators a belief that "it is a pernicious illusion to imagine that they [philosophies and religions] cannot be studied scientifically." But their common ground ended there, as Hook attacked the early ideas of University of Chicago chancellor Robert Hutchins for reforming the college curriculum: "The college as such is not called upon to formulate, or impose, or indoctrinate its students with either a philosophy of life or a philosophy of society. Neither money nor metaphysics should serve as principles of organization."[51] Hook used Cardinal John Henry Newman's *The Idea of a University* to ground his critique of Hutchins's plan, as if to show Hutchins he could dismantle the proposed Chicago plan using a Thomistic thinker of the previous century:[52] "The practical function which Cardinal Newman assigned to the university is to train good members of society, not members of the good society.[53] I would modify this, in a way which Newman's theological commitments would not allow, to say that it is to train 'better' members of society, that is, individuals *who can make their own discoveries and decisions* about the nature of the good society."[54]

Hook wanted neither ancient philosophies nor present-day religious ideologies to become the centerpiece of liberal arts college curricula. His ideal method of education relied on the independence of social science, and its goal was to train better citizens. What he shared with those who wanted to establish religion departments as part of the curriculum was a concern for "civilization" and the belief that understanding religious ideas better would serve students well.[55]

Bertrand Russell, the mathematician and philosopher whose writings shared many philosophical motifs with Hook's, was less tolerant of a place for religion in higher education. Winner of the Nobel Prize and well known for his anti-Christian stance, Russell also wrote about the need for educational reform. But while most Protestant educators placed "nationalism" in opposition to "religion" when considering solutions for college education, Russell saw them both as destructive forces for education: "Our world is a mad world. . . . The cure for our problem is to make men sane, and to make men sane they must be educated sanely. At present the various factors we have been considering all tend towards social disaster. Religion encourages stupidity, and an insufficient sense of reality. . . . Nationalism as taught in schools implies that the most important duty of young men is homicide."[56] Thus for Russell, religion was not an answer to the problems of education but rather one of the problems itself.

If there was one representative of new religious humanism's philosophy against whom the Protestant educators who founded religion departments at midcentury struggled most, it was philosopher and educator John Dewey, professor of philosophy at Columbia after sojourns at the University of Michigan and the University of Chicago. Dewey, in *A Common Faith*, claimed that the presence of the Christian religion within modern university life amounted to merely one more philosophical system clamoring for a place at the table: "For the first time in human history, religion is now a special interest within a secular community . . . thereby the community is deprived of that marriage of intelligence and emotion."[57] The advocates for establishing new religion departments acknowledged that this area of knowledge was one among many, but understood the establishing of those departments to be a necessary response to this fact.

Dewey felt that too much intellectual energy had been spent trying to make ancient doctrines fit modern circumstances, to no avail:

> It is probably impossible to imagine the amount of intellectual energy that has been diverted from normal processes of arriving at intellectual conclusions because it has gone into rationalization of the doctrines entertained by historic religions. . . . The modern liberal version of the intellectual content of Christianity seems to the modern mind to be more rational than some of the earlier doctrines that have been reacted against. Such is not the case in fact. The theological philosophers of the Middle Ages had no greater difficulty in giving rational form to all the doctrines of the Roman church than has the liberal theologian

of today in formulating and justifying intellectually the doctrines he entertains.[58]

Dewey also took aim at the primary intellectual trope that midcentury Protestant educators invoked to strengthen their position in the university—namely, the idea that there are two distinct areas of knowledge. One is natural knowledge, which is best understood and best advanced by scientific methods and reasoning. The other is revelation or religious experience, which is unintelligible, or less intelligible, to scientific methods than to religious sensibilities: "The implication is that in one territory the supremacy of scientific knowledge must be acknowledged, while there is another region, not very precisely defined, of intimate personal experience wherein other methods and criteria hold sway."[59] Dewey blasted this idea as one more attempt to show that because science had not yet "invaded" an area, it was not capable of doing so and would not ever do so: "Apologists for a religion often point to the shift that goes on in scientific ideas and materials as evidence of the unreliability of science as a mode of knowledge. They often seem peculiarly elated by the great, almost revolutionary, change in fundamental physical conceptions that has taken place in science during the present generation. . . . But in fact they miss the point. Science is not constituted by any particular body of subject-matter. It is constituted by a method."[60] While Kent, Wooster, and Sperry displayed disagreements within a general framework, and Gilkey, Mathews, and Aubrey revealed new ways of imagining religion taught to college students, Dewey, Russell, and Hook provided counterarguments to every dream the former group of educators had for college education as regards the teaching of religion. Nearly every foundational argument and future fault line in the formation of college religion departments can be found in the ideas, institutions, and disciplinary arguments made by these nine thinkers. Moving into the second third of the American century, Princeton and Chicago took the lead in different directions. Reinhold Niebuhr and Paul Tillich were added to this group of nine in becoming leading lights whose influence was felt intellectually and institutionally within this story.

For most elite colleges in America in the first third of the twentieth century, religion was considered neither the primary transformative answer to problems faced by civilization nor a significant hindrance to social progress. Rather, it was a vestige of times past, a foundation previously built upon. Mandatory chapel had, for the most part, faded away when it was not removed by rowdy student protest. Governing boards had either removed or diminished denominational or religious restrictions on their membership. Low-quality or purely confessional courses in the Bible or theology were generally tolerated by a faculty and administration who either ignored them or appreciated their mollifying effect on pious alumni. Material of a religious nature was often covered in art history, literature, and philosophy courses, but with no special mention of the practical nature of such religious subjects. Such a time had come, however, by the mid-1930s, that Princeton University felt it necessary to examine what exactly the role of Christianity or "religion" should be in the classroom. Humanities professors, recently categorized as such and leery of the fact that a growing number of research scientists were found on campus, were looking for ways to boost their own curricular productivity and usefulness. All eyes may not have been fixed on Princeton, awaiting the outcome of their examination, but the conclusions that did emerge were cited for decades, with special attention paid to their great innovation—the separation of chapel from the realm of religion courses in the curriculum.

Chapter Two

Princeton Department Founding Pushes Pious Centralized Study

In April of 1935, Princeton University professor Theodore M. Greene and five faculty members presented a *Princeton University Report of the Special Committee of the Faculty on Religious Education*.[1] Committee members besides Greene included P. A. Chapman, Charles G. Osgood, R. M. Scoon, and T. J. Wertenbaker; Professor A. M. Friend Jr. acted as chairman for the committee.[2] The report does much to confirm that what midcentury religious educators sought was not the study of religion from other disciplinary perspectives. The new or renovated religion departments did not spring so much from an academic desire to study religious individuals, texts, communities, and movements in greater depth. Instead, these departments were born of a desire to make the chaplain's religion programs and courses more scholarly so as to be acceptable to other departments in the university. Scholars throughout the university were already studying various aspects of religious art, history, ideas, and so forth. These scholars were not, however, studying religion as a useful source for enriching students' spiritual lives, and that was the ultimate focus of the report.

Each of these professors had either taught or written directly about matters related to religion, but they had not focused on religion in the way they hoped the new religion department professors would. Of the six committee members, Theodore M. Greene became the most outspoken and prolific about religion and higher education, authoring several articles, chapters, and essays in the 1930s and 1940s.[3]

The Princeton report of 1935, authorized and approved by the faculty and board of trustees,[4] established a standing committee of the faculty that in turn was charged with creating two religion courses: "The Development of the Religious Thought of the Hebrews" and "Religious Thought in the Gospels." The most striking aspect of the report, an exercise repeated at many colleges during the 1930s, 1940s, and 1950s,[5] was its emphasis on the distinction between the study of religion and the practice of religion. If there was one characteristic of earlier college educators' rhetoric about religious matters, it was that it exhibited little appreciation for a distinction between religious practices and religion as a subject of study.

The Princeton committee revealed its own confusion by emphasizing the need to separate chapel and inculcation from the teaching of religion while also declaring that inculcation and moral training be part of courses in religion. It was suggesting that the chapel and religion departments separate so that the latter could simultaneously attempt to become academically legitimate and offer chapel-like religious direction in its courses. In so saying, the Princeton committee joined Yale, Harvard, and Robert Maynard Hutchins at Chicago in agreeing with the separation of the teaching of religion and chapel so that one could legitimately perform chapel-like functions in the classroom—not through prayer, reflection, and practice but through teaching, research, and examination. Chapel and classroom were separated not to remove the inculcation of values from the religion courses but rather to encourage such activity.

When a college reevaluated its "religion program" in the first third of the twentieth century, the chapel program, we can safely assume, would have been the focal point of a plan to meet student needs. By the middle third of the twentieth century, however, things had changed. The fourteen-page Princeton report wasted no time in explaining why the mixture of chapel and the study of religion, two different aspects of campus religious education, was problematic: it "bred a suspicion that has in the end driven the study from an independent place in the curriculum, and left the practice isolated from the rest of the life of the university."[6] The "practice of religion" on campuses may have never fully recovered from this isolation, but the health of religion as an academically taught subject did by the 1950s after being separated from its formerly inseparable twin. As for the phrase "driven the study from an independent place in the curriculum," we should note that such an independent place never existed.

In much the same way that Yale professor Erwin R. Goodenough and others came to emphasize the distinction between what the "professional" or divinity school did and what the new religion departments would be expected to do, the Princeton report acknowledged the importance of the chapel to the Christian religion while distancing it from the curricular experiment: "The study of religion . . . is an intellectual discipline, and as such has a proper place in the curriculum of instruction of a university which pretends to devote itself to liberal studies." Such distinctions did not imply, according to the authors, any "antagonisms or opposites," because the study and "practice of religion certainly supplemented one another and aided one another."[7]

If the practice and the study of religion were to be separate, program founders had to determine exactly what they meant by *religion* and the best method for studying it. Because the committee members at Princeton were adamant about religion's irreducible nature as a phenomenon, the historical method was seen to be the only appropriate one. Since the work of the historian was the recounting of what happened in the past, religion would not be in danger of being reduced to an epiphenomenon of another descriptive category or academic discipline so long as the historical method was used: "What is so necessary today [is] to make clear that religion is not literature, not art, not philosophy. . . . It is an independent power. Religion is a part of the humanities and historical methods must be used for investigation and demonstration."[8]

For this notion of religion as a "power" or "force" in history, the committee relied on the observation of British historian Lord Acton that "all understanding of history depends on one's understanding of the forces that make it, of which religious forces are the most active and most definite," and called for the "understanding of these religious forces in order to restore religion to its proper place in the curriculum of the University." The committee continued in its report, "The religious forces in history are distinct with their own essence, developments, and effects. Consequently, the study of them is a study in itself and not a by-product of the study of other phenomena."[9]

It is worth stressing that the committee report consistently used the words "religious forces" to describe religion as an object of study. They were convinced that the previous study of religion had really been the study of epiphenomena and not the real forces behind them.[10] A knowledge "of the periphery lacks coherence, meaning and value when the heart of the matter is simply not taught." If readers of the report found "religious forces" to be too vague or too broad a notion to teach, the authors made it clear that "the central religious force in the culture of which we are a product is, and has been, without dispute, Christianity. So the object of the study of religion for us should be first the understanding of what Christianity is—a difficult but fundamental goal."[11] While religion was for them something more than Protestant Christianity, Protestantism was its highest expression and the one most understandable to students. The study of religion was therefore understood as the investigation of Christianity as a powerful force within the lives of individuals and the nation.

The Princeton committee generally, and many other Christian educators, understood Judaism and the Hebrew Bible to be important primarily because they gave rise to Christianity. For the most part, their understanding of the "Hebrew tradition" did not amount to an appreciation of Judaism as a viable, interesting, or useful religious movement in America apart from Christianity and Jesus. This was not, therefore, the beginning of Judaic studies in Protestant institutions of higher education.

The committee also insisted that Jewish and Christian "origins" were the wrong place to begin the study of religion. They remarked that "we go to the Old Testament and the New to find the best presentation of what Religion is, but not at first in order to study the origin of these religious forces." This and other passages indicate that they wanted students to see and appreciate the glory of religious forces before being introduced to arguments related to their anthropological origins. After all, there were citizens throughout the country wondering, "Has history any meaning—any purpose? To him who asks, . . . Judaism and Christianity answer an emphatic yes. 'It is of the utmost importance today that the student have a knowledge of that culture whose notion of history itself gave hope, courage, and action.'"[12] Christianity was the great hope of civilization because it offered purpose and meaning. If such a resource for humanity existed in a time of so much hopelessness, it should be studied and mined for its benefits.

Many Protestant educators of the day shared this understanding that, properly taught, the study of religion in colleges and universities could be a source for overcoming the general societal malaise. When discussing the paucity of knowledge that the new religion professor would encounter in religiously illiterate students, the Princeton committee members added, "Yet this vacuum is not without its value since it makes so apparent what may be done and offers so little resistance to the doing of it."[13] Students would be eager to learn about Christianity, they believed, because their very lack of knowledge forestalled any resistance to its overwhelming power. And what the students would learn would give them the capacity for religious experience, a power of sympathetic appraisal, and an enlightened sense of values in personal and public life.

In sum, the Princeton committee had two concerns about teaching religion properly that were evident throughout the document. The first was the separation of the study of religion from religious practice—a liberalizing, independence-creating move. While the committee wanted to foster an awakened interest in the subject of religion for the values and meaning that could be conveyed, it clearly stated that there should be no compulsory courses in the study of religion.[14] The second was the concern that if religion were subsumed under another discipline such as psychology, anthropology, philosophy, or comparative religions, teachers might explain away the capacity of religious forces to offer hope to a society concerned about the meaninglessness of history—a conserving, protective move. Both concerns, liberalizing and conserving, were central to balancing the creative tensions inherent in the process of carving out a proper curricular place for the study of religion.

The report concluded with the recommendation that, although the founding of a religion department would at that time be premature, it should be considered a future possibility depending on student interest and the place religion might come to hold within the newly defined grouping of departments known as the "humanities." Five years later, such a time came. The search for a faculty member to fill the position of department founder and religion professor brought George Thomas, philosophy professor at the University of North Carolina, to Princeton in 1940.

Princeton was not alone in seeking to establish a religion department as part of its overall curriculum.[15] In colleges and universities across the country, religious educators—including philosophers, biblical instructors, and theologians—were developing rationales for the creation of similar programs or departments. There were many differences among such rationales, but what they shared was a commitment both to teaching religion as an independent course of study and to promoting Christianity as the source for those values most coherent with the goals of higher education.

The early 1930s were a time of significant social upheaval in the United States of America and across the growing higher education sector. Colleges were opening their doors, along with land grant universities, to more students who were eager to reap the benefits of further education, even as Jim Crow laws ensured racial segregation while gender restrictions and anti-Jewish quotas, among other restrictions, pushed against this general democratization of collegiate life. The world wars provided a common cause, the Spanish flu epidemic a common enemy, and the Great Depression a deep fear while expansion of the scientific method offered both hope and concern, as the post–Scopes Trial country seemed divided between rural religiosity and urban culture.

If varying forms of fascism were able to take hold in the cultural heart of the Enlightenment (Germany), the home of literary riches such as Cervantes's *Don Quixote* (Spain), and the geographical center of the Renaissance (Italy), what were Americans to make of their future, especially given France and England were now in potential danger? Immigration in the United States had paused between waves of millions of newcomers while Jewish intellectuals from Europe were seeking safe haven in universities that benefited from their scientific and philosophical excellence.

Higher education was increasingly federally funded, with the collegiate unit of credit having been established in preceding decades by the Carnegie Foundation. Carnegie also participated in the 1906 move to establish pensions for teachers but with a demand that schools with religious requirements could not participate. During periods of relative cultural and financial calm for statecraft or community, there is less of a need for reconfirming one's identity as a school, church, or country. Both institutionally and theologically, higher education administrators and professors became convinced that this was a time during which to reconfigure pillars of meaning in the form of religion departments. Such departments in the college only became necessary when it was discovered that Christianity, understood as the best form of religion in general, was no longer pervasive. It needed a home base from which to operate during this time of upheaval. The college model in its most ideal form, to these leaders, was fraying and being pushed to become only one part of a larger project that could no longer have religion as its center as easily as in a college. The university model considered faith to be, at best, simply another story humanity told about itself, however true or important. Religion was beginning to be lined up against other stories instead of being the story under which these others (science, professionalism, careerism, capitalism, power) need to exist. The college model found it difficult to withstand these changes, and the formation of religion departments at elite institutions was one attempt for white, mainline Protestant elites to grab ahold one last time to what they considered to be the theological and cultural center of their project writ large.

In 1928, the University of Chicago, with its divinity school dedicated to educating Protestant ministers and teachers, reorganized itself, establishing graduate divisions of the humanities, social sciences, and physical sciences that were separate from the college. The college, however, did not include a religion department, a fact that was of concern to several professors, notably William Clayton Bower, a University of Chicago Divinity School professor of religious education. Bower argued for the creation of a religion department at the university's new college, asserting that the importance of religion in the undergraduate curriculum lay in its understanding of "man's experience." Appreciation of religion, he said, should be taught "as a fundamental aspect of man's adjustment to this world and of his spiritual insights and achievements."[16]

Bower detailed religion's importance for historians, psychologists, sociologists, anthropologists, and other university faculty. But he also believed that the academic study of religion was in fact becoming a science, with unique methods. Bower's understanding of the word *religion* included educators' ideals in creating a renewed sense of appreciation for spiritual life, church work, and Protestant theology. They sought to use this religion to weave together a curriculum, synthesizing mere facts that had brought students and faculty to a pedagogical dead end.[17]

Bower's reasoning reflected the reality of a dual role of religion departments but without any acknowledgment of the difficulties of religious instruction fulfilling these dramatically different, if not contradictory, roles. He claimed that "religion needs no defense." It needed none because, according to him, religion could provide the synthesis that education requested of students' lives.[18]

Seven years later, at the University of Chicago when President Hutchins surveyed the landscape of colleges and universities in 1935, he reported what he saw as chaos. Schools were obsessed with vocationalism because of their "love of money" and with empirical data gathering because of their "love of facts." What they ignored was a "metaphysical" structure with which to interpret those facts. He admired the medieval university for its unified purpose under the authority of theology: "The insight that governed the system of the medieval theologians was that as first principles order all truths in the speculative order, so last ends order all means and actions in the practical order. God is the first truth and the last end. The medieval university was ordered, and for its time, it was practically ordered too."[19] Yet such an ordering of the university under theology was no longer possible in modern times, according to Hutchins. Because theology was "based on revealed truth and on articles of faith," it was not a viable unifier for a "faithless generation" who took "no stock in revelation." For Hutchins, theology implied "orthodoxy and an orthodox church." Since modern America had neither, to use theology "to unify the modern university is futile and vain."

President Hutchins was convinced, therefore, that theology or religion per se was unable to answer the university's need for unification. Still, order and synthesis were necessary for a university to be a university:

> It is impossible to have social order without intellectual order. I am not here arguing for any specific theological or metaphysical system. I am insisting that consciously or unconsciously we are always trying to get one. I suggest that we shall get a better one if we recognize explicitly the

need for one and try to get the most rational one we can. We are, as a matter of fact, living today by the haphazard, accidental, shifting shreds of a theology and metaphysics to which we cling because we must cling to something. If we can revitalize metaphysics and restore it to its place in the higher learning, we may be able to establish rational order in the modern world as well as in the universities. . . . Metaphysics, the study of first principles, pervades the whole. Inseparably connected with it is the most generalized understanding of the nature of the world and the nature of man. Dependent on this and subordinate to it are the social and natural sciences. . . . It is possible to get one [an education] in no other way, for in no other way can the world of thought be presented as a comprehensible whole.[20]

Further alarming members of the social and physical sciences faculties who were less metaphysically inclined, Hutchins announced that "prospective clergymen" would graduate "under the faculty of metaphysics."[21] Here Hutchins tipped his hand as to how exactly he envisioned metaphysics. It was to be the new overarching and ordering principle of the university, prospective clergy would study under the metaphysics faculty, and it would provide social and natural sciences with their principal questions.

Union Theological Seminary professor and Yale Corporation board member William Adams Brown envisioned theology as the center of the university curriculum. His ideal was not widely accepted throughout the 1930s in higher education, but his arguments in *The Case for Theology in the University*[22] represented the deepest hopes for many Protestant educators who had witnessed what they considered to be a secularization of the landscape in colleges and universities. Brown claimed to have been inspired to write the book by Robert Hutchins's misunderstanding of theology in *The Higher Learning in America*.[23] Brown was most interested in countering Hutchins's dismissal of theology in the university because the latter's book was a very influential volume for leaders of higher education.

Hutchins put on alert his entire faculty when he added that "a university is concerned with thought and that the collection of information, historical or current, had no place in it except as such data may illustrate or confirm principles or assist in their development."

Understandably, more than several faculty members were anxious to know which principles Hutchins wanted to "illustrate or confirm" and which he wanted to develop. His call to abolish all departments, allowing only "those who are working on fundamental problems in the fields of the three faculties [metaphysics, social sciences, natural sciences] to remain professors in the university" caused even greater alarm.[24]

Although Hutchins did not directly address professor William Bower's recommendation for an undergraduate religion department, he did make clear his position on all departments when he declared "the departmental system, which has done so much to obstruct the advancement of education and the advancement of knowledge, will vanish. . . . Members of existing departments who are exclusively concerned either with data collection or vocational training will be transferred to research or technical institutes. . . . The professional schools would disappear as such." This rhetoric was a stick of dynamite whose explosion was heard on campuses across the country.[25]

Theologian William Adams Brown, however, believed Hutchins misunderstood the nature of theology insofar as he rejected its efficacy in the curriculum. Brown argued that Hutchins was correct in assuming that theology as "revealed religion" or "faith" would not be a viable basis for unifying the modern university. However, Hutchins had not properly considered "theology" as "the philosophy of the Christian religion, or, in other words, the sum of the attempts to use the clue which Christian faith provides to bring unity and consistency into man's thought of the universe."[26] In answering the questions why universities had removed theology from their midst and "how far this secularization has gone," Brown used Hutchins's own assessment: "'Theology,' he tells us, is banned by law from some institutions. It might as well be from the rest." Brown lamented this situation, highlighting that for a "state-supported institution . . . to give no place to theology we can understand." However, "that Harvard and Yale, not to speak of the University of Chicago, should be content to think of it [Christian theology] as but one special interest among others must be due to other factors than the separation of church and state."[27] Brown, who knew Hutchins at Yale when the former served on the board of trustees and the latter was dean of the law school,[28] asked Hutchins to reconsider theology as a potential unifying principle for the university, an argument Brown would later make to Yale University's faculty and administration as commissioner of a faculty report on teaching religion to undergraduates.

Hutchins's response clarified what he had meant by metaphysics: "When, in *The Higher Learning in America*, I said that theology could not assist us, I was thinking only of dogmatic theology, which rests upon faith, or super-natural knowledge. Since a secular university must be open to a diversity of faiths, dogmatic theology cannot unify it; metaphysics, which includes natural theology, may. Everything that Mr. Brown puts in the category of theology I should call natural theology."[29] Having agreed with Brown's assessment that more clarity was needed about his understanding of the word *theology*, Hutchins wrote further about what particular metaphysics he considered to be vital to a university: "There are a Christian philosophy, a Christian metaphysics, and a Christian natural theology which in all their central points are a great advance over the Greek accomplishment. I should hope that if universities attempted to achieve intelligibility through metaphysics they would arrive at the best. The best, as far as I know, is the Christian achievement."[30] Hutchins also emphasized the connection between "those who naively identify science with progress" and the devastating results this leads to—that humans are no different from animals. If this were the case, Hutchins argued, then "why should not Hitler and Mussolini and Stalin use men as they are using them today?"[31] Implicating philosophical nihilists as complicit in the immoral political regimes of Europe was not uncommon on the parts of Protestant educators in the late 1930s and early 1940s.

The significance of Brown's and Hutchins's arguments for the renewal of Christian theology or metaphysics as unifying principles for higher education was not lost on Protestant educators, and their arguments were only strengthened as they began to articulate their rationale for the renewal of teaching religion to undergraduates. Moreover, for Brown, a seminary professor, successfully to have cajoled the outspoken University of Chicago president and general education proponent to clarify his position on the value of Christian theology in the university was no small victory. Hutchins's words about metaphysics as a unifying principle for universities were not interpreted as mere rhetoric by his own faculty, however. Indeed, his description of what he saw as a fragmented, vocationally focused university curriculum, devoid of a philosophical center and coherence, was met with considerable criticism.

As already noted, in *The Case for Theology in the University*, Brown attempted in part to explain how Hutchins's metaphysics might be better understood as theology and that such a basis for education was necessary, useful, and practicable. In describing the place that theology occupied in higher education in 1938, Brown wrote that "theology still retains its modest place in the list of university studies as one among other departments in a professional school which is still maintained out of a decent respect for the past, though it exercises little or no influence upon the educational policy of the university as a whole."[32] This description of theology's place in the university made clear Brown's hopes for its recognized role in the curriculum. It also hinted at the place religion as a positive force would be called on to have in the 1940s and 1950s on various American flagship campuses. Brown's arguments were not entirely dissimilar to those made by educators during and just after World War II, though theology was renamed "religion" and its place would not be so glorified as Brown had in mind.

As a member of the Yale University board of trustees, Brown was influential in ensuring that religion was taught as part of Yale's undergraduate curriculum. But sixteen years before William F. Buckley Jr. wrote his well-known diatribe against the religious atmosphere on Yale's campus, *God and Man at Yale* (1951), the acting chaplain of Yale drafted a memorandum to President A. Whitney Griswold, "On the Status of Religion on the Yale Campus." His reflections were based on his nearly four years on campus, from 1930 to 1934.

The memo contained little of the optimism that college chaplain Merrimon Cuninggim would convey ten years later in his review of the wartime campus he knew so well. The chaplain began with the observation that "religion, in any sense in which that word has been used in the past, is at a low ebb upon the campus." In a revealing passage, he clarified the role of Yale's campus chaplain: "Leaving aside the Roman Catholic group which is under the charge of Father Riggs, where the condition is not quite so bad as among the Protestants, and also omitting the Jewish students who are left largely to themselves, and confining ourselves to the Protestant group, it may be said that the University Church, Dwight Hall and the Berkeley Association are not touching more than twenty to twenty-five percent of the students."[33] The problem was an atmosphere of indifference that was frustrating all those whose responsibilities included religious life at Yale. He concluded that "there is no doubt that this atmosphere is responsible for the dearth of interest in the courses in Religion."[34]

What, then, were the causes of this atmosphere on campus? First, the chaplain acknowledged there was a "general wave of irreligion throughout the world" that had only worsened since World War I, and which was understandable to a degree because past wars had created a similar "irreligious movement." But it was the influence of naturalism that was his primary concern because it had become "subtly entrenched in the various fields of knowledge." In much the same way that Princeton's George Thomas understood the development of religious thought in the early twentieth century, this chaplain believed that naturalism was not the welcome product of a long and arduous search for the most accurate description of reality—nor was it the most tenable hypothesis for understanding the human and societal condition. Rather, it was an incorrect, corrupt, and amoral enemy of truth because it eliminated the realm of religious experience and knowledge.

The second cause for the ebb of religion on Yale's campus was cited as the failure of the Protestant church to teach religious thought, "those objective aspects of religion." Instead, it had emphasized "the moral life, the practical social activities . . . the value of an inner experience." In a passage representative of much of neoorthodox thought, the chaplain explained the situation: "In its desire to be tolerant it has been indifferent to religious thought, and so it has raised up a generation of religious people who are unprepared for the present onslaught of naturalistic philosophy. The only creeds they know are those they are unable to accept, and hence many are being carried away in the wave of irreligion."[35] Protestants had not been concerned enough with teaching their youth, or themselves, about religious thought to be able to fight back against the challenge of new philosophies. This concern and critique were not uncommon at mid-twentieth century.

The third cause noted was a college campus that was "hostile to religion." The chaplain admitted that universities always contain some measure of such hostility because it is inherent in the process of educating young people, but at Yale, it seemed to dominate. Students "see no meaning in truth for its own sake, nor do they feel any sense of vocation in life, and college life has ceased to be a serious affair."[36]

His suggestions for turning Yale toward religious revival included establishing colleges (residence halls) "on the basis of a religious interest, or if it were preferred, that some be established on the basis of a lack of interest in religion." These might provide encouragement to students to think through their hostility toward religion. He also recommended requiring that students take a course entitled "The Christian Religion," complementing the course in classical civilization. "The western world draws from Greece, Rome and Judea for its civilization, and the University has required knowledge of only Greece and Rome."[37] These recommendations, however, were not implemented and undergraduate enrollment in religion courses remained insignificant until the mid-1940s.

Courses in religion had always been taught in colleges across the country. Religious literature, figures, and history had been in varying degrees part of the curricula of universities and colleges from the beginning. But what such courses did not offer to many administrators and most Protestant educators was the chance to encourage and explain the practical impact of religious activity, to show its importance to the students' lives. Rather, the topic of religion was subsumed by other disciplines of study—sociology, anthropology, history, and literature. Bible departments, many of which were staffed by undereducated teachers, could not stand up to the materialist explanation of religion given by these other areas of study.

While Princeton University would be attempting to separate chapel from courses taught in religion in order to bring greater effectiveness and credibility to such courses, and Chicago had decided to create no religion department (having its own divinity school and Hutchins' disdain for departmental specialization at the undergraduate level), Stanford University in the 1930s moved in the opposite direction under its director of religion courses, D. Elton Trueblood, a Quaker theologian. Convinced that Christianity was of greatest importance to undergraduates, Trueblood regularly taught courses in the philosophy department during his tenure as chaplain of the university. Since its founding in 1891, Stanford had attempted to educate its students in religious thought and feeling, though it claimed to do so with no interest in denominational

partisanship. The courses Trueblood taught on a regular basis throughout the 1930s included "Survey of Religious Literature," which sought
to examine "the development of religious thought as seen in its classic
expressions," understood by him to mean the Old and New Testaments
of Christian scripture. Students also read more contemporary authors,
such as Cardinal Newman and Enlightenment thinkers like Blaise Pas-
cal, who were described as "characteristic products of the religious consciousness." Trueblood also conducted a philosophy of religion course
that was more directly aimed at helping students understand that their
"worldview" should be "consistent with religious experience." It was in
this course that Trueblood introduced students to the "rational basis
of belief in God." To further ensure that students understood religion
courses as merely a dry recitation of the facts of world religions, he
offered a course entitled "Human Values." It was here that Trueblood
encouraged undergraduates to seek and "discover the deeper meanings
of human life and thus provide a basis for wise living." This course was
designed specifically for "teachers and others who feel the need of help
in the development of a consistent personal philosophy."[38]

While Trueblood's colleagues in history, literature, and philosophy
also offered courses that covered topics that could be distinguished
as religious in nature, Trueblood understood his mission to be one of
teaching Christianity to students, who would personally benefit from
its content. Christianity was taught "as a form of religiosity," but it was
also understood as the best that religion had to offer.[39] Stanford formed
its own department of religion decades later under the direction of New
Zealander and youth ministry evangelist Alexander Miller (the development of which is chronicled in chapter 8).

The explosion in the founding of college and university departments of religion that would come in the 1940s was not in response
to an absence of the study of religious texts, people, or movements but to
an absence of the study of religion as a subject in its own right. It was
important to many teachers of college religion courses that the reality of
religion as a historical force or power be made clear, not explained away
by other disciplinary theories. So while college religion courses were
not lacking in the 1930s, Protestant administrators and local church
leaders were interested in strengthening the perceived curricular legitimacy and impact of such classes in the face of the dangers posed by

the rise of secularism, which would later be blamed for the lack of personal and social values throughout the Western world. These Protestant educators directed their energies toward helping students move beyond what they understood to be shallow scientism and vocationalism. To do so, they sought to improve the quality of teaching religion in colleges and universities, which meant establishing a faculty of teachers with earned doctorates and training from leaders in the field, mostly at the divinity schools of the day. Many department founders believed that as the University model became ascendant, the teaching of religion could bring back some of the values of the college model, the true ends of college discovered in the beginnings of a stand alone religion department.

The scapegoats for the lack of proper religious teaching in colleges became the new humanists, social and natural scientists, disciples of German theologian Karl Barth,[40] and proponents of other forms of sectarianism. If these conflicting ideologies could be defeated by a reasoned approach to religion, then college students and faculty would respect and themselves benefit from this new emphasis on religion (or for some, "metaphysics"). From Princeton and Chicago to Stanford and Yale, elite colleges and their administrations were wrestling with different options for improving and strengthening religious instruction. These curricular experiments and their rationale are the story of higher education during the 1940s.

Two dynamics are important to clarify: one was for the movement from college ideal model to university ideal model, and the second for the various ways in which religion was operating (mostly Christian faith and theology at this point). There are at least fifteen stages in the move from college to university, many overlapping and occurring during various decades depending on whether institutions were somewhat national or completely regional, whether Protestant or Catholic, private or state, or historically African American, women's colleges, and so forth. The transformations of institutions' ideals as they moved from the college to the university model were

1. from comfort with subjectivity to a goal of objectivity;
2. from morally focused to focused on research and the scientific/practical/useful;
3. from received to created;

4. from molding cultured citizens to turning out professional producers;
5. from listening/receiving to speaking/engaging;
6. from primarily church/private supported to government/industry/ private supported;
7. from having an elite constituency to democratization;
8. from small house residencies or homes to large dorms;
9. from a one-school structure to a multiple-school structure, including graduate;
10. from rural geographically to suburban, urban, or exurban;
11. from appreciative of sociopolitical context to skeptical of institutions;
12. from peripheral support of US national power and identity to becoming central to economy and federally sponsored research;
13. from generalist full-time professors to part-time specialists;
14. from church and seminary–trained to research university–trained; and
15. from primarily shared moral, ethnic, and class commitments to a commitment to a process of inquiry, such as the principle of noncontradiction.

Regarding the stages of the study of religion that can likewise be detected in the arguments and in the institutional curricular shift in the teaching of college religion (again, mostly Christian thought), there are at least ten stages visible here:

1. Religious belief is so integral to the school, it doesn't need special mention, as it is primarily about that content from the start.
2. Religion is so central that it is constantly noted but now needs to be reinforced.
3. Protestantism is important enough to be present throughout curricula, but staff do not need to be steeped in religion.
4. Christianity receives/needs special emphasis in chaplaincy and there are required courses focused on it, but some faculty need not be religious.
5. Faith is appreciated generally, and there are courses to take, and faculty for those courses need to be religious.
6. Religion needs a department with dedicated scholars, as faith is needed for students in times of crisis.

7. Religion is an important subject that needs to be studied but merely one among many subjects.

8. Specialized courses in any number of religions are possible within curricula but need regular rationalizing.

9. Religion/religions must be understood in order to interpret what is happening to society outside college, especially as regards the strength of the country.

10. The specialization (and thus fragmentation) of higher education institutions' subject matter and later its operations.

The way in which religion functions in those institutions moves, as noted here, from implicit to explicit. Put another way, the theorists and institutionalists of this period were negotiating how religion is central and organizes, or how religion does not belong, or how religion is merely a part of other disciplines, or how religion has a place all its own as a taught subject.

There was also a set of dynamics at play more internal to Christian thought. Namely, Christian thought (noted as "religion" by them) is based on reason, revelation, science, philosophy, or social utility, in which case pedagogy is of great importance. The skeptics questioned teaching religion ("Christian theology") to improve or practice it. The pious true believers protected it as life-giving while wanting to improve the rigor of research, teaching, and publication. Balancing between these two were reconcilers who tried to explain each group to the other. Types blended too, as they must when institutional structures like college religion departments are formed within or alongside the influence of myriad cultural phenomena and varied partners such as philanthropy, internal politics, alumni, and faculty.[41]

CHAPTER THREE

Wartime 1940s Faith Presses Scientific Secular Skeptics

A symposium in 1950 gathered by the periodical the *Partisan Review* proclaimed that there had been a turn toward religion among intellectuals during the 1940s. This was asserted with no small amount of surprise, given that science and materialism were as philosophies considered to be ascendant on campuses earlier in the twentieth century. In the years just after World War II, thinkers, writers, and public intellectuals were invited to reflect on if or how this could be the case. John Dewey, Marianne Moore, Sidney Hook, Paul Tillich, Hannah Arendt, W. H. Auden, I. A. Richards, and others each opined on how modern intellectuals could accept religion, given the previous generation's critique from the perspective of atheism.[1] As the writer Norman Mailer noted, concentration camps, wartime ethical dilemmas, and the specter of nuclear war itself shaped the consciousness of every individual who was engaged in cultural or intellectual work at midcentury. Professors arguing for the formation of religion departments during that period were deeply affected by this, and discussion of those ethical and national dilemmas comprised their rationale for teaching religion.

Western and central Europe were by 1940 in the grips of several disastrous political and military campaigns. University of North Carolina philosophy professor George Thomas and other Protestant educators joined national leaders in expressing their concern for the welfare of Western civilization. Thomas believed that a proper knowledge of philosophy and religion had something important to offer those in the United States who were confused by the economic, political, and spiritual turmoil of the day, and he relished the thought of being part of a project that might assist in bringing about a solution to such problems.[2]

In that same year, Theodore M. Greene of Princeton University's philosophy department, a friend of George Thomas's from the American Theological Society, inquired as to whether Thomas might be interested in building a department of religion from the ground up. After investigating exactly what the Princeton Faculty Committee on Religion and president Harold Dodds had in mind, Thomas decided to move to New Jersey to help create Princeton's religion department, for which, according to him, there were no models save the great university-related divinity schools (those of Chicago, Harvard, and Yale as well as the Union Theological Seminary of New York City / Columbia).

Thomas realized he had little training for such a venture. Confessing his lack of theological preparation to University of North Carolina president Frank Porter Graham,[3] he asked for and received a nine-month sabbatical to study at Yale Divinity School in order to improve his theological preparation and to "fill the large gaps in his training in the Western Religious Tradition." In an autobiographical account of his decision to move to Princeton, Thomas recalled, "[I felt] our secular civilization was threatened with disaster and that what our American society needed most was not philosophical analysis and speculation, but religious faith and a way of life based upon it. For these reasons, I finally accepted the invitation from Princeton."[4]

Religion in an Age of Secularism

At Princeton, although educators avoided claiming Christianity's superiority, it was tacitly assumed. Theodore M. Greene described the role of the study of religion in college in a tone that was somewhat more pious or confessional than the 1935 Princeton curriculum report he had helped author:

To divorce the study of morality and religion from actual moral conduct and religious worship, or to believe that an understanding of what morality and religion really involve can be achieved by mere external observation, without sympathetic insight, would be foolish and uninformed. A liberal study, however, involves no such divorce or belief. Liberal schools and colleges can and should provide moral and religious instruction which will enable students to escape from slavish conventions or complete ignorance, by putting at their disposal relevant facts and by teaching them to interpret these facts in a rational and informed manner.[5]

The Princeton report sought to separate the practice and study of religion in hopes that religion would flourish as a subject in the curriculum, not primarily through campus ministries or the chaplain's office. But Greene and Thomas shared a vision of religion on campus that required greater advocacy in the classroom. When they proclaimed, "religion matters," they did not mean that it was critical to understand how religion functioned within societies or affected human behavior or social movements. It would be well and good to study this, but religion mattered most to individuals in their personal lives, and teaching it meant introducing students to the ways religion might meet that need. They did not consider this to be a violation of the mission of a liberal arts college. On the contrary, this was exactly what such an education must address, and Princeton administrators were ready to infuse the curriculum with a new religious emphasis.

George Thomas's inaugural lecture, "Religion in an Age of Secularism,"[6] delivered October 24, 1940, in Princeton University's McCosh Hall, was viewed by other college educators as a foundational document legitimating the teaching of religion in colleges.[7] It also contains the best explanation of Thomas's own rationale for teaching religion and the ends he hoped to attain by creating a department for that purpose. Princeton University president Harold Dodds remarked at the time, "I believe that this occasion will in years to come be considered as an historical moment marking a long and significant step toward the accomplishment of a program of the very first importance to this university and to the nation which it serves."[8]

Though Dodds's statement may appear somewhat grandiose, we should remember that during the 1940s, Princeton's faculty and administrators came to view Princeton as a national university with a constituency much broader than the northeast of the United States.[9] There is every reason to believe that Dodds and others at the time did have grounds for being hopeful, even if the tone of "service to the nation" was a practiced attempt to reimagine Princeton as a leader in higher education in much the same way that Harvard considered itself from at least the 1880s onward.[10] Dodds then added the almost obligatory comment about "the needs of the time," an oblique reference to the turmoil in Western Europe: "Princeton's historic position and present conviction and the acute needs of the time place on this University a heavy responsibility of developing in our students a fuller understanding of religion and its significance."[11]

Thomas's lecture covered four basic areas of concern: secularism's lethal grasp on culture, religion's ability to bring unity to fragmentary existence, democracy's relationship to religion, and the importance of teaching and studying religion: "It was because of my conviction that the program was important and might have consequences far beyond this university that I agreed [to take the position]. . . . At a crucial time in history such as our own it is imperative that this task be undertaken." Religious instruction was intended to turn back the tide of "religious illiteracy in educated circles since the Great War. Such illiteracy is both a product of a growing secularism and ensures that it will continue unchecked, with the survival of culture hanging in the balance."[12] Secularism, according to Thomas, was responsible for individuals' sense of incompleteness, frustration, purposelessness, and lack of meaning or value. He defined it as "the theory that men should seek ends which are exclusively human and natural . . . that all ends which claim to transcend nature and human life are illusory . . . [and it is] opposed to any form of philosophical Idealism which takes seriously the uniqueness of the human spirit."[13] Secularism's twin, materialism, also troubled Thomas because he felt such a philosophy left humanity with nothing more than what the eye can see or the mind detect.

Much of Thomas's writing career was spent attacking the philosophy of naturalistic materialism and what he perceived to be its implications for Christianity, the human spirit, and the meaning of human existence. Though many of his writings suggest that the primary problem was that this corrosive philosophy wreaks havoc on humanity, he made the claim in the inaugural lecture at Princeton that materialism was also false dogma. Not only was it destructive; it was not true. He articulated the familiar argument that the scientific method is productive but has its limits and that the human spirit and religious sentiment are effectively out of bounds, according to science's ostensibly empirical grounds. Douglas Sloan's account, in *Faith and Knowledge*, of Protestantism's midcentury attempt to affect higher education through campus ministry and church policy illuminates Thomas's thought on this point. Sloan explained the "realm theory of truth" as one option available to religious educators at that time: "This is the view that there are the truths of knowledge as these are given predominantly by science and discursive, empirical reason. On the other side are the truths of faith, religious experience, morality, meaning, and value. The latter are seen as grounded not in knowledge but variously in feeling, ethical action, communal convention, folk tradition, or unfathomable mystical experience."[14] Thomas believed Christianity could be studied for its truths of knowledge and not be found wanting. This was not, however, the only or most important benefit that the academic pursuit of the subject had for students. Thomas felt that Christianity's communal call to ethical action and feeling would also be beneficial to students, Princeton, the nation, and civilization.

For Thomas, secularism (the result of naturalistic materialism) was not the inevitable realization that there is no spiritual realm—no God, meaning, or purpose for life. Secularism was an inaccurate philosophy of life that had to be countered with a better account of reality, which Thomas believed was possible through the teaching of religion. Neither was secularism merely the unfortunate situation in which we found ourselves; it was a spell under which many in the West had fallen. The spell was, to him, reversible if the appropriate efforts were made. The particular manner in which Thomas argued against its corrosive effect was representative of a generation of Christian scholars who delivered repeated attacks on secularism.[15]

The lack of unity in modern life was seen by Thomas as a signal warning of the "disintegration of culture." In fact, disintegration was what troubled him most: "Perhaps the most striking thing about modern secular culture is its lack of homogeneity. It has divided itself into a plurality of activities which are unrelated to, and often at war with, one another."[16] This was the case because secularism ensured that religion was denied the opportunity to function as the unifier of all human activity. Without religion as an integrative agent, the various aspects of human life remained separate, often opposed to one another, and lacked any semblance of unity.

Thomas joined Robert Hutchins in looking back both longingly and critically to a medieval synthesis, noting that "the only interest which can justly claim superiority to all others is not an interest in any single finite good, but an interest in the infinite source of finite goods which includes and gives meaning to them all."[17] Once again, the price to be paid for the lack of unity or disintegration was meaninglessness, or at least less meaning. Thomas was aware that in holding up "religious man" as the model that most accurately represented the truth about reality, he was rejecting "economic man" and other models. For him, these alternative views were an important part of describing humanity but were unable to give an overall account of human life that included spirituality. Not oblivious to the fact that great gains had been made in economics, science, and medicine because autonomy had been given to these independent areas in the wake of the Enlightenment, he lamented that such a state of affairs ensured that "organic unity" would never be reached—thus the need for the teaching of religion: "It is the search for such a synthesis which explains the demand of college students for courses which will serve to integrate the truths gained from several departments into an inclusive system of truth. . . . Any synthesis which is attained by combining truths and values arrived at in independence of each other can be little more than a sum of parts in external relation to one another."[18]

The disunity of the various truths required a creative principle to bring all areas into a coherent relation with one another. According to Thomas, "The secular ideal of autonomous interest cannot provide such a creative principle. Only two alternative principles can rescue the meaningless disunified life: the political and the religious."[19] Of these two options, the political and the religious, the former ran the risk of lapsing into totalitarianism because the political implied no fundamental ethics to keep it from violating the principle of individual freedom, a violation that religion, correctly taught, would not commit: "One of the major tasks of a professor of religious thought in our secular age should be to restate and reexamine the claim of religion to provide a basis of organic unity." In his most pithy formulation, Thomas stated that "religion brings our fragmentary truths and values into unity by relating them to an infinite Reality and Goodness which transcends them all."[20]

Many educators of the 1940s made the connection between the current crisis of Western civilization—the cradle of the Renaissance was fascist and the birthplace of the Enlightenment was home to Nazism—and the effects of secularism. But this supposedly causal connection between the problems of civilization and the secularized college and modern world frustrated others, notably the secular philosopher Sidney Hook.

In Praise of Secularism and against the Tide of Religiosity

Sidney Hook surveyed the cultural tendencies "of our own times" that pointed to a new failure of nerve in Western civilization. One instance of this dynamic was in the "refurbishing of theological and metaphysical dogmas about the infinite as necessary presuppositions of knowledge of the finite . . . and the belief that myth and mysteries are modes of knowledge; a veritable campaign to 'prove' that without a belief in God and immortality, democracy—or even plain moral decency—cannot be reasonably justified."[21]

Hook was unsparing in his attack against advocates for establishing college departments of religion: "In the schools, the churches and in the literary arts, the tom-tom of theology and the bagpipes of transcendental metaphysics are growing more insistent and shrill. We are told that our children cannot be properly educated unless they are inoculated with 'proper' religious beliefs; that theology and metaphysics must be given a dominant place in the curriculum of our universities. . . . Fundamentalism is no longer beyond the pale; it has donned a top hat and gone high church."[22] The reference to "metaphysics" was a direct assault on University of Chicago chancellor Robert Hutchins's program to bring Aristotelian first principles to the center of that institution's life. And by mentioning "Fundamentalism," Hook did not mean Baptist church leaders in the South or the National Association of Evangelicals' attempt to revitalize Christian colleges. Rather, he was referring to the professors at Princeton who were creating a new department of religion and to Reinhold Niebuhr,[23] whose courses were included in Columbia University's curriculum and whose advice on curricular matters was sought by Harvard University president James Conant.[24]

Hook explained the origins of the failure of nerve as multiple and obvious: "Economic crises, world war, a bad peace, tragically inept statesmanship, the tidal waves of totalitarianism." Such were the reasons that educators had turned to a "theology of despair and the politics of wish" in hopes that a new "transcendental consolation" might save the colleges, the nation, and civilization. He described the purveyors of the new programs of religion in higher education as "the motley array of religionists filled with the élan of salvation and burdened with the theological baggage of centuries. . . . As interpreters of divine purpose, they have now become concerned with social healing, with the institutions of society and with the bodies of men, as necessarily involved in the healing of individual souls."[25]

Hook understood these educators and religious leaders to be using political and social crises as vehicles to improve the position of religious ideologies, communities, and authority:

> The world-order is to become a moral and religious order. Plans for the post-war world and for social reconstruction are coming from the Pope as well as from the humblest Protestant sect. They are now at flood-tide. . . . It is characteristic of the tendencies hostile to scientific method that they reject the view that the breakdown of capitalism and the rise of totalitarianism are primarily the result of a conjunction of material factors. Rather do they allege that the bankruptcy of Western European civilization is the direct result of the bankruptcy of the scientific and naturalistic spirit. The attempt to live by science resulted in chaos, relativism, Hitlerism and war. . . . The only implication that can be drawn from this strange state of affairs is that religious groups are seeking, as they always have, to make of God an instrument of national policy.[26]

The fear of Nazism, communism, and the fall of Western civilization— as well as the threats posed by science and relativism—were indeed the

clarion calls of educators across the nation. Founders of new departments of religion argued that these political maladies and ideological
threats demanded a response equal to overcoming them: namely, the
Hebraic-Christian tradition.

Sidney Hook aimed his ideological guns directly at the two most
common arguments espoused by George Thomas (Princeton), Clarence
Shedd (Yale), Edwin Aubrey (Penn), D. Elton Trueblood (Stanford), and
others. First, he argued against the suggestion that "if the beliefs of faith
were false, the world would be a terrible place: therefore they must be
true. Or since the beliefs of faith are consoling, they cannot be false."
Second, he attacked the proposition that "because not everything can
be proved, since even science must make assumptions, some faith in
something is unavoidable if one is to believe or do anything. Therefore faith in the absurd is justifiable. But only our faith, not the other
fellow's!" In arguing against these fundamental tropes of midcentury
religious educators, Hook, a longtime self-described leftist, focused his
attention on socialist Reinhold Niebuhr, with whom he shared many
political outlooks. Hook regarded Niebuhr's theological beliefs, which
Hook understood to be the basis for many of the arguments of the Protestant educators, as reactionary: "[His theology] is an eloquent combination of profound disillusionment in human action and a violent
belief in human ideals . . . [emotionally] moving rhetoric that breathes
passionate conviction about something whose very sense is in doubt.
Indeed, if we look closely at Niebuhr's theology, and take it out of the
language of myth and paradox, we find that whatever is acceptable in
it to critical thought is an obscure retelling of what was known to the
wiser unbelievers of the past."[27] Hook's criticism of Niebuhr was based
on what he considered to be a flawed definition of religion, one that
automatically lumped everyone in the camp of the religious. When religion was defined as "the primary and ultimate act of faith by which
life is endowed with meaning," everyone must necessarily be religious
because "to be alive is to be religious."[28]

Hook did not disagree with this part of the formula so much as with
what followed—that this kind of faith required for life is "necessarily
faith in God," the Christian God. Regardless of whether such a faith in
the Christian God makes life more tolerable or whether it is acceptable
because one must believe in something, such arguments for Hook were

not convincing enough to base a renewal of civilization or higher education on. A turn toward such arguments was for him, in fact, a "failure of nerve" and a distraction from the real roots of life's problems and practical solutions. Hook further argued that this twofold definition of religion seemed, paradoxically, to be based on a pragmatic equation—if believing in a religion is effective or can be effective, it must be true:

> We are asked to accept religious dogmas as true mainly on the grounds of their effectiveness in combating Hitlerism. This in turn rests, as we have seen, upon the notion that Fascism is the consequence not of economic conditions, nationalist tradition, and disastrous political policies inside Germany and out, but of the spread of positivism, secularism, and humanism. Why Fascism should then have arisen in such strongly religious and metaphysical countries as Italy and Germany and not in such scandalously heretical and positivistic countries as England and America, is something that the neo-Thomists and their fellow-travelers do not explain.[29]

Here Hook turned on its head the argument of religious educators and reformers—that humanism and positivism were the true culprits of the world crisis—by arguing that Italy and Germany had a longer, more deeply embedded tradition of religion and metaphysics than America and England, and yet it was there that fascism arose.

Neither Hook nor the Protestant educator apologists stood on middle ground. Hook heightened the decibel level one notch more when he argued that not only would America not fall to "Hitlerism" because of humanism, secularism, or positivism, but it would be more likely to do so in a frenzied search for a new piety:

> The new failure of nerve in contemporary culture is compounded of unwarranted hopes and unfounded beliefs. It is a desperate quest for a quick and all-inclusive faith that will save us from the trouble of thinking about difficult problems. These hopes, beliefs and faiths pretend to a knowledge which is not knowledge and to a superior insight not responsible to the checks of intelligence. The more fervently they are held the more complete will be their failure. Out of them will grow a disillusion in the possibility of intelligent human effort so profound that

even if Hitler is defeated, the blight of Hitlerism may rot the culture of his enemies.[30]

The Necessity of Christianity at College

In direct opposition to the views held by Hook, Yale professor of theology Robert Calhoun presented his analysis of religion's role in the life of the university, Yale in particular, in "The Place of Religion in Higher Education," a paper delivered at the University of Pennsylvania's bicentennial celebration. For Calhoun, essential or high religion "needed" critical inquiry from the academic world because religion's emotional content had to be kept in check. The university benefited because research specialists without a framework in religion could not operate credibly: "High religion, in short, and intellectual enterprise belong together. . . . The two in conjunction, but neither one by itself, can move with hope toward more effective conquest of the chaos that again and again threatens to engulf human living. That way lies whatever chance we may have for a more humane world."[31] For Calhoun, religion was the only answer to the crisis of "chaos" facing Western civilization, and higher education was the means to inculcating its values: "With civilization cracking, why trouble ourselves just now about higher education? . . . Because without the things it stands for, there is no civilization worth the name. . . . The primary aim of unregimented colleges and universities is to help produce disciplined free persons. . . . To this end they need religion, and religion needs them—or at least the things they stand for: trained intelligence, free inquiry, a critical temper, a clear-headed world outlook."[32] As many institutions underwent the transformation to modern research universities, at midcentury, many educators, including Calhoun, were concerned that students would become, in sociologist Max Weber's words, "specialists without hearts." This could be prevented, it was felt, by the unifying framework found in religion, which contained both an "intellectual perspective" and "religious devotion": "Without them its [education's] work is patchwork, not the making of unified persons, fit to bear civilization."[33] It is worth stressing that for American intellectuals and educators during the 1940s, it was indeed civilization that was at stake. The fall of France, the coopted German church, the hijacked Italian government, and the threat of an invasion of England were harbingers of Western civilization's weakening condition, if not of its destruction.

The greatest danger in training specialists with fragmented disciplinary knowledge was that an individual might become an "onlooker at the human scene, the victim of an 'academic' detachment grown into an obsession." The research university model itself, in part a creation of German society, government and culture, privileged a more detached analytical focus than the morally centered college ideal for many educators. As if speaking directly to the European adherents of fascism, Calhoun declared that "thinking machines, no matter how accurate, are not men."[34] This was another way of pointing out the creative tension between discipline and freedom that was central to discussions concerning education and religion. While the fact that religion was often associated with emotionalism was held in check by the rigors of academic discipline, the danger of academic detachment was considered to be offset by religion's unifying framework. This dynamic ensured that the possibility for the personal encounter with new ideas could exist: "Against these various dangers of the intellectual life there is no panacea, but there is a powerful antidote, once more prevalent in higher education than it has been recently. Religion of the right sort can provide a dynamic unity of experience more inclusive even than the theoretic unity of a metaphysics."[35] "Essential religion," for Calhoun, jolted one out of the mode of passive onlooker.

Calhoun's understanding of religion was akin to Rudolph Otto's *mysterium tremendum* and Schleiermacher's notion of the religious experience of total dependence or awe: "It is man's response to a Presence in his world so overwhelming to him that he cannot disregard, escape, or control it. This is for him 'the holy,' his God. . . . whether it be a naturedeity, a deified monarch or Führer, an exalted nation, class, or people or a transcendent God of justice." The only genuine response to such an impulse or reality is faith, and for Calhoun, the Christian narrative and faith response seemed to be representative of religions at their core.

Calhoun insisted that Christianity or high religion was the only effective alternative to Nazism. He disregarded other social or political options for countering the dangers of state-elevating "religions" such as fascism: "Once they have said to God (or to the state or the Führer), 'Not my will, but thine be done,' they have ceased to be ordinary ego. . . . They have become bondservants of their God, who find in his service a new kind of self-realization that men can neither give nor take away." The choice was not between religious and nonreligious worldviews.[36] Rather, nihilism and its relatives naturalism, secularism, and materialism were in fact "fierce religions of our own day gone wrong."[37]

One irony resulting from the tension created by the dual role of program founders (both to instruct students in being religious and to examine religion academically) was that many pious students and alumni felt that professors were not straightforwardly Christian enough, while the same professors struggled to fulfill the role of more objective "academics." For example, Yale student William F. Buckley Jr. was disappointed that Calhoun did not make his Christianity more pronounced in his introductory course for the college. The divinity school, according to Buckley, got more out of Calhoun than did the college. Among those seeking a more "objective" interpretation of religion, however, Calhoun was criticized for holding up Christianity as the best that religion had to offer.[38]

Tiring of the hyperbolic rhetoric flowing from both sides of the "return to religion debate,"[39] Harvard University literary theorist I. A. Richards launched his own appeal that some middle ground be found. Richards's perspective is important to these debates because he was one of the leading authors of Harvard's 1945 report on general education, where he argued that neither religion nor antireligion should be the unifying principle for higher education: "It does seem monstrous to suggest that this issue—on which the fate of Christendom (to speak with one party) or the destiny of Western man (to speak with the other) is presented as turning—is largely unreal; that it does not touch, or no longer touches, the questions through which thought grows. . . . Both sides agree that religion today is having a great comeback. Whether we are to praise the Lord for this or be anguished is a decision which, for me, waits on other questions."[40] Richards (a reconciler in this model, to Calhoun's true believer and Hook's skeptic) was most disturbed that dialogue between the two sides was not possible. He reminded both Sidney Hook and the Princeton group that they would do well to recall that "the distinctive mark of Germany and Japan alike has been a mixture of phony science and phony religion conjoined. . . . We shall have more such mixtures if the guardians of factual inquiry and the guardians of human purpose keep up this fight between them." Richards clearly represented the two sides—not only of the larger cultural discussion but of the debate about the role of the college religion department, which seemed forever to be in conflict. Both "factual inquiry" into religion and "human purpose" provided by religion were important characteristics in the creation of programs at Yale, Princeton, Columbia, and later at Stanford and Penn. Richards noted that the extent to which they were able to come together would be the extent to which problems could be resolved: "A Marriage between the houses and a new generation seems our best hope."[41]

Chaotic Wartime Campuses

From the winter of 1942 until the spring of 1945, many campuses across the country were transformed into military-training facilities. The four-year undergraduate curriculum was replaced with an official wartime accelerated program, allowing student soldiers to complete programs in two years while integrating their wartime training needs into the curriculum (engineering, languages, sciences).[42] Many elements of the traditionally "bright college years" were left behind as faculty, staff, students, and parents read the names of fallen soldiers in the student papers. Yale Divinity School faculty member Clarence Shedd expressed the concerns of many educators when, in 1942, he wrote, "Obviously, total war forces the colleges to abandon the 'ivory tower' and make radical changes. . . . The exigencies of the moment, however, pose a deeper problem for the college: will they be so overwhelmed by the demands of the armed forces for training that they will betray the vocation of the college?"[43]

The overnight transformation of so many colleges for military purposes gave presidents cause for reflection: "If we orient and rigidly align our students in war work . . . we will become a trade school. The universities have a responsibility to turn out citizens who can function in a democracy as well as to train 'fighting men.'"[44] This crisis of identity was acutely felt by colleges, forcing them to look at their mission and answer questions of ultimate loyalty. Colleges were supposed to be servants of the public, but not enslaved to public demands. Wartime pressures seemed to dissolve such differences. Shedd was convinced that higher education had never faced a more serious crisis. He called for administrators to consider a five-step plan to avoid betraying the mission of higher education: prepare students for citizenship broadly defined; retain distinctions between technical officer training and "education as usual"; support premedical, dental, theological, and other regular students; continue arts and humanities courses with female students in mind; and assert colleges' true vocation as keeping "the lights of civilization" burning in order to "mold men and women who can fight through to victory."[45]

Moreover, Shedd was not alone in criticizing the US government's reversal of policy on September 17, 1942, to lower the draft age to eighteen, further altering the college curriculum by requiring all "non-essential" courses be dropped. Brown University president Henry Wriston, Macalester College president Charles Turck, University of North Carolina president Frank Porter Graham, and University of Chicago chancellor Robert Hutchins each spoke out against the new policy. Chancellor Hutchins, addressing entering students on September 22, 1942, declared, "I reject in strongest terms [the War Department's] Mr. McNutt's assertion that non-essential courses must be replaced by subjects of immediate utility in winning the war. . . . Technology will not solve all our problems . . . nor will technology establish a just and lasting peace. What will win the war and establish a lasting peace are educated citizens."[46]

Against this background of tensions and radical curricular and campus changes, many colleges went about the task of revising their curricula in the mid-1940s. During this time of transition, educators were faced with the tasks of preparing citizens for a vibrant democracy and keeping the humanities alive within a research science institution, as they were convinced that the moral and academic mission of schools was of paramount importance. One way of meeting these challenges was to focus on those areas of teaching that might bolster the morale of the nation, and religion seemed to be such an area.

Wartime Rationale and Experimentation

Among the curricular experiments undertaken during the war was Stanford chaplain Elton Trueblood's attempt to encourage the teaching of theology not only to students but also to the faculty. Trueblood was inspired by the rationale given by George Thomas at Princeton for teaching religion in college. Trueblood cited Thomas's inaugural lecture, "Religion in an Age of Secularism," as formative for his own thinking, noting that not only were students "not up-to-date" on current theology but that professors also were ignorant of such matters: "The greatest harm comes from the flippant, smart remarks about religion from professors who may be educated in their own lines, but who are wholly ignorant religiously. Many are still fighting the old battles of their youth, judging the Christian religion by some feeble small-town church and worrying about old struggles between science and religion. How tired Galileo must be of being mentioned! . . . Often they know nothing of the teaching of modern men like Reinhold Niebuhr and William Temple and would be surprised to know of the intellectual integrity of such persons."[47]

Trueblood proposed seminars for faculty members to counteract their lack of understanding of modern theology and its methods in the hopes of correcting their tendency to poke fun at religion. It was well known, he remarked, that one way in which a professor could quickly become popular was to make "remarks which are supposed to shock his students or at least to shock the more pious among them. This easy road to popularity is taken by many, but with a terrible price. The students who are very young and tender begin to suppose that there is something laughable about faith in God."[48]

Trueblood's first attempt to institute a "religion" seminar for faculty was his invitation to Union Seminary theologian William Adams Brown to lead such a gathering at Stanford. It was, according to Trueblood, such a great "success that we hope to expand the practice in the future."[49] Such seminars did become a model for Stanford and were coupled with the more traditional "Religion Weeks."[50] The faculty were encouraged to participate in these activities by the chaplain's office, which referred to them as examples of the "advanced study of religion."[51]

Trueblood was not striving for a detached teaching of religion to either faculty or undergraduates, nor was he interested in the Princeton model of separating chaplaincy from the teaching of religion. Indeed, he praised Harvard dean Willard Sperry's proposal that the chaplain also be a teacher of religion: "Our best insight is that religion should be taught in a religious way, just as science should be taught in a scientific way. . . . We should think very poorly of the medical school in which the professors of medicine were men who never did practical work and we ought to think equally poorly of a university in which the practical university life and the academic teaching of religion are essentially unconnected." Universities were, for him, a great bastion of "pagan culture, places of immense danger."[52]

Trueblood had drawn the battle lines between the religious and the antireligious, not among the various religions. "The omission of theology from a university because of fear of sectarianism has practically no contemporary justification. . . . As one president remarked, they all say the same thing whether they call themselves Methodists, Baptists, Quakers or Jews. The same could be added for many Catholics and representatives of other groups."

In February of 1942, Trueblood hosted the Stanford Conference on Religion in Higher Education, which drew together college and university teachers and administrators, and ministers. Among the speakers was British theologian and educator Arnold Nash, who joined Unitarian theologian James Luther Adams in interpreting the critical importance of the war for higher education and religion. Adams asserted that "the war is being fought to determine what should be the relation between higher education and the state, and whether education and religion are to be merely instruments of political power." He criticized the false authoritarianism of "liberalism and humanism" and questioned the "Catholic denials of free inquiry" in higher education.[53] Adams went on to compare Catholic education to the Fundamentalist notion of education seen in the Scopes Trial in Tennessee, where Clarence Darrow and William Jennings Bryan had faced off to argue the legality of teaching evolution to schoolchildren.

Nash seconded James Luther Adams's praise of Robert Hutchins's experiment with the new scholasticism at the University of Chicago but mounted a diatribe against separating out religion as a discrete course of study from education as a whole. Nash, who paradoxically would later establish the University of North Carolina's religion department as a base from which he planned to reach "every professor and student" with his Christian gospel, argued that religious practice and study should not be separated in this way: "If religion becomes a specialized subject it is neither religion nor education. . . . therefore, the establishment of departments of religion in universities is a calamity. We should not train economists or doctors who are also but separately trained to be Christians, for this involves a clash of categories. There is need for Christian categories which will permeate other fields."[54] Nash and other educators were sympathetic to Hutchins's call to arms against vocationalism and overspecialization in college education because these represented the eclipse of the humanities and the reign of either a fragmented curriculum or the natural sciences. Nash, however, stood alone among the Protestant educators in his criticism of the Princeton and Yale projects. He was troubled by the dual role that the religion department was expected to fulfill, primarily because it subsumed Christianity under the heading of religion as "just another subject." There was little reason to teach "about" a religion if teaching the supreme religion itself was an option. For Nash, all genuine or proper education is essentially religious. Nash's early stance against religion departments in 1942 reflected his belief that the movement toward a revival of Christian beliefs and practices in America was strong enough to demand not just one department but the entire school. The Christian way of life provided the strength for democracy, and it should be afforded the highest place in education. He would later come to moderate his view with the understanding that, if he could not have the whole university, then a department of religion from which to approach the whole university would have to suffice.

Trueblood saw little tension between the dual roles of the religion department, because to teach about religion and to teach religiously were, in his mind, necessarily paired. They represented the synthesis of a dialectic in which religion in the university had first been "theology dominant" before becoming "theology excluded." The third stage, Trueblood now proposed, was that it be "theology respected."[55] He cited Princeton's new religion department as "evidence of the widespread reopening of the subject" on college campuses, and hoped that this would mean a "reintroduction of an important discipline into our academic experience."[56] Such a reintroduction was necessary because of the threat of "Hitler, who is certainly the leader of a religion." Since the hope of destroying Hitler's malignant religion was left to "Western Civilization," which had been "so largely founded on Christian principles," it was incumbent upon universities to teach Christian theology in "an objective manner."[57]

In response to the challenges presented by the war, Princeton philosophy professor Theodore M. Greene (later at Yale) led faculty members at Princeton in creating a special course to underscore the importance of the Christian tradition to democracy. The two-semester course, given first in 1942, was entitled "Man and His Freedom in the Western Tradition." This course was only possible, according to Greene, because of this shift on campus toward religious questions: "Another encouraging fact worthy of record is the very notable change of attitude among college students since Pearl Harbor. Prior to Pearl Harbor the dominant undergraduate mood on our liberal arts campuses was one of cynicism, frustration, and indifference to serious questions, including religious problems."[58]

This change in mood convinced various departmental faculty to join Greene in lecturing on "the central beliefs of the developing Hebraic-Christian and Graeco-Roman traditions, the infusion in the Middle Ages and the Protestant Reformation." Readings included "long assignments in the Bible," Augustine, Saint Francis, Luther, and modern writers such as "Marx, Dewey, and Reinhold Niebuhr." Greene noted that "our students, both in and out of uniform, have been electing this course in increasing numbers."[59] Not only had students' attitudes changed, according to Greene, but faculty members had also been deeply affected by the war, prodding them to direct their teaching toward "urgent problems and vital issues," seeking solutions to such issues in order to "deepen and enrich" the lives of students.[60]

Wartime concerns, military-led science-based projects, campuses full of student soldiers participating in accelerated courses, and later veterans all philosophically and practically aided in shifting these schools further away from the old collegiate model and toward the university model practically, while drawing on the college ideal in the midst of the national crisis. Religion departments were in their earliest forms a place where the Christian beliefs of professors were shared with college students who were able to study Protestant theology in the context of the less specialized, more morally focused residential programs that embodied the collegiate ideal. Administration

and faculty concerns about materialism, nihilism, preprofessional-
ism, and the ethos of the university model made the creation of such
departments a temporary repository for the college model that represented a turn back to the humanities, a more personal and to many a
more reasonable response on campus, given the coming turn toward
religious piety.

CHAPTER FOUR

National Religion Turn Finds Odd Ally in Hutchins

The debate over the importance of the Judeo-Christian tradition in college teaching reached high pitch with the attendance of many leading Protestant educators at the most important series of meetings of academics during this era—the Conference on Science, Philosophy, and Religion (CSPR) in New York City in the mid-1940s.[1] A majority of the participants in the multiyear conference believed that a broad societal and cultural turn back to religion—to the traditions of Christianity and Judaism—was the only way out of the crisis of loss of values and meaning then facing Western civilization. George Thomas and members of the Princeton faculty along with a few Yale, Harvard, and Chicago professors were staunch supporters of the need for such religious renewal, while Erwin R. Goodenough, Sidney Hook, John Dewey, and other skeptics saw it as a disingenuous, self-serving, and dangerous failure of nerve.[2]

Hook, in one of many diatribes against the conference, noted that "only occasionally a lone voice speaks up like that of Professor Goodenough: 'Over and again the various absolutist philosophies suggested in the Conference have shown that once in power they would be dangerously like the closed systems (at least in being closed) which we want to oppose.' But these voices are relatively feeble and are drowned out in the chorus of fundamentalism." Hook continued to criticize the Princeton group, quoting part of their report to the CSPR that he found particularly reprehensible and inaccurate: "It [naturalism] leads inevitably to pride and egoism. The individual having nothing higher than himself to worship or serve worships himself, his reason, culture, or his race. . . . Totalitarianism is the historical result of the weakening of the Greek and Hebraic-Christian traditions."[3]

The Princeton group quoted unfavorably by Hook was composed of the leaders of the move to create and develop the department of religion at Princeton.[4] Its presentation to the CSPR was entitled "The Spiritual Basis of Democracy," and in it, the group developed a rationale for the renewal of democratic society through an educated acceptance of the "spiritual conception of man." The spiritual life, the group argued, was "not identical with any of the phenomena and laws of nature described by the natural sciences; and whatever description of them the natural sciences may be capable of giving cannot affect their reality and their value." Although biological and physical processes conditioned the human spirit, the spirit was in need of its own "distinctive methods and categories suitable to its distinctive nature."[5] In addition to claiming that the nature and reality of the spiritual realm was out of the range of the scientific tools of empirical verification, the Princeton group affirmed the superiority of the intellectual "Hebraic-Christian" tradition's understanding of the human spirit. The "modern naturalistic view of man" was deemed inferior because it divorced humans from the moral and spiritual order.

This naturalistic view, according to the Princeton group, was the culprit in the decline and potential fall of Western civilization because its adherents in many democratic countries were "unaware of the dangers of their position: Influenced by the last remnants of philosophical Idealism, romantic Transcendentalism, or religious Theism in our day, they act as if they still believed in the spiritual conception of man which they have intellectually repudiated. They try to maintain their feelings for the dignity of man, while paying homage to an essentially materialistic philosophy according to which man is simply a highly developed animal. . . . In short, they are living off the spiritual capital which has come down to them from their classical and religious heritage, while at the same time they ignore that heritage itself as antiquated and false."[6]

To complete their argument against the strains of naturalism then pervading much of Western civilization, the group stated that the ultimate political and social end of this philosophy was in fact the dangerous ideology sweeping across Europe at that very hour: "Totalitarianism is the historical result of the weakening of the Greek and Hebraic-Christian traditions we have described. As awareness of an objective moral and spiritual order has grown dim, other 'orders' have captured men's imaginations." In conclusion, the Princeton group offered their solution for checking the spread of naturalism. Scholars, teachers, writers, and religious leaders needed to "succeed in arousing the minds and hearts" of students and citizens. According to the group, scholars and teachers everywhere should bring the truths of the spiritual and moral life to every citizen before naturalism and skepticism proved to be "the death of democratic society and its culture."

Only a few months later, in early 1943, philosopher John Dewey fired back. Having read Thomas and the Princeton group's attack on naturalism, Dewey condensed their argument to one assertion: "The rights and freedom which constitute democracy have no validity or significance save as they are referable to some center and authority entirely outside nature and outside men's connections with one another in society."[7] Dewey countered that naturalism revealed the "value and dignity of men and women, founded in human nature itself, in the connections, actual and potential, of human beings with one another in their natural and social relationships." Furthermore, he asserted that naturalism maintained that the importance of this argument "is a much sounder one than is alleged to exist outside the constitution of man and nature."[8]

Dewey viewed the Princeton group's assertion of a transcendent authority to be reminiscent of a time when "the Church had the power to protect the faithful from 'science falsely so-called,' and from dangerous thoughts in scholarship." Those who had a sense of history, Dewey predicted, "might well smile at the innocence of their colleagues who imply that inquiry, scholarship, and teaching are completely unhampered where naturalism has not obtained a foothold."[9] He believed that unhampered scholarship was more likely to occur where naturalism prevailed over authoritarian attempts to impose an external transcendent order on scholarship.

Between the Skeptics and Pious, Edwin Aubrey

Writing in the *Humanist*, a journal not in the habit of publishing Protestant theologians, Edwin Aubrey responded to Hook's and Dewey's criticisms of the CSPR's papers asserting the preeminence of the Hebraic-Christian tradition. Aubrey admitted that the conference was heavily weighted toward "the side of dogmatic theology," and that Mortimer Adler's acrimonious proclamation that liberal professors were more dangerous than Hitler was disturbing but also "irrelevant." However, Aubrey argued that the counterattack on the Hebraic-Christian tradition was one-sided:

> It is always possible to bring the charge against the Christian churches that they do not live up to their professions; but this does not alter the fact that the doctrine of agape in Christian ethics mitigated Roman slavery and made the Christian groups a powerful ferment in the antislavery movement in both England and America. That the monastic brotherhoods were democratic within their limits; that the sixteenth and seventeenth century sects gave an impetus to modern doctrines of political freedom; and that our churches even today are admitted by active social reformers to be their most productive source of personnel—all these facts need to be in the picture too.[10]

Aubrey showed his own independence from both the Princeton group and such Roman Catholic theologians in attendance as Jacques Maritain by agreeing with Hook that a major obstacle to dialogue at the CSPR was the clinging to a "theory of revealed truth," which precluded genuine intellectual cooperation with empirically minded thinkers.[11]

In the aftermath of the CSPR controversies, Yale's Erwin R. Goodenough wrote his first article on the usefulness of teaching religion for the Study of Man series in the American Jewish Committee's journal *Commentary*. Goodenough understood religion to provide "final answers to such basic questions as 'Where do I come from?' . . . 'If I don't do what is right, what will happen to me?' 'If I do it, what reward may I expect?'"[12] Because science did not provide sufficient answers to such questions, the innate quest for certainty prompted humans to seek that certitude in religious explanations.[13]

George Thomas, the Princeton Group, and many other thinkers influenced by neoorthodoxy understood what they called religion to stand in stark contrast to the scientific worldview and to the political systems of fascism and communism. Conversely, Goodenough's contrast between science and "religious explanation" was arranged so that the latter was lumped together with the political ideologies. Religious explanations, according to Goodenough, had to be studied "scientifically" just as the ideologies of politics had to be. Scientists, having rid themselves of their oppressor religion, "have not recognized that in their new enemies, the totalitarian ideologies which now again threaten to choke them, they only face—in a new uniform—their old enemy, the human craving for certainty in an uncertain world."[14]

For Goodenough, the scientist of religion must necessarily ask the questions "What is this craving for certainty?" and "What are its assets and liabilities?" Having inverted the often-expressed apothegm that religion gives science new hope, Goodenough joined with many founders of religion departments of his day in characterizing the value of teaching religion in practical terms—"religion, like other human forces, needs to be understood if it is to serve man." In this, he resonated with the pragmatic undertones of many of the founders, which they might not have recognized: "Religion must serve us, wither or change." Such an ultimatum to the gods may have seemed irreverent to the more pious of Protestant educators, but much of their rhetoric regarding the uses of religion for undergraduates consistently made the case for such an ultimatum: it must be useful in serving humanity.

Religion, according to Goodenough, needed to be studied and taught scientifically, and he wasted no words in giving his estimation of teachers in the field of religion at midcentury: "The apologists of religious scholarship take proper pride in the tremendous energy and critical acumen that have gone into modern biblical study . . . and that biblical scholars should be fully as ready as scientists to accept conclusions violating all their prejudices and emotional commitments, whenever the evidence seems to compel such conclusions. I am convinced, however, that few religious scholars have ever had this kind of experience." He went on to decry scholars who replaced a concern with the certainty of Scripture with the certainty that "Jesus would lead man into the golden age of democracy or socialism."[15]

Erwin R. Goodenough embodied the struggle between the desire for a new discipline of religion and for instruction in a religion classroom that would help students better appreciate why religion is important to practice.[16] This twofold purpose was integral to his and so many others' conception of how such courses could best serve the students and the college ideal. The new teaching of religion he proposed would promote a scientific study of religion that would also accommodate the desire to make religion count in the classroom. Goodenough believed in the efficacy of prayer and the importance of an appreciation of religion's power, while simultaneously scoffing at the chaplain-like role that many professors and administrators at Yale and Princeton suggested for the department of religion. Goodenough's position against pious advocacy teaching in the college at Yale and his contrarian voice at the CSPR ensured continued debate about the renewal of departments of religion at midcentury and their role in retaining the college ideal amid the university model's march forward.[17]

Unlikely Ally for Nonskeptics, Robert Maynard Hutchins

Robert Hutchins was listed as a participant in the CSPR but in absentia. Professor Mortimer Adler and others represented Hutchins's general perspective on the need for a metaphysical or religious stance within the university to offset the dangers posed by nihilism and overly zealous "scientism." Hutchins nevertheless continued to clarify his own thinking on the importance of religious instruction in colleges. However much he despised the departmental model and that of the traditional four-year college that was so full of vocational and professional aspirations, he did argue for the importance of religious instruction and research in higher education. On October 25, 1943, Hutchins delivered an address entitled "The Place of Theological Education in a University" as he inaugurated the Federated Theological Faculty at the University of Chicago. This was a cooperative effort among the university's divinity school, the local Unitarian and Congregationalist seminaries, and the Disciples Divinity House of the Disciples of Christ (Christian church). Hutchins saw the mission of the project as one of working "together on the common problems of Protestant theology."[18] His conviction that religious faith should be central to the college enterprise was clear: "Any true community must have a spiritual basis. The brotherhood of man must rest on the father-hood of God. If God is denied, or man's spiritual nature denied, then the basis of community disappears. . . . Unless we believe that every man is the child of God, we cannot love our neighbors."[19]

Mainstream Protestantism's news and commentary organ, the *Christian Century*, commented with immense joy that Hutchins had "gone further . . . passing beyond the limit of metaphysics which he had previously espoused as the unifying discipline of academic culture and has come out in the clear light of religious faith. . . . It is something new in modern education for theology based on revelation to be recognized as an integral part of the culture which a university is set to re-examine."[20] The *Christian Century* editors had either not studied or chose to ignore Hutchins's own denouncement of revelation-based theology, written as the response to William Adams Brown's *The Case for Theology in the University* (1938), as they declared him to be in favor of more than a divinity school that trained ministers: "It is evident that President Hutchins had something more in mind than merely to welcome into the university's institutional structure a professional faculty which would attract only those who intended to enter the Christian ministry. He could hardly have spoken as he did if he had not envisaged a time when the general student body would be attracted to theology as an essential part of a liberal education. His welcome was addressed to theology itself, and was extended on behalf of the cultural life of the whole academic community."[21] This was not the first time that Hutchins's powerful rhetorical had been misinterpreted, as it was by friends and enemies alike. It was questionable whether he had any plan of making theology, as understood by the editors, the queen of the university, as he made clear in his preface to Brown's jeremiad. However, his dream of basing all humanities and sciences education on an unchanging set of first principles, a metaphysic, had been well publicized by the national media, and he was forever qualifying his intentions, not least of all to his own faculty at Chicago.

Hutchins was fully cognizant of the predominant liberal perspective that frustrated many neoorthodox thinkers of the day. He rejected that perspective, characterizing it as one in which the individual proclaims, "I am a humanitarian and a liberal. I will help my fellow-men without worrying about whether we have a common Father." His counter

to such a proclamation was to paraphrase Reinhold Niebuhr: "Because
men are animal, because the flesh is weak and life is hard, the virtues
[of Aristotle] cannot be consistently practiced without divine aid."[22]

Hutchins implored graduating students to revolutionize society,
emphasizing at the same time the critical need for a clearly articulated
monotheistic religious perspective: "Improve the world, promote a
moral, intellectual and spiritual revolution throughout the world. To
try to get all we can, to breed more barbarians, to regard one another
as so many animals, rational or not, will lead us inevitably to the final
catastrophe. It is very late; perhaps nothing can save us. . . . But if we
can gain for ourselves a coherent system of ideas concerning the world
and humanity; if we can mean the fatherhood of God when we say
the brotherhood of man, then we may have one more chance."[23] Not
unlike George Thomas, Clarence Shedd, and many other founders of
programs in religion, Hutchins was deeply troubled by the modern
understanding of human beings as animals with some mores, which
for him smacked of the basic philosophy that allowed a Hitler to flourish. Hutchins was even more troubled to be the leader of a university at
which such views were taught every day.[24]

In his roles as head of a leading university and a national figure who
elevated the part morality had to play in the life of the college and society at large, Hutchins regularly corresponded with other educational
leaders. For example, the chaplain of Occidental College in Los Ange-
les, Herbert Nobel, wrote asking for information about "the new development that" Hutchins had "set underway at the Chicago University in
putting theology at the center of the university curriculum": "It seems
to me that you have taken a step in the right direction." Nobel went on to
say, "I do feel that there is a great deal of confusion in this field of relation of religion and education. I wish to clarify my own thinking and
also develop a policy for the religious program and activities here on
our own campus."[25] Hutchins wrote Nobel back, not to say that there
must have been some misunderstanding, but to give him a copy of his
speech at the inauguration of the Federated Theological Faculty.

The president of Mills College in Oakland, Lynn White Jr., also
wrote Hutchins about his Federated Theological Faculty speech,
remarking, "I have never felt that one could 'save souls' by even the best
system of education, but something must be done at least to remedy

the appalling religious illiteracy which is normal among college graduates. Your insistence upon the necessity of re-incorporating theology into the general structure of education naturally warms the heart of a renegade medieval historian like myself."[26] These educators were appreciative of Hutchins's straightforward encouragement of the role that theology could play in a university's curriculum. And from him, they were seeking clear words of guidance on a matter that had become difficult to assess.

Historically religious colleges were faced at midcentury with faculties whose perspectives on religious thought increasingly were not in line with the original missions of the schools' founders, and many administrators felt they had to address the lack of a positive religious influence on campus. George Rosser, a teacher in the department of biblical literature at Wesleyan College in Georgia, exclaimed in a letter to Hutchins, "Hurrah and hallelujah! Thank you, thank your splendid father and especially thank God for your wisdom. The blessing of Heaven will abound unto you and unto the great university. . . . I have earnestly and intensely followed your utterances concerning the nature and stupendous and central value, and proper and logical place of the 'Queen of the Sciences.' God bless you and the great university. And He will."[27]

Hutchins expressed his thanks to admirers such as these but was somewhat taken aback by the attention given his speech, which to him must have seemed a rather straightforward exposition of where universities should stand on the question of the teaching of theology.[28] The *Christian Century*'s editorial referred to previously, announcing Hutchins's change of heart about theology in the university, indicated that he meant something more: "If the university—if just one university—is awaking at last to the fundamental place of theology in a liberal culture, is it not high time for Protestantism to bring theology out of the cloister and make it something more than an esoteric possession of a professional class?"[29] For all this acclaim, however, it is important to remember that teaching the Christian religion to undergraduates through a theology or religion department was not part of Hutchins's plan. He did not favor discrete academic departments, which according to him, led to overspecialization far too soon in the life of a college student. His argument, again, was that metaphysics was the foundation for all the important questions of life and thus of university inquiry. Specialized research must come after this foundation had been laid.

Hutchins was frustrated most by the influence on the university community of the materialist view of humankind, emanating principally from the sociology, anthropology, and economics faculty. When the university teaches only truths and not Truth, then might makes right, educators can become little dictators, and there is no authoritative and final resort to morality. It was not Hutchins's intention that undergraduate education be given over to the specialists of the various departments, but that it be a general education, of which his own brand of theology was to be the focus. Such a theology had been described as based on Aristotelian first principles with some Aquinas added for good measure.

As carried out by University of Chicago philosopher Richard McKeon, Hutchins's educational program was not welcomed in many corners of the campus. Humanist Harry Gideonse believed, for instance, that universities were for research, not inculcation of values, and that imposing such a dual role on higher education was confusing and wrong.[30]

This difference between research and inculcation, or between theory and practice in the teaching of religion, was at the very center of the rationale for the creation of departments of religion as well as the shift from college ideal to university ideal. Courses that examined all manner of religious topics were plentiful in the prewar colleges. One of the "Seven Sisters" (elite women's educational institutions), Mount Holyoke College, for instance, offered no fewer than eighteen courses throughout its academic departments with such titles as "Religion and the Social Order," "Literature of Private Worship," "Modern Religious Movements," "Philosophy of Religion," "Interpretation of Religion in America since 1918," "Greek Testament," "The Reformation and the Rise of Modern States," "Medieval Philosophy," "Metaphysical Systems," and "Theory of Value." Such courses were deemed by many Protestant educators, however, to be focused primarily on theory, not the thoughtful practice of personal religion. What then might the founding or renewal of a department of religion mean for such a curriculum?

Edward Blakeman, the University of Michigan's research consultant in religious education and a promoter of religion departments in state universities, explained why such courses did not have the impact that a strong, purposeful, and separate religion department might bring to the college:

> They [courses] emerge in the departments of history, literature, philosophy, psychology, political science and sociology. In other words, religion as a phase of culture persists. . . . On the other hand, partly due to the fact that the ecclesiastical sects or denominations are excluded, many scholars interested in spiritual values, have given definite attention to the conserving nature of higher education so that within current departments the contributions of religious experience shall be carried to youth. Whether religion so presented can come to them freighted with the emotion which a church or fellowship of believers can supply is always a debatable question.[31]

Protestant educators in the mid-twentieth century were increasingly concerned that professors in separate departments who taught courses focused on religious theory or history were unable to have as strong an effect on students as might be possible by a department of religion that had a practical mission. In the same way that religion and religions were being taught "about" at Princeton long before the 1940 founding of its religion department, many other colleges offered courses that were a combination of pious offerings of the Bible department and more secular, critical considerations of religious topics by other departments. But none of these was satisfactory to those who wanted to create new religion departments in elite colleges. Secular philosophers and social scientists were not to be trusted with the time-tested truths of Christianity, but neither were the ill-trained local ministers whose courses were not respected in the colleges. Separate religion departments filled with confessionally focused, Christian PhDs were what was needed.

Henry Nelson Wieman and the Incompetence of Religious Thinking

As we have seen, however, several religious educators and thinkers at midcentury were unhappy with this dual role—teaching about religion and teaching to inculcate Protestantism—that was expected of the proposed departments of religion, from Erwin R. Goodenough's call to return to Max Müller's *Religionswissenschaft* (science of religion) to Alexander Miller's proposal to teach Christianity outside of the category of religion. Another concerned voice was that of philosopher, theologian, and University of Chicago professor Henry Nelson Wieman, who also called for reappraising the place that religion might have in the modern university. Wieman was frustrated, along with Goodenough, that religious thought was not able to enter the "educative process" because it was so weak in its academic or disciplinary structure within colleges and universities. His great hope was to "put religion into higher education on a parity with other disciplines" by first fighting the "incompetence of religious thinking." This incompetence resulted from the isolation imposed on it by "a great army of men in the universities who are devoting all their powers to disinterested research in the attempt to solve problems." For Wieman, the religious thinker did not regularly rely on higher education as a resource upon which to draw, and for that reason it was "no wonder religion lags far behind every other branch of human inquiry."[32]

Wieman sought "certain standards of critical intelligence for religious concepts so that they can be made a part of the educative system." He called for the use of "modern thinking under secular auspices" as the way best to pursue religious truth within academe. This would, according to him, be the most effective way to aid religious communities, individuals, and civilization itself. Even though, at bottom, his primary concern was for the renewal of religious life in America, he felt that "religion" (which he used interchangeably with "the best that Protestantism had to offer") should be subjected to rigorous academic criticism in order to strengthen it: "Such criticism may be able to distinguish the mythology, which may be pragmatically required for religious living, but which cannot meet the tests of truth imposed by critical inquiry. These latter only can be put into higher education on equality with other areas of instruction and research. Such instruction, established first in the colleges and universities, might then be extended to secondary and primary schools—and into the churches—revitalizing religion at every level."[33]

Wieman's explanation for why the teaching of religion had to make a clean break from the professional schools (as Goodenough proposed at Yale) and chaplaincy (as Thomas implemented at Princeton) was that they were "caught in a vicious circle. They must minister directly to people, or train men to minister to people." For its own good, he thought that the academic enterprise of teaching religion should be one or two steps removed from inculcating the practical aspects of religious life. Without this distance from practical ministry, he argued, the help that academic criticism could provide to strengthen religious thought in the eyes of the secular world, in the classroom, and in the life of the churches would remain at bay: "[Most people get] a good part of their religious thought from half an hour a week in Sunday school under the instruction of a sixteen-year-old girl who received her religious education from another adolescent of the previous generation. . . . The vicious circle which requires the theologian and the professional school of religion to develop only those ideas which can be used to engender religious living in people whose religious thinking is so crude, serves to insulate the intellectual framework of religion still further."[34]

Wieman wanted to put religion back into the classroom, but in a different way than had been imagined by University of Chicago chaplain Charles Gilkey, whose focus was more pastoral. What the two Chicagoans seemed to share, however, was the goal of strengthening Protestant thought and the churches that depended on it. Wieman's hopes were not at cross-purposes with those of divinity school professor and later dean Bernard Loomer or Robert Hutchins, but they had different foci. This was one of the reasons that Chicago never instituted a religion department and never directly articulated the role of the divinity school in teaching religion to undergraduates as Harvard did. Hutchins, as already noted, was wary of the departmental system in the undergraduate setting and of professional schools, seeing in them the danger of overspecialization and undue professionalization. For his part, Gilkey, more than any other educator at Chicago, saw the divinity school's role as being much larger in the lives of undergraduates. But in the end, these various proposals produced only an inconclusive recommendation about the teaching of religion in the undergraduate college, though there was no lack of interest in the university-wide implications such proposals engendered.[35] And certainly, Hutchins's thought was known and examined throughout the national community of Protestant educators and was used by many of them across the country to further their own plans to revive religious instruction on campuses.

No Common Faith of the Skeptics

Taking aim directly at philosophers John Dewey and Sidney Hook, George Thomas put forth his strongest statement about teaching religion to college students in 1944, making comments that might have seemed out of place in his 1940 inaugural lecture at Princeton University.[36] Six years before the *Partisan Review*'s series on Religion and the Intellectuals, Thomas cited with approval Lewis Mumford's book *Faith for Living* and Walter Lippmann's writings on morality and modernity. He took these as indications that "our literary men are taking more seriously the deeper foundations of society." Thomas quoted Lippmann's assessment of education's most critical point of failure as a summary of his own thinking about why religion should be taught in college curricula: "Colleges have . . . been sending out into the world men who no longer understand the creative principle of the society in which they must live. . . . Modern education rejects and excludes from the curriculum of necessary studies the whole religious tradition of the West." Not that religion courses did not exist, of course, but as Thomas explained, "They are no longer regarded as important, much less necessary."[37]

Thomas's article includes the line of reasoning, the call for action, and the plan for reestablishing religion as an important subject taught in colleges that had been articulated by a long list of educators. He recognized that, although it was taught in many schools, religion on campus was often considered by many to be unimportant and unnecessary. For this reason, merely increasing the number of religion classes offered to students would do nothing to affect its status. What was needed was a demonstration of the importance of religion by rigorous research, writing, and argument. That such a demonstration was necessary was clear from the mood of the times. The goal was for religion, as a subject of study and a way of life, to become a "common moral and intellectual discipline" in an era Lippmann defined as having "no common faith, no common body of knowledge."[38]

Thomas believed there were three basic reasons for religion's neglect on the nation's campuses: legal concerns, secularism, and naturalism.

Questions of its legality applied only to state colleges and universities, where the "establishment" of religion was unconstitutional. But he dismissed any legal objection by borrowing Clarence Shedd's observation that religion had been taught in public schools for years—if not in religion departments, then certainly in English courses studying the biblical literature and in Greek courses translating the New Testament. And they had done so without crossing the line separating church and state. Thomas made no specific legal argument save this reliance on precedent. Namely, if the teaching of religious content was happening in enough places without being challenged, either it was being taken for granted or it must not be wrong. Moreover, it was mistaken to think that "a person who has been specially trained in religion and who takes it seriously must be sectarian or dogmatic" and therefore should not be teaching religion.[39]

For Thomas and many of his colleagues, however, the most disturbing reason for the lack of interest in religion was the "secularism of our age." He did not mince words in defining secularists as those who believe that religion—which they understood to be the belief in and devotion to an eternal source of good that both fulfills and transcends the natural goods of human life—is a "delusion." But secularists were not antireligious, he argued, as much as they were participants in the new religion of humanism, whose confession of faith Thomas imagined in these words: "Of course, Christian morality is a good thing, and the school should inculcate its ideals. But we have to separate the moral ideals of Christianity from the erroneous or at least speculative religious beliefs which have been associated with them. Churches may still try to defend these beliefs or to get rid of irrational elements in them, but they are doomed to disappear. We now know that science alone can establish true beliefs; beliefs arrived at in any other way are mere guesses and fancies."[40] Though he may not have agreed with University of Chicago professor Mortimer Adler's claim that "ninety percent of all professors actually believe the scientific method is the only way to discover the truth about something," Thomas did feel that for many professors science had become a "sort of religion." But he was unconvinced that the scientific method, strictly adhered to, could satisfy the natural desires of human life.[41]

As a teacher of young men who had been called to active military service in World War II, Thomas was acutely aware that a strong faith would

be necessary to "maintain and defend the civilized life, one of democracy."
He found it tantamount to treason to accept the humanist's utilitarian
moral philosophy extolling "the greatest happiness of the greatest number." Thomas countered with the heroic Christian ideal of "self-giving and
self-sacrificing love for all men." Teaching young men otherwise, particularly to teach them a humanist religion of "earthly happiness," was too
dangerous given the wartime challenges faced by the nation.[42]

It was easy to be deceived by the apparent political and social implications of this new religion of humanism, Thomas felt. Humanism
claimed to be "most suitable to democracy" because, as humanists
explained, "religion, by its very nature, insists upon certain absolute
beliefs and values [whereas] men in a democracy must be free to revise
their beliefs." Thomas agreed that holding absolute beliefs was dangerous, but he countered that the "absolute beliefs asserted by Christianity
have to do, not with social policies in specific situations, but with the
general purposes of human life in society." Further, the most fundamental element of democracy was a "sense of responsibility, a willingness to
fulfill one's duties to one's fellow citizens." Without the undergirding
of democracy by individual responsibility, something that humanism
could not provide, democracy degenerated "into a struggle between
individuals, classes, or regions. Each class will press its own rights to
the limit without regard for those of others, and anarchy will result."
Thomas's third reason religion had been neglected on campuses was
"the dominant philosophy of naturalism." Naturalism was the enemy
of religion in college life because of the strength of the natural sciences
and the students' preoccupation with "earthly happiness, comfort and
prosperity." Naturalism, in Thomas's reading, flatly denied the reality
of humans' spiritual nature. And if humans were not spiritual creatures, they were merely animals with rational, social, and imaginative
capabilities. The result of such thinking, which he thought to be most
dangerously represented by John Dewey's *A Common Faith*, was to consider nature to be the only ultimate reality.[43]

Thomas admitted that "such a naturalistic religion was having a following of some of our most unselfish men," adding that it was "behind
the practical idealism of many doctors, teachers, and others." He nevertheless faulted it for "making an idol of man while leaving his spiritual
aspirations and moral efforts swinging in the wind."[44] And he registered

this fault while knowing that his alternate explanation of humanity could no more be proven true than the humanist outlook. "Reality of a divine spiritual life cannot be proved with certainty"; rather, it takes an act of faith. Knowledge cannot be substituted for faith. This was the crux of the problem religion faced in finding its proper place within college education. Though not blind credulity, faith must go beyond reason without contradicting it. The natural and social sciences are the best ways to investigate those phenomena accessible to the senses, whereas in the spiritual life, we experience "ourselves . . . through direct insight and feeling."[45]

This extrasensory experience of reality was humanity's spiritual nature expressed in religion. Through such an experience, individuals become "aware of a holy Presence, sometimes by itself, but more often as manifested in a beautiful object, a natural law, or a generous act." Thomas defined faith as "affirmation of the Reality [one] sees and feels in these high moments." It was clear, then, why Thomas advocated the study of religion in college: students would be led to investigate a realm beyond that accessible to sense perception as ordinarily understood. Such a claim must have seemed incredible to many of Thomas's colleagues at Princeton University, but his conviction was that a claim to this kind of knowledge "deserved to be examined carefully and sympathetically in colleges devoted to truth."[46]

Finally, Thomas described the features of a college that treated religion as an important and necessary subject worthy of teaching:

> In such a college, the religious view of life would be taught not only in the department of religion but in all departments. The departments of literature would show how the great writers, such as Milton and Wordsworth and Shelley, have interpreted human life in terms of its relation to something higher than itself. The department of social sciences would judge all the institutions and policies they study by the standard of an ideal community, ruled by the law of love. The department of history would explain the real triumphs and tragedies of humanity by reference to deeper factors than economic greed and political ambitions. The departments of natural science would, at suitable times, point out those intimations of divine wisdom and power behind nature which have always aroused man's wonder. The practical arts and professions,

finally, would be taught as opportunities to minister to human needs not for profit but for love. In short, knowledge in every department would be taught for its own sake, and also for its contribution to the spiritual life. . . . Every citizen of our democratic society can do something to make this dream for education come true.[47]

This somewhat grandiose way of envisioning the university struck Sidney Hook, John Dewey, and other academics who were not religiously focused as misplaced zeal. Dewey, writing in the fall of 1945, spoke directly to such attacks against so-called materialism, which amounted in some quarters to an attack of science: "The attack rests upon calling the sciences 'materialistic' while literary subjects are identified with whatever is idealistic and 'spiritual' in our traditions and institutions. This position rests back upon belief in the separation of man from nature."[48] Dewey compared the then current "spiritual humanities versus materialistic science" debate to the "earlier movement that bears the name of 'Conflict of Science and Religion.' . . . It can hardly be said that the scientific doctrines won a complete victory. Fundamentalism is still rife in both Roman Catholic and Protestant denominations. But upon the whole the climate of opinion became adjusted to the new views." Dewey was especially critical of the claims of religious humanists that science should not "trespass upon the moral domain of humane concerns."[49]

The somber, reflective, and often crisis-oriented mood of many citizens from the late 1930s to late 1940s manifested itself in the sort of educational reforms and curricular reexaminations that were undertaken by leading institutions and educators, which included a rethinking of the place of religion in college curricula as such schools were shifting toward the University ideal. Undoubtedly the mood of the nation affected institutions in a variety of ways. One constant, however, was the way in which founders of departments of religion strengthened their position within colleges by arguing that the teaching of religion was needed in order to bring about a resolution to the crises facing Western civilization. Universities may be focusing on research, the creation of new knowledge and shifting away from the inculcation of values toward the critical examination of values, but religion departments would be able to bridge the college and university ideals by both examining moral values and enhancing the academic quality of instruction about and for religion.

In the attempt to fulfill their dual role as teachers about religion as well as inculcators of religious values, religion department founders discovered that both were complicated by wartime curricular cooperation between school and government; the complexities of ecumenism; the fear of "the bomb" and the developing Cold War;[50] and by the need to come to terms with the democratization of American higher education and the emergence of the modern research university.

Successfully balancing these various interests and concerns that were part of American life through the first half of the twentieth century would have been difficult enough for Protestant educators, but serving both church and a fledgling academic field or department during this time made matters all the more difficult. And yet they persevered, motivated by a powerful vision of the relationship between theology and human experience, and the institutions that mediate that relationship: "They conceived of theology less as doctrinal studies grounded in specific confessional traditions than as an ecumenical inquiry into common human experience and the transpersonal forces that challenged and nurtured that common experience. They were institution builders who believed in the power of institutions to better the human lot. Their confidence arose not so much from a sense of personal righteousness as from the conviction that the values to which they aspired were congruent with the heart of things."[51]

The crisis atmosphere of World War II exacerbated the tension between teaching about religions and religious education from a Christian perspective. Each discipline in the university was scrutinized for how it could further the national war effort. Teaching how to better understand various religious perspectives was not at the top of the list. Most of the prospective religion teachers were graduating from seminaries, and the undergraduate departments and graduate departments in which they would be teaching were all based on a divinity school curriculum. The nation's colleges were generally less interested in dissecting religion to examine it and more willing to support it while also looking for resources within religion by studying it with new methods.[52] The tension between bringing religion to the undergraduate curriculum as a healing, unifying, nourishing force and bolstering a new

research discipline has already been clarified as the foundation for religion departments by those who wanted them and those who proposed
to create them. The wartime university was seemingly in greater need
of the former nourishing kind of religion, but academic legitimation
still needed to be ensured. The tensions inherent in the dual role of the
religion department founder and Protestant university educator grew
during this period.

While professors and academics of other disciplines sought how
they might best serve the nation, many Protestant religious educators
were interested in finding the proper role for religion. The role they
found was putting religion in the service of the country, just as colleges
were assumed to be in the service of the nation.

CHAPTER FIVE

Atomic Cold War Faces
Yale Christian Hope

On August 5, 1945, the front page of the *New York Times* carried a twenty-paragraph story on Yale University's decision to create a new department of religion. Such an article would not have achieved front-page billing a few days later, as reports of the *Enola Gay*'s mission of atomic devastation dominated the news.

Accompanying the article was a letter from the Yale committee recommending the creation of the department of religion. It stated, "We repudiate Nazism, but many of us are not at all sure what we really do believe in. The urgent practical importance facing that question is, nevertheless, beginning to be recognized. The university has a responsibility for helping in this area." The committee added, "Yale University exists today not to propagate a single philosophy, or creed, but to seek the truth."[1]

Yale's struggle to place religion more forcefully into the undergraduate curriculum was an almost perfect example of the tension inherent in forming an academic department with the sort of dual mandate examined in the preceding chapters. Its function was both to serve humanity by strengthening Christianity (however veiled) in the West and to carve out a place for itself as a legitimate enterprise within the modern university, which increasingly was adopting the research model for its curricular self-understanding. Certainly the presence of the divinity school made Yale a distinctive example among the elite universities reconsidering the role of the study of religion, but even at Yale the challenge of the dual role had to be faced by the faculty of the new religion department. Each member of the new department was expected to bring both a demonstrated competence in an academic discipline and their own spiritual practice to bear on the subject of religion.

The composition of this department of religion, formed to bring hope and understanding to the world through the study of religion, was wide-ranging. The list of sought-after faculty members included a psychologist, an anthropologist, a historian of Christianity, a specialist in Near Eastern religions, a scholar of Jewish tradition, a scholar of Islam, a modern linguist, and a philosopher. The committee's language was as lofty in setting forth their plan for the department as it was sobering in explaining why the department was deemed to be so important: "If Yale is looking for a venture which will be acclaimed for its leadership and vision in the country and in the world we believe that this is the venture. . . . Yale is committed, as is all the modern world, to a belief in the value of unprejudiced study of man's problems; it must therefore believe that such a study of prayer, faith and deeds will be no less profitable than the same sort of study in economics and agriculture."[2] The committee's tone conveyed a guarded hopefulness, but less certainty than some professors at Yale had hoped for.

The Yale report had been commissioned by the university's president, Charles Seymour, and the Fellows of Yale. They asked a committee of nine to examine the place and function of religion at Yale. The committee's recommendations for improvements in religion in postwar life at Yale were divided into three areas: religion as worship, religion in undergraduate life, and religion as knowledge. Unlike Princeton University's committee, the Yale committee was asked to examine the practice and study of religion together. The subcommittee responsible for the third area—religion as knowledge—was chaired by Erwin R. Goodenough, professor of the history of religion.[3] Goodenough was the only scholar of religion on the committee, other than Yale's chaplain, a fact that was not overlooked by several of the divinity school professors.

Religious educator and divinity school professor Clarence Shedd was frustrated because of his conviction that the work of the already existing divinity school was for the most part ignored in the committee's report. No divinity school faculty members, for example, were asked to serve on the committee. Moreover, Goodenough was part of a Yale faculty faction that wanted religion to be studied with more detachment than divinity school professors, who had professional interests in training ministers, could provide. In Goodenough's eyes, this committee report, recommending a new department to study religion, was an opportunity for a fresh start at Yale.

The report of the committee began with an acknowledgment that modern colleges had broken away from the theological authoritarianism of colonial New England. Modern education, the committee noted, had given rise to a "gulf that is fixed between the religious and the secular approach to knowledge." The "clear result" of that gulf, it declared, "is anarchy, moral and intellectual, which it is imperative for us to order from within lest it come to be ordered from without, as it has been in the totalitarian state." The committee's admission that the modern university was as aimless as the sectarian college was dogmatic echoed earlier critiques of the value-neutral German university, which was left powerless when the state made value-laden demands. Referring to a European university's recent statement about the importance of positive spiritual values in courses, it called for the rejection of a "neutral university, without character and principles."[4] In addition to calling for a new religion department at Yale, the report of the committee encouraged other colleges to follow Yale's lead for the good of society. Other schools needed a department, the argument went, for reasons similar to those at Yale. Colleges across the nation had lost their moral center. That center could be regained only through the renewal of religion's role on campus.

Chapel attendance at Yale had become voluntary in 1926, and since 1933, the university schedule had not been designed to include a free period during the day when every student would be able to attend chapel. Although the university had appointed a full-time chaplain in the 1930s, the committee hoped to point out what it saw as past encroachments on religious life at Yale as part of its goal of leading other faculty to see "religion as an important body of knowledge."[5] But the committee also wanted to distinguish between the issues of the past (mandatory chapel and religious instruction) and of the present (cooperation among campus ministers and the academic study of religion).

The report pointed to two trends on campus that were at odds with one another: the ecumenical spirit among Protestant groups generally, yet a fierce denominational loyalty among some of the larger Protestant groups. As Douglas Sloan explained in *Faith and Knowledge*,[6] the leaders of the larger Protestant denominations during this period increased the attention they paid to campus ministry. But the Yale committee discouraged the tendency to stress denominational identity on campus: "This impact of sectarian interests upon a nonsectarian university like Yale . . . is fraught with difficulties. . . . This Committee disapproves any organic duplication on the campus of the many sectarian divisions which characterize the present body of Protestantism."[7]

In the second section of their report, an examination of student religious life on campus, the committee addressed the campus spirit at Yale as it existed between the two world wars. They complained of a "mood of cynicism and aggressive secularism which was evident throughout the life of the nation" and worried about those on campus whose "religious convictions appeared to be intellectually discredited."[8] Moreover, the committee made it clear that not only was religious belief endangered by this mood but there was a natural connection between religious belief and citizenship, and so the understanding of citizens' moral obligations to the community was also threatened. When citizens do not share fundamental religious beliefs and assumptions, society cannot hold together, they argued. Or, more forcefully put, individuals would have no reason to fight to preserve a society when few notions about that society were held in common. When, as the committee wrote, "the very nature of moral obligation became obscured," no one could predict what would happen.[9]

This part of the committee's report was a reaction to the earlier waning of religious sentiment and its importance that had taken place on the campuses over the 1920s and 1930s. By April 1945, they could note "the disappearance of strong antipathy against religion" and less "prejudice" against the religious presence on campus. These were days of hope that the place properly accorded to religion might be renewed.

This was not, however, the primary concern of Erwin R. Goodenough, leading contributor to the third part of the report and longtime adversary of the university's divinity school professors. This concluding section of the report, "Religious Scholarship in a Modern University:

The Need for Research in Religion," went through several revealing drafts. An early draft of the opening paragraph began as follows:

> America has spent a great deal of money upon religious faculties and institutions. . . . But the religious scholars of the country are, with a few sporadic exceptions, dedicated to the task of propagating some religious point of view, Jewish, Protestant, Catholic. . . . [They are] uniformly committed to one or another religious tradition. Meanwhile, in the rest of its study our modern world has taken a different path. . . . Its loyalty is to fact, not to any explanation of fact. In religious study, on the other hand, men are still protagonists of traditional major premises. Of course we all work from preconceptions. But the preconception of modern scholarship is that we may, perhaps, through careful study, come to a clearer understanding of ourselves and our environment; the preconception of religious scholarship has been that by study we may better understand, propagate, and adapt to each new generation the religious traditions, in whole or in part, of the fathers. . . . To frightened and perplexed humanity they must be able to say with complete confidence, "We have the truth."[10]

In both style and content, such a proclamation was vintage Goodenough. The subcommittee, however, was not in full agreement with such a bold statement and opted for a straightforward but potentially less offensive beginning: "The modern university and its scholars, like the sages of every civilization, must transmit the classics of the past together with their ideals and values. But the modern university has an obligation in addition which is new in the history of learning. . . . The modern university recognizes no ultimate authority but facts, and its final loyalty is to these, not to any given explanation of them. Religious study has never adequately adapted itself to this new approach."[11]

Whether the earlier draft or the later is taken as the better expression of the committee's intent, the message was clear. A new and better way to study and teach religion was now possible. The committee was careful, though, to distinguish between the training of ministers, which was the province of the divinity school, and this new form of undergraduate and graduate study: "In suggesting such an approach to religion we have not at all in mind 'killing in order to dissect.' . . .

Understanding and reinterpreting the truth of a specific religious heritage has an essential place in our civilization, and no completely objective study of religion could pose as a substitute for it."[12] This respectful dismissal of the divinity school's work as it related to modern research was, again, classic Goodenough and proved irritating to Yale Divinity School professors Robert Calhoun and Clarence Shedd. Calhoun and Shedd understood all truth to be God's truth, and the symbolic or actual removal of the divinity school from the broader mission of the college and graduate departments was frustrating and philosophically unintelligible to them. According to them, Goodenough and the other committee members had simply erected an ill-conceived wall between the college and the divinity school in the attempt to divide what in fact was not divisible.

The arguments put forth by the committee show clearly how the expectations of a dual role for the religion department created a fault line at the base of the foundation of such departments. One might have thought that if any school were to be successful in attempting to create a department of religion separate from the practical advocacy of religion, it would be one whose divinity school handled such matters at the graduate level. Professors like Goodenough, who believed there was no need for an undergraduate department that encouraged religious belief and practice, had little to gain by including practical religious concerns with the search for academic truth about religion. It is important to note that Goodenough and the committee did not argue that the study of religion should have nothing to do with the practice of it. Rather, they contended that the practice of religion should be studied not to *improve* the practice but to *understand* the practice. Clarence Shedd and Robert Calhoun, on the other hand, needed the divinity school to retain a role in the academic search for religious truth in order to keep a place in the realm of university discourse in the first place.

In drawing a firm line between university and seminary, Goodenough posited that "it is only the universities, not the churches or seminaries, which can hope to discover how we may, without destructive schizophrenia, at once pray and question, and so be fully men." Such a study of the practices of prayer, worship, or Scripture would finally help determine what exactly constituted religion, "the hope and inspiration of mankind . . . [or] the opium of the masses. . . . One of the most urgent needs is an investigation to find out where the truth really lies."[13] These words reveal that lying alongside the concern with religious truth (if not actually underlying that concern) was Goodenough and the committee's concern for the practical needs of students.

The committee asserted that the study of religion "must begin not with God but with man" and that the only reason to study religion was "to get understanding."[14] The authors of the report put forward this humanist argument throughout. It was, of course, the same argument that George Thomas and other neoorthodox thinkers had denounced in their jeremiads against modernity: namely, that humans are inherently worthwhile and should be respected as such; they are fascinating creatures capable of good, evil, language, music, love, jealousy, religious expression, and disbelief. The appeal to a transcendent reality is not required for ethics and beauty.[15]

After composing a list of the most important subdisciplines that were to have made up this ideal undergraduate and graduate religion department, the committee twice called upon other universities to do the same. They added, "Religion is so important an aspect of human life that no university is doing its duty toward young men which does not offer them the best obtainable instruction in the field . . . and best results are obtained from instruction which approaches religion and its problems with objectivity."[16] Objectivity was the battle cry that frustrated many divinity school professors at Yale, but such an ideal was not considered by Goodenough and the committee to be in opposition to practical religious wisdom, only the sectarian teaching of Christianity.

Objectivity in approaching religion and other research data was the intent of many academics, but most college religious educators during this era had two problems with such an approach. They claimed it was both unattainable and undesirable. Objectivity was unattainable because every professor approached his or her work from a certain perspective, and religion teachers were bound to have the perspective that religion was a good thing for the most part—at least that the best kind of religion was likely to be thought helpful to students. Objectivity was undesirable because the crisis of Western civilization, however one defined it, demanded not the cold objectivity of a Nazi university, but a renewal of values that were central to civilization and democracy.[17]

Religious Facts and Moral Values

On February 9, 1946, the Yale Corporation voted to create the new religion department on recommendation of the "committee appointed to Study Spiritual and Moral Aspects of Post-war Campus Life."[18] The old Department of Religion, the Faculty of the Divinity School, became the Department of Divinity. The new Department of Religion was designed to be responsible for the undergraduate majors and for work leading to graduate degrees. The next week, Erwin R. Goodenough wrote President Seymour with further advice for those who would lead the department: "If we want real advance in religious knowledge it must be not by developing more and more elaborate techniques for rationalizing a revealed code of right and wrong, whether it be the code of Christianity, of Confucianism, or of the Southern Gentleman, but by getting down to the real facts of religious and moral motivation."[19]

Goodenough was asked to join the executive committee of the department. He hoped the department could leave behind the old model of Protestants, Catholics, and Jews teaching students to be loyal. According to Goodenough, "they had a commitment to a type of conclusion in their research which marks all of their work as ultimately sectarian."[20] The university was not the place for such indoctrination. Yale was a university that hoped to lead the way in the creation of new knowledge but also possessed a concern for passing along the great traditions of Western civilization and Christianity to college students.

President Seymour expressed his own hopes for the department, significantly at odds with Goodenough's, when he wrote to a potential contributor to the university's new religion department: "I sympathize with the desire that something more than an abstract study of religion is necessary to strengthen the faith of our students."[21] His press release for the Sunday papers on May 5, 1946, focused on the practical goal of giving students an appreciation of "the religious background of contemporary life and its relationship to contemporary problems." Explaining the department's formation, Seymour stated,

> The University has always recognized the role of religion as central to its life and history. The war has only made more apparent its place in world thought and culture. The young men who through their service

in the armed forces saw the impact of religion upon varying traditions and cultures expect the college to help them understand and interpret their profound spiritual experience. It is our hope, in creating this department, that these young men who think so deeply about the future of the nation and of the world may, through their knowledge of the religious tradition, see its power in the creation of a civilization illumined and strengthened by its insights.[22]

Seymour's statements contained the basic elements of a rationale put forth in the 1940s for the teaching of religion to undergraduates—namely, that religion should have an important role in the university because it helped form character for a democratic civilization. The experience of the war focused educators on religion's importance. Students had changed and would require or need instruction in religion. The future of the nation and civilization depended on knowledge of and insights from religious traditions.[23]

In 1947, the Reverend John Schroeder was chosen to lead Yale's new Department of Religion. A graduate of Union Seminary in New York City, Schroeder served as minister of the State Street Church in Portland, Maine, and was considered by the Yale Corporation "qualified for this post both by virtue of his theological background and by his intimate contacts with undergraduates, as Master of Calhoun College." His style of teaching at Yale College was described as a "sympathetic and understanding approach to undergraduate interest in religion."[24]

Clarence Shedd's ideas for Schroeder's new department were clarified in a letter from Shedd to divinity school dean Luther Weigle. Shedd wanted to supplement the new department "with some courses that in the hands of a scholar with evangelistic interests might have deep religious consequences in the lives of students." Shedd wanted a new faculty member "whose scholarship gives him standing with his faculty colleagues and who at the same time has a real passion for using his teaching as a means of Christian evangelism." Shedd praised several courses that lent themselves "in a special way to evangelizing purposes. I think for example, of a course like that which George Thomas is giving this year at Princeton on contemporary religious ideas." Shedd's son had taken the course while at Princeton. Shedd was most enthusiastic about the potential for New Testament courses that focused on the "great throbbing religious ideas—the kind of course that inevitably confronts the students with the personality of Jesus Christ in such a way as to make a decision about him an inescapable matter rather than a matter of intellectual option."[25]

Schroeder's own concern for students enrolled in religion courses was evident in his comments to President Seymour the next month. Seymour had requested information about the usefulness of religion courses, as he was planning to discuss the department with a potential contributor of a faculty chair. After reading students' comments on his course, Schroeder wrote, "They have persuaded me, as many [students] asked me to do, to give them a more precise view of my own religious belief. I've tried so hard to be objective with them."[26] He included the students' answers to his final exam question: Have your ideas about religion changed as a result of this course?

A Catholic student explained how his mind had changed: "I believe I am today a believer in a God and in the value of a moral ethical life. . . . These ideas are definite changes from a religion which worships Christ and his family [Catholicism] to the first enlightened thought I have ever done on the subject." Another student, a veteran of World War II, wrote, "Before I was an agnostic, and I still remain so; but I am convinced that there is some force, varying in different degrees amongst different men, which pervades . . . our entire world. So, Mr. Schroeder, I have you to thank for opening my mind to a great many things which are extremely important." Yet another veteran commented, "If a person goes into the course with the usual rather unreasoned belief, it should strengthen rather than weaken it. Religion is a . . . changing force in life and as such should be understood by the student."[27]

The students' answers are themselves rich with raw observations, but more interesting still is that these were responses Schroeder considered exemplary of his work in the classroom. These answers give insight into Schroeder's own hopes and dreams for his courses and department. For instance, another student's reflection exemplified the general feeling of Protestant educators in universities: religion should be respected because it is that which cannot truly be known: "Prior to entering the course I had a vague conviction that man could somehow gradually explain away the unknown, but after pouring [sic] through the comments of many great minds, I am all the more impressed with the 'unknown' and am convinced that everything can not be known–that there will always be some unknown influence." Schroeder also tracked the nature of criticisms directed at the religion courses in the new department. He noted that one typical complaint was that the professor's approach was "too objective."

Caught between a group of students and some divinity school faculty members who wanted more advocacy in the classroom, and other students and faculty members who desired less, Schroeder pondered how he might change the nature of the courses: "The students are searching for a personal faith. I think I would rather have criticism of this sort than to hear that our courses are merely evangelical. However, I am planning this summer to revamp my own course, Religion 10, and weight it more heavily in terms of personal faith." He remarked on "how much help they need in organizing the knowledge they get in college into a functionary philosophy," hoping that courses such as his would "enable them to find more specific answers to some of their religious questions."[28]

Other criticisms of the Yale department included student concerns that its courses were not as popular as Princeton's offerings. The Department of Religion at Princeton was held up as a model by faculty and students alike in documents throughout the archival record. Department chair John Schroeder, in his first report to President A. Whitney Griswold, successor to President Seymour, brought this to his attention: "I am concerned about our standing in the college. As you may know, the Yale Daily News editorialized against the department this spring. The burden of the News' attack was that the Department of Religion at Princeton is one of the most popular departments there, while our own department limps behind the procession here." Schroeder decried the "invidious contrasts the News made between the two departments."[29] Whether Yale's religion courses were as "popular" as Princeton's is difficult to determine, but both did share a focus on students' personal needs for faith. It was just such a model for the new religion courses that leading Protestant foundations wanted to replicate at colleges across America. The goal was to populate college campuses with respected academics and intellectuals whose credentials would be accepted by their counterparts in other disciplines but whose personal commitment to the Christian faith would allow them to teach mainstream Protestant theology (often neoorthodox thought) as "religion."

What Brand of Christianity for the Departments?

This question was a matter of great concern to college teachers on both sides of the dual tension within religion programs on campus. For instance, Clarence Shedd responded to the Yale committee's report in a letter to President Charles Seymour. Shedd took issue with the implication that the document was a "comprehensive report on the 'place and function of religion in the post-war life of Yale University.'" He explained that the committee appeared to have had no awareness of what place the divinity school held in the wider university: "It seems to assume that the Divinity School is a typically sectarian 'seminary,' and that its relation to the University is that simply of dependence upon the University for 'support.' . . . The facts are just the opposite." Shedd pointed to the divinity school's participation in the existing graduate religion department's successful production of PhD candidates, more than 120 between 1925 and 1945. He assessed the divinity school's scholarship as being "as soundly critical and objective as those of any other department in the Graduate School."[30]

Shedd's strongest critique was saved for the proposed "utopian" department of religion: "The so-called 'ideal department' reads like a throw-back to the closing decades of the 19th century or the first decade of the 20th, with their proposals of a new religion based upon science." An examination of their correspondence reveals that President Seymour apparently took this particular criticism of Shedd's directly to Goodenough, as the latter argued this point with President Seymour in a letter to him in early 1946: "That what is proposed smacks of the vintage of '1909' is right, but to call it such is high praise." He went on to explain that "before the war, at its height in '1909,' there were a great number of brilliant scholars using, as was suggested, what was very close to the method we proposed." What happened, in Goodenough's estimation, was the First World War: "It was a time when in all humanistic and spiritual studies the world began the great reaction away from a critical study of data, to put authority in its place."[31]

Using Union Seminary as an example, Goodenough pointed to the "dogmatists" who ensured that historical studies were at a low ebb: "Niebuhr, Van Dusen, Tillich (who is better than the others by far)." After detailing the abysmal situation in Old and New Testament studies, Goodenough lambasted *Formgeschichte* as "basically a game of academic checkers." His final argument to Seymour, which he sent to each member of the committee, took issue with the advocative nature of religious scholarship: "The belief of your Committee was that if we want real advance in religious knowledge it must be not by developing more and more elaborate techniques for rationalizing a revealed code."[32] Responding to his comments, President Seymour explained to Goodenough that he would "want to re-study and to put [Goodenough's letter] into the hands of the committee."[33]

The undergraduate department of religion increasingly concerned divinity school professor Clarence Shedd, and he felt that the committee had "failed dismally in the section which I have assumed to be its primary concern. . . . It presents no coherent plan; it simply assumes that undergraduate instruction in religion may be left dependent upon the presence in the University of the research faculty."[34] According to Shedd, the committee did not pay special attention to the differences between faculty research and the teaching of undergraduates, in part because they did not consider the latter to be as important as the former. The report was indeed expected to have covered this area of undergraduate life more fully than it did. He was quick to point to the 1935 Princeton report, on which George Thomas's departmental work had been based: "I can send you a copy of the much better report which was adopted by Princeton University ten years ago." The suggestion was curious because the Princeton report draws an equally strict distinction between the work of a divinity school / seminary and a university.[35] Shedd also made recommendations about the publicity of the Yale religion report of 1945, which was highlighted in the *New York Times* later that summer: "I earnestly hope that the sections of the present report which I have criticized may not be favorably considered or reach the stage of publicity. It would be a real blow to the Divinity School." Finally, Shedd remarked to President Seymour that his colleague Robert Calhoun had also written a memorandum regarding the report, and he offered to send Calhoun's comments to anyone who might wish to see them.

Professor Calhoun's comments filled fifteen pages. He took issue with several aspects of the report: the call for "objective study," misconceptions about the scientific method, an assumption of the inferiority of

Christian scholars who research Christianity, the advocacy of a strict Baconian basis for a university, the statement that modern universities are based on facts, and the desire to have humanities and social sciences discover evidence as physical sciences do. He disputed the claim that outsiders could understand Christianity as well as Christians, and he was not convinced that research scholars would be able to teach undergraduates well.[36]

Shedd's analysis of the postwar situation as it related to religion and higher education was similar to many call-to-arms articles stressing the importance of a liberal arts education.[37] Many professors agreed that science and practical technological training were necessary to prepare for and win the war, but that a liberal arts education would be necessary for surviving the aftermath, which was just as important. Shedd was encouraged by the number of educators who had acknowledged a religious or theological foundation as necessary for maintaining meaning and unity in higher education: "The growth of this conviction augurs well for higher education, but these affirmations will remain pious platitudes unless we do the hard thinking required for their implementation in the aims, structure and curriculum of our colleges and universities."[38] Shedd wanted religion to become integral to the whole life of the college, and he made recommendations to that end.

For Shedd, religion was "the golden thread that draws together all the separate aspects of culture. . . . Faith is that which helps individuals place all the facts learned in education into a meaningful whole, the light of the wisdom of the ages."[39] He peppered his comments with references to Catholic thinkers such as Cardinal Newman and scholars from "the Hebrew-Christian heritage." Shedd listed faith in God and "long devotion to . . . goodness, beauty, justice and brotherhood" as the by-products of a good college education. He encouraged all professors to strive to include religious interpretation of their materials when the materials seemed to demand it.[40]

With language similar to that of the Yale committee statement on a religion department, Shedd called for the college to be a community of teachers and students who seek truth. Shedd was convinced that if truth was sought and religion given its place, then education could be whole again, offering its wholeness to students and the country, even to civilization. Shedd was fond of the saying, "Religion is both caught and taught," a catchy phrase that can be found in numerous articles throughout religion and education literature of the 1940s and 1950s. Shedd and his colleagues were not concerned that religion (i.e., Western religious traditions), if subjected to the "fair" kind of inquiry that their "believing" colleagues had always given Western religious life, would somehow come up short. They believed that their brand of modern Christianity would not be found wanting if studied more rigorously. The dual role of such a department was primarily of concern to those who may have had an appreciation of Christianity in general, but who dreamed of a more objective search for truth among the religions. Erwin R. Goodenough at Yale was just such a scholar.

Professor of the history of religions at Yale from 1919 until his death in 1965,[41] at Yale, he never integrated into the life of the divinity school. The fact that he was chosen as the only religion scholar to be a member of the Yale religion committee that delivered the much-publicized report in 1945 did not endear him to Clarence Shedd or Robert Calhoun.

For Goodenough, not only was the act of investigating religious devotion, formation, or community imperative for the academy—it was a spiritually enhancing activity. He wanted nothing to do with the "democracy, freedom, and religion" group of religion teachers who felt that Christianity was the best religious form for a free democracy, especially America.[42]

He was distressed not only by the piety of religion teachers but also by the irrelevance of much that biblical scholarship brought to the table during the first half of the twentieth century: "The pressure of contemporary problems is too great for it to matter much whether Q was in one piece, or was a series of disconnected leaves . . . or whether there ever was a Q at all or not." Other scholars in the fields of sociology, psychology, and theology were offering something to people that would directly affect their lives, but he feared that biblical scholars were "doomed to be superseded like the old herbalists." Aware of how disciplines had arisen and disappeared or changed, he wrote, "We cannot be alchemists endlessly repeating the same experiments." Then, in a refrain that was repeated at midcentury by many of the founders of religion programs who longed for relevance after the government's wartime use of their campus made humanists and social scientists appear less useful, he proclaimed, "The only excuse for biblical scholarship, like all scholarship, is that it promises to tell men, directly or indirectly, something important for their way of life. New Testament studies has 'failed' in this regard."[43]

Studying Christianity was of interest to both Goodenough and George Thomas because it was of inherent historical interest and because American society was still Christian enough to warrant better understanding it, but he pleaded with Society of Biblical Literature members regarding their method: "We cannot go on simply . . . asking questions we know now we shall never answer, questions in which society has lost interest. We must begin afresh."[44] To summarize Goodenough's rationale for teaching and studying religion as a subject, religion must be studied not because it offers a more credible view than science or other modes of knowing but because "people do not feel that they can wait for the truth . . . and [so they] look for their final values in ways that are recognizably religious."[45] Goodenough's world produced new faiths because people must go on living with meaning, beauty, and truth. New faiths were not undesirable so long as adherents and scholars knew this, understood this, and avoided creating new forms of absolutism. Studying and then teaching religion as a subject was beneficial not because life would be necessarily richer with a deeper understanding of religion but because the modern individual must be made aware of this desire for certainty and authoritarianism: "We cannot live by [science] alone. We must live also by ideas and ideals, Beauty, Freedom, Intelligence, Justice, the Good . . . At least we must feel that we are living by them, if our moral stamina is to remain. Can we live by these—and this is the real question before civilization at the moment—in the full consciousness that they are necessities for our functioning but not necessarily for the functioning of nature about us, and that for all we know these and other supreme 'values' are only projections of our desires?"[46]

Erwin R. Goodenough was not a radical empiricist, nor did he deny the importance of religious activity, communities, or texts. He was suspicious of teaching religious values to undergraduates with the expressed intent of claiming their lives for the church. He was even more concerned that such teaching would detract from his grand vision for the future of the study of religion. He understood the dual expectations of new religion departments during a time of national crisis, and his goal was to deliver better citizens to the world through deeper understanding, not necessarily through religious conversion. It was a fine and difficult line to walk, one that Princeton assistant professor and ethicist Paul Ramsey knew well.

Religion department founders and administrators, faculty colleagues, graduates, and local religious leaders who supported such developments were faced with a difficult choice. They were able to create departments at their elite institutions because of the combination of the upheaval of the wartime campus, societal and academic chaos of other sorts, the beginnings of a turn toward religion, the last gasp of Protestant educators' hopes, the desire to instill meaning into the lives of a changing type of student, philanthropic support, and other opportunities made possible by the state of the college ideal within the humanities crises. However, they also wanted to gain academic respectability for their subject (Christian theology or philosophy, church history or biblical studies) and thus the dual role of religious departments—or the dual challenge—was to create a department with a set of expectations that were more value-laden or pious (their way into the school) and attempt to create academic legitimacy while still using the divinity school curricular model, given that most faculty or potential faculty were coming from such training. Each school and founder saw varied results, and Harvard was no different.

CHAPTER SIX

Harvard Dissents Feature Tillich, Niebuhr, and White

At least two problems remained for those professors who held the belief that religion might hold the answer to a civilization in crisis. First, how could something so particular as a religion, much less one particular religion (Christianity), be called upon to unify a curriculum or university community in the modern world? Second, what exactly would "religion" have to amount to for it to provide the basis for a renewal of higher education? Besides underscoring the importance of the dual role that undergraduate religion programs generally were asked to play, these two questions were at the center of the postwar curricular soul-searching on the parts of Harvard University and the University of Chicago. Both decided not to create separate departments of religion, but only Harvard relied heavily upon its divinity school for a renewal of the teaching of religion to undergraduates.

Although Harvard and Chicago at midcentury steered clear of founding a department of religion in part out of concern for the unavoidable tensions in the dual role such departments faced, that dual role was present regardless, whether as part of a separate religion department or not.[1] The argument at Harvard against religion becoming a guiding force for the undergraduate curriculum was laid out in *General Education in a Free Society: Report of the Harvard Committee*

1945 ("the Redbook"). The authors of the report argued that democracy leads to creativity and thereby freedom, but also divergence. General education, it was hoped, would prepare students for an informed and responsible life in the service of the nation: "Education seeks to do two things: help young persons fulfill the unique, particular functions in life which it is in them to fulfill, and fit them so far as it can for those common spheres which, as citizens and heirs to a joint culture, they will share with others."[2] The Harvard report pointedly did not acknowledge any role for the church in this educational goal: "The sphere of the family or the church is not the sphere of educational institutions."[3] But the Harvard committee did point out that the church and religious life could be valuable resources for the university so long as they did not prove divisive.[4]

This divisiveness was, of course, the primary reason for discerning the tension emanating from the teaching of religion within universities and even within religion programs, where those existed. If the spheres and roles were overlapping and neither belonged wholly to the other, but they were each helpful to the other, how could one serve both spheres and play both roles from within one department? Harvard officially decided to leave this problem of the dual role of undergraduate religion instruction to a relatively weak divinity school with a small faculty working from an ill-defined mission. Harvard also relied on Willard Sperry, an overworked divinity school professor who was also dean of the chapel and responsible for the religious life of undergraduates, to resolve the tension of academic instruction versus pious advocacy. In the chapter entitled "The Search for Unity," the report committee proclaimed, "The spirit and intention of General Education is training in what unites, rather than what divides modern man."

According to the Harvard report of 1945, not only could religion not unify a curriculum, but the very subject was thought likely to undermine the unity of an educational mission because it proved divisive. On the other hand, the committee also wrote that "these are exceptional times and we must have something at our core, so even though religion shouldn't be the center we need it for the moment."[5] Thus the committee's report can be seen to have been ambivalent, dismissing religion's importance to the university while asserting its value. On balance, however, the committee was decidedly negative about religion's role in the curriculum. For example, regarding the sad state of affairs they found higher education generally to reflect, the Harvard committee agreed with Robert Hutchins's complaint about the dangers of vocation specialization:

> This condition, which seemingly robs liberal education of any clear, coherent meaning, has for some time disturbed people and prompted a variety of solutions. Sectarian, particularly Roman Catholic, colleges have of course their solution, which was generally shared by American colleges until less than a century ago: namely, the conviction that Christianity gives meaning and ultimate unity to all parts of the curriculum, indeed to the whole life of the college. Yet this solution is out of the question in publicly supported colleges and is practically, if not legally, impossible in most others. Some think it the Achilles' heel of democracy that, by its very nature, it cannot foster general agreement on ultimates, and perhaps must foster the contrary. But whatever one's view, religion is not now for most colleges a practicable source of intellectual unity.[6]

Thus they could not agree with Hutchins's solution to the situation, a solution that entailed subscribing to a fixed curriculum of general education focusing on the great books and perennial questions. Such a plan hinted at too much of a predetermined educational system. Harvard spurned not only official institutional religions' answers to the vocational problem but also Hutchins's own "religious" answer based on Aristotelian first principles cum Aquinas.

If Not the Center, Then a Central Role

In 1947, two years after Harvard decided that religion could not be central to postwar curricular reform, a committee including public theologian Reinhold Niebuhr and president of the University of Chicago Ernest Colwell studied religion's place in the curriculum and reported on a new initiative at Harvard.[7] They recommended that Harvard establish a "center of religious learning whose quality and prestige will be worthy of a warm welcome from the other Departments of the University."[8] The report illuminated the latest compromise between church and university. Church leaders agreed to have all the presuppositions of their faith put under the scientific microscope in return for having the facts of such a faith on display for all to see. The committee wrote that "the most helpful intercourse between the religious, the philosophic, and the scientific elements of a culture can be attained in the atmosphere of freedom prevailing in our great Liberal Arts centers of learning . . . [where] neither any modern nor ancient presupposition of faith which imparts meaning to life should remain unexamined."[9]

The authors of the report were convinced that Christian doctrine would hold up under such a close examination of its effectiveness and logical coherence and were confident the university would proclaim it to be so. They were also assured that the only scholars included as examiners who had doctorates were Protestants with seminary credentials. The committee generally was satisfied that if religious presuppositions, whether liberal or conservative, were found to be logically coherent, they would be recognized as such.

This committee was aware of the new cultural bend toward religious interests of varying kinds. They made special mention of the fact that "the new interest in religious questions in academic communities" was related to the tension between the need for scientific study and moral reflection.[10] The committee asserted that the importance of teaching religion to college students arose from the observation that religious faith was necessary in the modern world, but that the modern world demanded that any claim to truth be held up to scientific scrutiny. The report contained signs that the struggle at Yale had been taken into consideration. Committee members saw the divinity school at Harvard as being integral to the undergraduate program in religious instruction, unlike at Yale, where the divinity school was kept at arm's length. The Harvard report was clear in its analysis of the need for undergraduate teaching in religion, though it held to the sentiments of the earlier report on general education by refusing to make religion the centerpiece at Harvard.

Niebuhr and the committee began with the observation that "everyone acquainted with university life is aware of the profound dissatisfaction felt by many thoughtful observers because, until very recently, most colleges have been following a policy of indifference to the whole

problem of education in the essentials of religious thought characteristic of Western civilization."[11] Such indifference was no longer an
option, according to them, because anyone who was "unacquainted
with the record of man's search for God has missed a most important
part" of humanity's education. More important, however, was that even
a "knowledge of the facts does not of itself produce the right attitudes."
There were right attitudes to be had, and without instruction in religion, even the most basic facts about life's meaning would be missed.[12]
It was not an absence of scholarship about religions, religious people,
or texts that was their concern. Rather, these committee members
wanted to encourage a particular kind of approach to undergraduate religious teaching, one that would produce these "right attitudes"
among students and an appreciation of Western civilization.

What then was their stance on the difficult tension between the academic freedom necessary to push beyond particular moral stances and
the presuppositions required by particular religious beliefs? They
argued that fear of violating "academic freedom may be pressed too
far." This was the case, they believed, because the "college or university
which dedicates itself to the search for truth does not by that fact evade
the responsibility for taking sides on a moral issue." In other words,
open-mindedness in the college does not mean "freedom from moral
commitment." They were committed to both an advocacy of Western
religious moral values and the advancement of knowledge about Christianity or religion in general in the classroom.[13]

The Harvard committee attempted to collapse the differences
between the dual roles of the religion program by highlighting their
complementary nature within the university. The division and tension,
however, remained: "To become aware of the authority of the intellectual ideal is to employ one means of discovering the authority of God.
To use the college classroom for the analysis and evaluation of the data
of religious experience is therefore not to lose touch with the strictly
academic task but to win a new understanding of what it is and new
insight into the unity of the spiritual life."[14] The committee saw no conflict between the dual roles given a religion program. The two necessarily work together because they need each other. Without religious
reflection, moral commitments were difficult to make in the academy,
and without academic rigor, the worst of religious belief would become

the ideal. The committee cited the new departments at Columbia, Princeton, and Yale as examples of "how the winds of opinion are blowing on this issue."[15]

Harvard was often the leader in curricular reform, but in establishing a department of religion, its review committee looked toward their Ivy League colleagues and similarly rigorous schools.[16] Schools such as the University of Pennsylvania, Stanford, and Washington University were also closely following developments at these four Ivy League schools as Harvard's leaders made their decisions, and each time one more school argued successfully for the importance of teaching religion to undergraduates, the case became that much stronger for the next school's advocates. The lack of undergraduate connection to the divinity school was the most important gap cited by those who wrote the Harvard report to make suggestions regarding what they considered religion's place at the university.[17]

In 1945, just two years before this report was released to internal constituents, Harvard's *General Education in a Free Society* had proclaimed that religion would not be the unifier of a curriculum regardless of how important it was to the entire university. The 1945 study declared early and often that religion would not work as a basis for curricular reform.

President Conant and the faculty may have vaguely appreciated religion's importance but could not fathom how to make it work for a pluralist university. The divinity school would have to suffice, though undergraduates took few classes there. Undergraduates did take courses regularly in the Harvard philosophy department, where Morton White was part of a revamped department himself—one that no longer carried the Christian water of the divinity school to undergraduates, as previous generations of philosophers had done.[18]

Teaching about Religions, Not Training the Religious

Professor White's concern about the dual role of religion departments is representative of the tension that such departments faced at their founding. He looked disparagingly on the "increasingly fashionable" effort to impart religious education to college students. He posed the perennial question about religious instruction in the university when he noted, "Those who wish to introduce religious instruction into the undergraduate college and who adopt this more recent way of construing religion must now ask themselves just what they mean by religion."[19] White's concern pointed to the dual role for departments of religion. In his view, churches and synagogues were the places that best inculcated belief, and religion departments should play no role in that. White disdained such a dual role but saw its reality clearly, noting that to encourage religious feeling or ideas was untrue to the aims of undergraduate education, if not untrue to the aims of religion itself. White saw religion as a complete way of life—take all of it or none of it. He cast doubt on the notion of religion as a subject worthy of teaching, questioning whether religion existed "generally," outside of religions as they were themselves practiced in particular.

This was the reason he referred disparagingly to a group of Niebuhr's followers as "atheists for Niebuhr." He claimed they loved Niebuhr's political analysis of human finitude and hubris-become-national-immorality but would not accept his foundational religious ideals. White would have none of this, claiming that one must be taken along with the other.

White fought President Nathan Pusey's new administration at Harvard as it turned its sights toward encouraging religious education on campus through the divinity school and any other department that would have it. Harvard professor George Williams recalls that White was not the only member of the faculty who felt this way: "Pusey's programmatic representation as a classicist of the older ideal of the Christian College would not go unchallenged by eminent members of the Faculty of Arts and Sciences."[20]

White concluded that "we should not make the effort [to inculcate religion] in colleges which are not religious institutions, and that we become frankly sectarian in our teaching of religion and therefore limit higher religious instruction to the divinity schools which are properly devoted to the study and the propagation of specific religions conceived as total ways of life, knowledge, emotion and action."[21] White ostensibly was not opposed to religion; rather, he wanted to protect what he saw as the integrity of both the undergraduate educational process and the process of religious indoctrination, and never the two should meet. He characterized the difficulty or tension inherent in this dual role for religion instruction in the college as the difference between being a teacher of feeling and willing and a teacher of knowing. He strongly advocated teaching students *about* religion, but he rejected the effort to teach them how to become more religious. White still believed that religion could be studied objectively, but not by those individuals who wanted to advocate religious experience and morality. Divinity schools would be excellent places for the training of ministers, but undergraduate teaching of religion could not be properly executed by these same professors without thereby suffering from their own advocacy and thus the dual and confused role of the religion department.

In its report of 1947, Harvard's "religion" committee decided that the divinity school would be the place to start the program of teaching undergraduates, since "it would be easier to attract able teachers for undergraduate courses in religion if they could be assured of the cooperative support of a large and vigorous group of colleagues in the professional school." The course for which they saw the greatest demand was "Christianity—its origin, its history, its sects, and its major ideas." Their work as a committee brought them to a point of agreement with the authors of Harvard's report on *General Education in a Free Society*, concurring that "the objective of education is not just knowledge of values but commitment to them. . . . Education is not complete without moral guidance; and moral wisdom may be obtained from our religious heritage."[22] The Harvard committee hoped that divinity school professors could provide undergraduate instruction. At Yale University, the divinity school had been given a much less active role in the process of creating a new undergraduate religion department than at Harvard. In a move not dissimilar to Princeton's separation of its chapel from the new religion department, Yale had marked a clear distinction between its divinity school and its new religion department, the exact opposite of Harvard divinity school's integral role in its proposed undergraduate program.

Postwar Princeton Developments

As early as 1947, Professor Ramsey wrote about the relationship at Princeton among its chapel, student ministries, and the religion curriculum. This triad, which Princeton hoped to keep separate within the institution, was understood by most religious educators and organizations to be part of a whole. Ramsey, hired by George Thomas as the second person in the department during the war, spoke on behalf of the religion department. He highlighted the importance religion courses had in the new core curriculum adopted by Princeton. He emphasized the "grass roots" faculty movement to create the department, the creation of "bridge majors" between history, philosophy, and English, and the participation of religion professors in the wartime course "The Western Tradition of Man: Man and His Freedom."[23] This course was, during the war, "begun as an emergency measure for men who had only a semester or so in college before being drafted to fight for a freedom they knew little about." Thomas also had remarked that such young men needed to know why and for what they were fighting.[24]

After the war, Ramsey wrote, this course became a distribution requirement, helping emphasize "the role of religion in western civilization and its part in man's long struggle for freedom." Ramsey echoed Thomas's understanding that freedom was both democracy's great achievement and its most endangered constitutive part. During the war, faculty of each discipline or area of study were required to think about the discipline's contribution to the training of military men, and religion's contribution appeared to be clear-cut. Ramsey wrote, "Members of the faculty in religion frequently assist in public worship at the University Chapel and in the daily devotional services. They serve as advisors and leaders of student forum groups under the auspices of the Student Christian Association. . . . Instruction in religion strengthens the leadership and indeed general participation in the student [religious activities] program."[25]

Princeton University joined many schools in reconfiguring its undergraduate academic program during the war, and this new curriculum was adopted in 1947. Religion courses were added to history and philosophy courses as one option for fulfilling a distribution requirement. These subjects were placed within the humanities division and as an upper-level concentration option. In the *Journal of Higher Education*, Professor Robert Root explained the purpose of the religion curriculum within the new Princeton college plan of study with no appreciation for the fine distinctions between the practice and study of religion: "Religion, more particularly the Christian religion, is a guiding and activating principle for the whole of human living and right thinking, embracing our social and economic duty to our neighbor as well as those high and pure aspirations of spirit, those glimpses of the divine Being appropriate to inheritors of the kingdom of heaven. It is expected that the requirement of study in history, philosophy, and religion will serve to inculcate in the student the recognition of the essential unity of all knowledge, the habit of organizing and systematizing all his intellectual activities."[26] Root's description did not place an emphasis on separating practice and teaching about religion as the Princeton report attempted to do, but his perspective was not far from the desires of those teaching religion at Princeton.

Merrimon Cuninggim, a graduate of Yale Divinity School and professor at Pomona College, captured the spirit of the mid-1940s' crisis mentality coupled with jubilation that religion was on the way back into the classroom. Cuninggim's *The College Seeks Religion* was referred to for decades after its publication, as it related to the formation of college religion departments. His assessment of the issues, institutions, and ideas involving religion on campus proved helpful and important for advocates and critics alike. Cuninggim also invoked the trinity of chapel worship, campus ministries, and curricular programs in describing religion at Princeton.

Regarding the teaching of religion, he noted, "The secular trend in higher education in the early years of the century was reflected at Princeton in the elimination of all instruction in religion. But gradually the need was felt and the omission was recognized." Cuninggim did not gloss over the main difference between Yale's and Princeton's initial intentions (though he was not aware of the disagreement between parties at Yale, as described in chapter 3): "An interesting contrast with Yale is furnished by the philosophy behind the establishment of the new teaching position [at Princeton]. Whatever was the original intention when Princeton embarked on its enlarged program in the twenties, the result has been that the worship and teaching function are separated. Dean Wicks [chapel dean] offers no regular courses, and Professor Thomas has no direct connection with the chapel program."[27]

Advocating greater unification of the three separate parts of campus religion, he wrote the following: "This theory of separation, which until recently involved the activity program as a third separate sphere, is not unanimously defended at Princeton today. The planning for the future, to which reference has already been made, implies that an effort will be made to integrate the various provisions into an interrelated whole, without losing any of the gains which the programs have achieved separately."[28] The attempted separation of teaching and practice at Princeton did not escape the observations of Cuninggim, though his understanding was that any advantage in separation was not worth the loss of integration. In fact, the reasons for keeping them separate seemed artificial to many who considered religion to be a viable part of study and life. Professors George Thomas, Theodore M. Greene, Paul Ramsey, Dean Christian Gauss, and others at Princeton were firmly committed to the benefits to be gained, in their estimation, by separating practice from teaching. Courses, however, were taught with an understanding that Christianity would be presented as the best of many options; religion department professors could not fathom ignoring the chapel and campus ministry programs when called upon to serve them; journal articles written for the faithful proclaimed great strides for advocacy in the classroom; and letters written to other notables in the field suggested not duplicity but eagerness to bring the Christian truth to students.

One of the most telling remarks about the state of the teaching of religion in this period came from the report that Edwin Aubrey and George Thomas delivered after having made their "faculty consultation" visit to Iowa's famed School of Religion (twenty years old at the time of the visit). In the annual report of the school for 1946, the department head wrote,

> The second observation I want to report was made by Professor George F. Thomas of Princeton University. . . . He said, "Would it not improve your School if in addition to having teachers who represent the various religious groups, you should have at least one other who would represent NO religious group and so who might embody an entirely objective approach to the subject?" I should add that he was not only very appreciative of the spirit and work of our school, but also more or less dubious as to whether the kind of additional teacher he had in mind could readily, or even ever, be found.[29]

George Thomas had been frustrated with models such as Iowa because they perpetuated the conflation of teaching religion and teaching the practice of religion. He admired Iowa's program, however, because unlike Princeton at that time, Iowa employed a variety of interfaith (not simply ecumenical) voices in the school. Thomas's analysis of Iowa's program further highlights the striking tension between having religious individuals explain, if not promote, their own religious data and, in this case, having "at least one" teacher who might "embody an entirely objective approach to the subject."

The University of Iowa's annual report from the administrative director for the teaching of religion to undergraduates documented that 1,811 students were instructed in religion for the academic year 1946–47. The college's core course in religion was described as "just made to order to reveal in a very scholarly and yet warmly fraternal way both the historic and contemporary differences and unities of religious faith. What a chance it offers in a state university to teach intelligent understanding and brotherliness at the same time!"[30] Founded in 1927, the Iowa School of Religion was one of the first, if not the very first, state university to create a religion department. Its program was distinguished by four features: religion professors having duties in leading student life religious groups, core courses taught to thousands of students not majoring in religion (those majoring numbered in the single digits), a belief and practice that interfaith work was meaningful to students and the broader community, and finally, an attempt to have each religion taught by the practitioner of that particular religion.

Iowa's religion department staff members, along with others throughout the country, were particularly sensitive to criticisms of their program, given the prescriptive versus descriptive nature of the religion teaching divide. One stinging exchange took place between a University of Chicago Federated Theological Faculty professor and the Iowa administrative director. The Chicago faculty member asserted "in a rather uncomplimentary way" that the Iowa school was bound to the authority of religions being taught: "I suggested that after all the principle underlying our School seemed to me to be fundamentally the same as that underlying the federation of theological seminaries at the University of Chicago. He answers, 'Not so, for all the seminaries at the University of Chicago stand for freedom of thought and inquiry, while the school at Iowa admits the principle of authority.' I did not answer him, but I leave it to you to say which plan is the more broadly and fairly conceived."[31] The administrator, M. Willard Lampe, was supported financially in his work by John D. Rockefeller Jr., and the curricular model became known for its success in reaching many students on campus. Professors such as Howard Thurman—the first African American to serve on their Protestant faculty, albeit as a guest lecturer—regularly passed through the Iowa school.[32]

Tensions felt by Iowa faculty and staff mirrored what Yale, Princeton, Chicago, Stanford, Penn, Columbia, and others faced. Lofty language regarding the importance of the teaching of religion and the humanities during the 1940s was echoed by Professor Lampe:

> It is not quite like me to write in this aggressive and expansive sort of way. While I have not shunned new things I am naturally cautious and prefer to make haste slowly. Moreover I no longer possess cantankerous youth. Yet I am impressed as I am sure you are too by the overwhelming testimony that never in all history have we been in such a clear "race between education and catastrophe," and if education is to win, it will surely need the help of the kind of education we represent and believe in who are in this room as "trustee"—*trustees* of what to me in a world-saving spirit and idea.[33]

Lampe regularly used veiled language as he balanced his program between church leaders who wanted their denominations to be seen in the best light and taught well to students, and academic colleagues who were distrustful of the "interfaith" model, which amounted to what is more accurately called a "Protestant, Catholic, Jew model" (well before Will Herberg's successful monograph of that title). It was interdenominational plus a Catholic priest and rabbi teaching their own traditions to students, with little thought and some defensiveness in private memos regarding what was coming to be thought of as a nascent teaching of religion qua religion.[34] Lampe was clear that "the great opportunity we here have in working out a course in religion which will be satisfactory both to the religious groups and to a public educational institutions" is most important. "There are many who think that this is one of the great needs of democracy in our times." The Iowa model for a religion department was clear in its intention to create a "sympathetic study, under competent leadership, of each separate faith."[35]

Christianity as Curricular Center

The Yale report confirmed the need for but questioned the current capacity of religion to become central to the educational program, while the Harvard report on general education in the end dismissed religion as a unifying force on campus. Princeton continued to draw thin distinctions between its chapel programs and curriculum. And while several deliberately pro-Christianity voices were heard in higher education at the time, none in the mainstream was more strident than that of British theologian and University of North Carolina religion department founder and professor Arnold Nash. Nash's vision of the university, a new one and yet oddly traditional, was one in which the influence of the religion department would be so great as to enlist the other departments in support of its goal of developing the Christian student. Nash was convinced that Western civilization was near extinction and had only one hope for its survival—a turn toward Christian values. His work was appreciated and cited even by those Protestant educators who knew their own institutions would never allow the religion departments such influence. Most other founders of departments of religion resolved the tension between academic rigor and practical advocacy of religious values in favor of the former; Nash turned this dynamic on its head by calling for the resolution of any tension between advocacy and academic rigor in favor of advocacy.

Arnold Nash, a theologian by training, had been invited to create a department of religion at the University of North Carolina in 1947. His British education and old-world manners impressed several college faculty members in the American South during the 1950s. But these did not restrain him from boldly stating his own conviction that the constitutional ideal of state and church, so often discussed as part of the mission of state universities, was ill-conceived. His monograph *The University and the Modern World*, an influential work among Protestant educators, was both a Cold War treatise and an apologia for an American academic freedom based on the "Christian" way of life.[36]

In his nationally influential work *The Totalitarian University and Christian Higher Education*, Nash posited that developments in communist Russia and Nazi German universities were an incorrect response to a correct diagnosis of "the malady that besets higher education in liberal democratic countries." The malady was that the sciences as subjects of academic study had no "sense" of life's meaning or of how history should be interpreted. Yet the modern university espoused a neutral objectivity while proclaiming that human nature was "slowly getting better and that if we can only have more research foundations spending more money on more research schemes, then sooner or later we shall control sun-spots and even get rid of death!"[37] This belief that science could save civilization sped the country further down the path toward disintegration. In the same way that Edwin Aubrey at the University of Pennsylvania argued for religion's role in tempering scientific hegemony, Nash believed that Christianity could humble the mighty scientist and provide resources for an understanding of life that was deeper than the atomic structure.

Nash echoed Reinhold Niebuhr and other proponents of a neoorthodoxy who condemned a naïve optimism about human nature. But he added to this familiar trope the call to arms for Christian faculty members who could offer something more than a dangerous neutrality on campus. He called on faculty members to "initiate a movement that over the next century can perform the task which another group of Christians led by St. Augustine did for another era: namely, to save the world of scholarship from a relapse into intellectual barbarism." For Nash, this meant throwing out anything that placed itself against the knowledge of God, "bringing into captivity every thought to the obedience of Christ."[38] This dream for a Christian curriculum and faculty made the choice to have him lead the University of North Carolina's new department a bold one.

Nash did not, however, limit his energies to founding a department of religion. He also advised that "in the spheres of psychology and the social sciences we must seek to understand man and society in terms of a specifically Christian anthropology. For too long have we taken our presuppositions in these realms from sources other than a Christian *Weltanschauung*."[39] Nash joined the chorus of voices we have earlier heard pointing out that, if no one in the university could really be academically objective, if everyone had presuppositions, then they might as well have Christian ones. Such reasoning was used at nearly every turn among the founders discussed in these chapters. It amounted to a call for students and faculty alike to proudly proclaim their worldview.

Nash, however, was open to insights other than those found in the Bible: "I am not, of course, suggesting that behaviourism and Freudianism are completely wrong. They have much to teach us; but their insights have to be baptized into Christ before their true meaning can be discovered."[40] Nash's great dream was to "Christianize" all of human knowledge.

It would be neither fair to Nash nor accurate to see him as an isolated case or an anomalous throwback to nineteenth-century parochialism within higher education. He was not alone in his views, and neither was his program challenged significantly at North Carolina, though he seldom retreated from engaging the science departments in debate. Nash was particularly bothered by the fact that when non-Christian physics professors proclaimed that God's creation of the universe was just a fairy tale, Christian professors tended to take this lying down. He most clearly stated his argument, and that of some other religion department founders, when he wrote that if a liberal-rationalist-Marxist professor could share his or her convictions in class, then the Christian should be allowed to do the same. Administrators at North Carolina and liberal Protestant educators across the country seemed to have little problem with this reasoning. But Nash possessed an apocalyptic fervor in that he foresaw a time when such Christian teaching on campus would not be possible. He noted that "the time is short: 'We must work . . . while it is day; the night cometh when no man can work.'"[41]

Nash was a clear representative of Christian triumphalism within the cadre of religion teachers in the mid-twentieth century. His fears of communism, the fragmentation of knowledge, and immorality on campus were certainly inextricably tied to his own interests in developing the department at the University of North Carolina. Because of his vocal insistence that Christianity be the foundation of every academic department, Nash was overlooked by the Hazen Foundation when it was choosing representatives to conduct "faculty consultations" at colleges across the country. Religion departments were already suspect in the eyes of other departments; the Hazen Foundation could not chance being further ostracized because of such a firebrand like Nash.[42] Just after the war, leading foundations such as Danforth and Hazen targeted colleges for study and assessment, and the colleges were encouraged to use the teaching of religion to strengthen students as citizens.

CHAPTER SEVEN

College Ideal Leaves Morals to Religion Departments

Leading the perennially influential Hazen Foundation's efforts, John W. Nason's description of the much-touted "Hazen Faculty Consultations on Religion in Higher Education" was very clear about its purpose: "It would be disingenuous to suggest that the participants were strictly neutral in their attitudes. On the other hand, it would be a mistake to assume a merely missionary purpose." Nason, president of Swarthmore, lamented that colleges had become much more secular, as the scientific method reduced the importance of thoughts of "God, human destiny, heaven and hell."[1]

He explained further that "this led to a kind of neutrality between right and wrong which at its best became the philosophical doctrine of relativism and at its worst a cult of indifference. . . . Its depressing influence on any teaching about values, human ends, or the insights of religion is obvious; and it undoubtedly played its part in the discrediting of religion as an integral part of higher education."[2] Nason's tone echoed that of so many self-described Christian administrators and faculty who were breathing a sigh of relief that finally Christianity either was back in the driver's seat when it came to the basic values of higher education or surely had an opportunity to be.

Nason chronicled the then-familiar plot of how the teaching of religion was making its way back into colleges. Old departments of religion, long before World War II, were filled with ministers whose academic training was inferior and with teachers who were not always welcomed by their colleagues in other departments. Since Charles Foster Kent at Yale created the Kent Fellows program, more scholarly professors of religion were being placed in colleges. Armed with both religious conviction and the doctorates in theology that would confer academic respectability, these professors could begin to chart the new course. In explaining why each college should be visited, evaluated, and encouraged to create a religion department, Nason focused on the role of the religion professor's convictions: "The Nazis taught us what fanatical conviction can do. The Russians are demonstrating what single-minded devotion to their own ends can accomplish. Do we have equally potent convictions about our way of life?"[3]

This way of life to which Nason and his colleagues were referring was, in short, the "Hebraic-Christian tradition"—the part of "our cultural heritage" that was the antidote to the Nazis and communists. This cultural heritage needed to be reckoned with in the classroom, according to this argument: "The place of religion in this process cannot be ignored. It may still be discounted on the basis of some intellectual belief; it may even be attacked as otiose; but it cannot be ignored, for the understanding of the ultimate ends of human life is illumined by religious history as well as by present religious experience and belief."[4] Nason and many of the department founders used the term *religion* as a less threatening alternative to "Christianity," though they believed the latter to be the best example of the former. Once you established that "religion" was important, it was obvious which kind of religion would be the best to teach, study, and use as an exemplar.

Nason was expressing the sentiments of an entire movement of Protestant educators who, though differing in their specific theologies and institutional contexts, agreed on the following characteristics of teaching religion. First, religion was necessary to bring America and Western civilization out of the crisis signaled by the rise of Nazism and communism.[5] Second, although the teaching of religion in colleges had previously been insignificant, inadequate, or challenged by the naive liberal optimism of the sciences, teachers of religion were now prepared to give

Western religious traditions their renewed attention as scholars with authority. Third, religion, understood primarily as the moral teachings of the Hebraic-Christian tradition, was sufficiently general to be used as the basis for all educational thinking about ultimate issues. According to many Protestant educators, parochial denominationalism was condemnable and, in any case, no longer a threat after most Americans had been united against the great common enemy of nihilism. Nason felt that the Christian religion offered great resources to colleges and their students during this period of great social turbulence, and in a great effort to spread these ideas to as many colleges as possible, several rounds of "faculty consultations" were arranged with a wide variety of schools.

The first round of faculty consultations took place during 1945–46, when four consultants visited nineteen schools[6] to determine how the teaching of religion might best be integrated into their curricula. The Hazen Foundation steering committee[7] chose the four: Princeton's department founder George Thomas, Penn's department founder Edwin Aubrey (formerly at the University of Chicago Divinity School), Yale philosophy professor Theodore M. Greene (formerly with Thomas at Princeton), and Harvard philosophy professor emeritus William Ernest Hocking. "Hocking, having retired from Harvard, was invited by faculty dean Donald Morrison to teach courses at Dartmouth from 1947-49 according to a brief history of the Dartmouth department of religion written possibly by Fred Berthold who was a department founder-type along with professor Wing-tsit Chan who also taught there in the 1950s."

According to their reports, the consultants were welcomed warmly, but they found the "teaching of religion was inadequate in nearly every instance."[8] They concluded that not enough courses were being taught and that departmental support, if it existed at all, was weak. Moreover, they explained, "In many institutions the majority of the faculty with whom they talked are either hostile to or indifferent toward religion. . . . In most cases, however, it is [due to] a fear of indoctrination."[9]

Nason concluded his assessment of religion's place in colleges with this common refrain: "An effective teacher of religion needs some personal conviction on the issues he is discussing." Nason remarked that critics often wrongly concluded that "such conviction invalidated the quality of the teaching." He then articulated the familiar argument that great literature professors will be possessed with a great passion for Shakespeare, social scientists with their own discoveries, and religion professors for their religion.

Nason was one of many spokespersons for the importance of religion in college classrooms and seemed, like many of them, either unaware or unconvinced of the concerns of fellow academics who suspected that the new religion courses might be used as tools for the teaching of (not *about*) Protestant ethics, values, morals, holy scriptures, and history. What is most surprising is not that these Protestant educators used such unveiled language or that they had these hopes and dreams for "religion" (i.e., Protestantism) in the college. Rather, what is noteworthy is that they believed they were conceding many things to the academy. Namely, they would (1) surrender their particularistic doctrinal beliefs; (2) come to teach with a doctoral degree; (3) teach only the sort of religion that could be agreed upon by anyone wanting to save democracy and fight the common enemy; (4) ask no more of their English, political science, or history colleagues than they would ask of themselves (as they saw it); and finally, (5) represent not the church but rather all that is true, having examined human nature, society, history, and "ultimate things."

At Harvard, no less than at Princeton, Yale, Columbia, Stanford, Penn, Washington, the University of North Carolina, and Chicago, the mandate to those who taught religion was one of dual purpose: study and teach religion with respectable academic scrutiny (such that the new university model's expectations could be met [research based and seeking truth]) but also with an eye toward encouraging the best that such a religious perspective might have to offer a citizenry and student body in need of moral refinement (such that the college model's features could be fulfilled). At the University of Chicago, the divinity school was larger, financially healthier, and more focused on its mission of training ministers and religious scholars than at Harvard.

The University of Chicago's Robert Hutchins, like Harvard president Nathan Pusey in his dedication to neoorthodox theology, promoted his own brand of "first principles," which the Chicago faculty either mostly tolerated or disdained. Harvard's general education report was in part a reaction against John Dewey and Hutchins, a kind of *via media* between the nondisciplinary, problem-and-solution-focused nature of the former and the Great Books–prescribed, Aristotelian philosophical absolutism of the latter.[10]

In his book *Morals, Religion and Higher Education*, originally a lecture given in 1947 at Kenyon College, Hutchins made clear that he had changed his mind regarding his view, espoused in the 1930s, that religion does not belong in colleges. He still considered college curricula no place for moral instruction, but he believed religion needed to be examined in courses.

> Most of our educational institutions are and must remain secular, in the sense that they are not controlled by any church and are open to everybody regardless of his religious faith or lack of it. But there is another kind of secularism the besets the higher learning in America, and that is secularism in the sense in which we say that religion is insignificant, it is outmoded, it is equivalent to superstition. This kind of secularism higher education can and should repel. If a college or university is going to think and think about important things, then it must think about religion. It is perhaps not necessary that all the faculty should be religious; it is necessary that most of them, at least, should take religions seriously.[11]

In the 1940s at Chicago, an important summary course debuted for fourth-year students in the college. "Methods, Values and Concepts" was to be the course that unified and integrated the entire four years of college. Its focus was "analysis and criticism of . . . the main types of human activity (science, art, morality, religion) together with the basic values associated with these activities; and the common problems and the fundamental ideas underlying these characteristic modes of behavior." The course was administered by the philosophy department.[12]

For each of these schools, however, the question remained, What kind of religion would be taught—or, more precisely, what manner of Christianity?[13] As we've seen, each of the schools' faculty members responded differently to the crises of education and civilization they faced. Harvard declared religion too divisive to serve as a unifying force, then moved to bolster its teaching to undergraduates by enlarging the divinity school faculty and giving them a mandate to teach college students. Yale entertained arguments and curricular structures that addressed the tensions of teaching religion but ultimately solved few problems among the squabbling camps as a weak undergraduate department was formed. Chicago's varying voices found the import of teaching religion to be both too foundational and too professional or specialized to offer much to undergraduates in department form. Princeton tried to separate chapel from the new religion department, but the professors there saw their mission as one of salvation and growing academic sophistication.

These educators' institutional locations encouraged different responses to their general desire to find a new place in the curriculum for religion, but imagining how the teaching of religion (Christianity, for most) would help them address intellectual, spiritual, and curricular crises was something they shared. They also shared a struggle with the tension between seeking knowledge and understanding about religion, and teaching how best to use such knowledge to save civilization through democracy or the self through religious practice. Naturally, the professors who had studied religious life, texts, and communities for so long would be those most likely to take interest in the students' needs. Most elite colleges at midcentury had an in loco parentis model for relating to students, and such an attitude would not have ignored the religion teachers, especially during a time of great cultural and social consternation in the West. But what would be the future of a department and professors whose goals were both to advance knowledge about religious life and thought and to advance religious life itself? These tensions did not go away during the next period in the development of religion programs in the 1950s. Struggles at Princeton and Yale over Catholicism and questions of Christianity's dominance at Stanford, the University of North Carolina, and Columbia would only highlight the dual role of religion in their newly formed departments.

College Ideal Fades as Religious Studies Begins

The 1950s marked a time of new confidence among educators who argued for religion's place in the college curriculum. Gone were the days of woeful handwringing and a curricular rationale based primarily on fear of nihilism and the demise of civilization. Neither a casual pluralism nor a dramatic emphasis on world religions was common on college campuses. Presenting a civilization-saving rationale for religion courses was of less importance in the 1950s than showing exactly how natural it was for colleges to present such a topic to their students. On this matter, conflict, dissent, and differences were more pronounced within the camps of Protestant educators than without. Nevertheless, the respectability of the study of religion seemed to be gaining ground among intellectuals generally. Regarding this turn toward religion by many intellectuals, John Dewey, writing in the *Partisan Review* series Religion and the Intellectuals, opined,

> The present loss of faith in science among intellectuals, and the accompanying reversion to moral attitudes and beliefs which intellectuals as a class had abandoned, is an outstanding event. . . . Loss of nerve and upset of equilibrium affect the mass of human beings. Indirect confirmation on this point is found in the position of those intellectuals who remained faithful to the old attitudes permeated with supernaturalism. In effect they are now saying in chorus: "We have long been telling you what would be sure to happen if you cut loose from the anchorage of supernatural authority. . . . Your only hope of security lies in return to the supreme authority of religions claiming supernatural origin and support."[14]

It was now John Dewey on the defensive, no longer asking how it was possible that a small group of educators from Princeton could believe in the efficacy of teaching traditional religious thought to students, rather explaining why so many intellectuals had turned to traditional religious practice during the new "Cold War."[15] Not many blocks from the *Partisan Review*'s headquarters and what many considered to be the intellectual center of the country, officials at Columbia University were moving in a direction that was applauded by many newly religious academics.

A New Department at Columbia

On June 30, 1950, Columbia University chaplain and religion professor James A. Pike[16] revealed the design and development of the newly renovated religion department. His analysis of this curricular development at Columbia was published in his annual chaplain's report to the president: "There are in the faculty and student body of the University persons of many different faiths, including the secularist faiths (humanism, materialism, etc.)—and quite properly so. But on the basis of its foundation the University as an institution is not neutral about the Judaeo-Christian tradition; it is *for* it and for its perpetuation and extension in our culture. As an independent university in a free society it is free to be *for* those forces on which a free society depends."[17] Pike cited the historical importance of Christian faith for the founders and early presidents of the college and reminded his colleagues that earlier in the twentieth century, Dean Van Amringe had declared, "Religion and learning are justified of their children. To extend and intensify their elevating and twice blessed power this College and University avowedly exist."[18]

Two years after the end of World War II, Columbia University joined the ranks of many universities reexamining the place of teaching religion to undergraduates. The committee responsible for recommendations included theologian Reinhold Niebuhr, philosophy professor Horace Friess, chaplain James A. Pike, two academic deans, and the provost, Albert C. Jacobs. With the assistance of Jacobs, a department was formed consisting of historian John Dillenberger,[19] religion instructor Ursula Niebuhr, and James A. Pike, an Episcopal priest and chaplain. Ursula Niebuhr was teaching religion at Barnard College, the women's college closely affiliated with Columbia.[20] According to Princeton professor John F. Wilson, she understood her role as that of bridging the gap between religious scholarship and the pluralism of higher education, a continual tension for which she felt her husband had less appreciation than he should have.[21]

Among the principles they identified in creating the department, they stressed avoiding the presentation of "a lowest common denominator, but rather [employing] the full presentation of the most distinctive elements of each tradition." Included was the mantra of midcentury religion teachers: "If an instructor believes in it, he is not a neutral [teacher]; if he disbelieves it, this too is a position, and he is not a neutral."[22] Thus teachers should be both Christian believers and potentially critical evaluators of their tradition.

At long last, Pike declared, Columbia University had come to the realization that a department of religion was a natural extension of this dedication to "the chief thing that is aimed at in this College . . . to know God." The creation of an undergraduate religion department was for him a confirmation that "the full implications of our University's heritage are being articulated in the realm of undergraduate instruction."[23]

His basic rationale for the teaching of religion was "the hope that we will provide fruitful resources for the thinking and living of our own students." The university's heritage demanded and "the nation" deserved it.[24] Pike proudly noted that, combining forces with professors Ursula Niebuhr at Barnard College and Reinhold Niebuhr at Union Seminary, "this fall [1950], the largest undergraduate curriculum in religion in the nation is being inaugurated at the University. Thirty-five courses covering every major field of religious thought are available to students." These courses were based on principles articulated by the professors and summarized by Pike:

1) The understanding as well as the maintenance of Western culture and its democratic institutions depends upon the transmission of that from which they were largely derived and on the vitality of which our common life so greatly depends: namely, the Judeo-Christian tradition.

2) This tradition should be communicated to those of this day with the same thoroughness of scholarship and the same maturity of approach as is assumed in other disciplines, so that the University does not turn out adults in physics or psychology who are children in religion and ethics.

3) The study of religion should not be confined to the categories of other disciplines, such as "the Bible as literature," or the philosophy of religion, or the history of thought, but should utilize the whole of the methodologies customary in theological study.

4) Although an institution with a heritage such as ours has a special responsibility for transmitting the Judeo-Christian faith, the study

of religion should not be limited to any one faith but should extend
to all significant religious systems, though especially to each of the
major traditions within Judaism and Christianity.

5) The University as an institution is not neutral about the Judeo-
Christian tradition; it is *for* it and for its perpetuation and extension
in our culture.[25]

According to Pike and the Columbia University administration,
Christianity should be privileged not because it was superior to other
religions but because such universities were founded on the Judeo-
Christian heritage. It was noteworthy that these principles were not
expressed as a plea for why Christianity should be taught and privileged within the religion department, as they likely would have been
in earlier decades. Rather, these were the principles of a confident new
department that had the backing of the provost, academic deans, and
colleagues throughout the university. This confidence, and the specifically Christian approach toward "religion" it encouraged, was not
pleasing to everyone at Columbia.

While at Columbia during the early 1950s, newly hired religion professor John Dillenberger was frustrated with the Reverend James A.
Pike's approach.[26] According to Dillenberger, Pike brought a pious
chaplain's perspective to a religion department already associated too
closely with nearby Union Theological Seminary.[27] Dillenberger warned
in a *Review of Religion* article that college religion teachers should avoid
demanding special status for religion, stating that "teaching religion
in a college or university is no different in principle than that of teaching other subjects."[28] Dillenberger tried to move the department closer
toward the "nonadvocacy teaching and research" pole of the dual role
of the department, but he found it difficult to keep Pike's more public statements of piety from being taught in the classroom.[29] Dillenberger had come directly from teaching at Princeton University, where
George Thomas and Paul Ramsey were developing a large department
on the premise that teaching about religion should be completely separate from the activities of the chaplain's office. Pike, on the other hand,
had done much to ensure the larger size of Columbia's department of
religion, and he believed that the energies of the two offices could be
combined to strengthen religion on campus.

Pike's faculty colleague Horace Friess described the growth in the number of undergraduate religion courses during this period as an example of the way in which the faculty was countering the "violent totalitarian challenge." He also described religious thought as having a "renewed confessional emphasis" during these years. Friess was encouraged by this "re-association" of society and the religious community. Friess himself had made a special effort to encourage Paul Tillich to come from Germany to New York City and he was a dedicated teacher of Reinhold Niebuhr's writings in the classroom. Friess and his colleagues were dedicated to "improving the historical study of religion in the general life of mankind."[30] He cited George Thomas and Theodore M. Greene's work in forming the Princeton department as inspirational for the founding of Columbia's own department.

It was not, however, Thomas's attempt to separate the chaplain's office from the department of religion that inspired James A. Pike and Horace Friess at Columbia. Rather, Friess cited Thomas's claim that to teach Christianity authentically, the teacher must be a professing member of the faith: "A religion could only be authentically understood and interpreted from inside, that is by those who experience it as adherents; and that the traditions of Judeo-Christian religion being historically central to our culture, their authentic interpretation should be central to the study of religion in our colleges. These two principles have had great influence since their enunciation."[31] Columbia administrators wanted the teaching of religion to play an important role in transmitting morality and democratic values, and Pike and Friess were willing to set aside differences between Protestant theologies and provide what the university wanted.

The program, developed extensively in the 1950s under the direction of Pike, introduced a large number of courses intended to bring the religious adherent's experience to bear on the training of undergraduates in the history and theology of the "Judeo-Christian heritage." Pike also took a page from the book of the Iowa School of Religion's curriculum by inviting Greek Orthodox, Catholic, and Jewish scholars to teach undergraduates.[32] To those who raised questions about the indoctrination of students in such courses, Friess explained that each college must decide what it finds important to pass along to students, and these decisions had already been made at Columbia.[33]

Chaplain Pike, explaining the origin of the new master of arts in
religion, attributed its creation to Reinhold Niebuhr's interest in the
new undergraduate department. Niebuhr envisioned Columbia's graduate degree as one that would prepare religion teachers for colleges and
prep schools, something Pike considered "a rapidly growing field due
to the expansion of curricula everywhere."[34] Having assisted Harvard
University administrators in their attempt to renew the teaching of
religion to their undergraduates, Reinhold Niebuhr had been asked by
Columbia University officials to join a committee that would prescribe
a blueprint for the newly formed religion department there, which later
evolved into a graduate program.

Niebuhr's efforts on behalf of undergraduate religion programs at
Harvard and Columbia were noted by Harvard philosopher Morton
White, who had completed his graduate studies at Columbia, where he
had experienced firsthand the work of Horace Friess. White was an outspoken academic critic of Niebuhr during the 1950s, arguing against
Niebuhr's attempts to expose undergraduates to the importance of Protestant Christianity and rejecting the attempt of Niebuhr's followers to
separate his politics from his theology. White wanted Niebuhr's admirers
(the so-called Atheists for Niebuhr) to understand that Niebuhr's theology
could not be separated from his political views, that one could not take
political Niebuhr and leave behind Niebuhr the theologian. White also
argued vigorously for the exclusion of Protestant Christian theology from
the college classroom and for the inclusion of teaching "about" religion.

According to White, the most important question for religious intellectuals had shifted from "Does God exist?" to "Should I be religious?"
This reformulation was at the center of higher education, where, White
argued, "it has become increasingly fashionable to urge the importance
of religious instruction for the undergraduate." By avoiding questions
about belief in God, Niebuhr, Thomas, and other Protestant educators
were able to recommend teaching religion because it was defensible as a
good policy in general. In answering the question "Why should I be
religious?" professors need not give arguments based on theological
evidence; they need only show that "it is good to be religious":

Those who wish to introduce religious instruction into the undergraduate college and who adopt this more recent way of construing

religion must now ask themselves just what they mean by religion. Having abandoned the straightforward and simple definition of a religious man as one who believes in God and defends his belief, they must set forth an alternative view. The twentieth century has witnessed a number of efforts to redefine religion in the light of this new religious distaste for traditional theology; they vary from an excessively narrow view of the religious life as a life of feeling (as opposed to knowing) to one that rightly regards religion as a total way of life—cognitive, esthetic, affective, moral and even political.[35]

The view of religious life as one of feeling, White believed, was not "true to religion," while the view of religion as a complete way of life, "if acted upon by those who are responsible in these matters, will be untrue to the aims of undergraduate education." White was convinced that this second option, disastrous for higher education, was more like teaching students "how" to be religious, not teaching "about" religion. White saw clearly that undergraduate religion departments and programs, as they were being founded were charged with fulfilling a dual role: training for the religious life and teaching about religious lives. White decried the former and supported the latter within college curricula. He was not opposed to the practice of religious life per se, but he saw the shift toward a more complex definition of religion as an attempt to "avoid identifying religion with *any* claim to knowledge that might have to run the gauntlet of scientific test." Religion was a complex concept, but the attempt to make it so complex as to be beyond knowledge was problematic for the scholar: "Religion has too often agreed to accept the role of a non-scientific spiritual grab-bag, or an ideological know-nothing, while science has promised to give up its control over feeling and will."[36] White was, to an extent, arguing against the application of the term *religion* outside the context of specific religions, which he took to be real religion. He believed that if we ask such questions at all, we should not ask abstractly "Should I be religious?" but "Should I be a Jew?" or "Should I be a Roman Catholic?" or "Should I be a Protestant?" Particular religions may be hybrids, composed of various cultural, aesthetic, or philosophical tropes, but one is not necessarily "religious" just because one admires religious art, music, or texts, according to White's narrow definition of religion. Religion was a superset of the particular forms that religions take, not a subset of the elements that are found in all religions.[37]

White's frustration with those who advocated teaching the religious life in religion departments was based on his understanding that one could not teach "religion," only religions that were too particular and too partisan for the college classroom. The term *religion* was being transformed by Protestant educators to serve the purposes of the particular religion with which they were affiliated, while they endeavored to mask their particular religion so it could be protected from scientific research. It was, White claimed, no time to "redefine 'religion' as the biologist redefines 'fish' to suit our present purposes": "Any educational effort to nourish religious feeling or to stimulate religious action by trying to present an abstract essence of religion, conceived as the life of feeling and willing (as opposed to knowing) must fail. From this I conclude that we should not make the effort in colleges which are not religious institutions, and that we become frankly sectarian in our teaching of religion and therefore limit higher religious instruction to the divinity schools which are properly devoted to the *study and propagation* of specific religions conceived as total ways of life, knowledge, emotion and action."[38]

White went on to explain that colleges must not abandon the "effort to help undergraduates to develop their emotions, to find themselves, to help them develop habits of practical decision, and to appreciate humane values. These are certainly admissible concerns of all scholars."[39] He agreed with these concerns for undergraduates with the advocates of a religion department, but he believed they could not be properly part of the teaching of religion in colleges.

Many Protestant educators had argued that scientists were teaching physics from a scientific point of view, and this affirmed the right of religion professors to teach Christianity from a Christian perspective. White confronted this logic with his own comparison of a physics professor and a religion professor. A physicist must "*believe* or pretend to believe the theory he teaches," becoming fully involved in "say, the theory of relativity, or quantum theory." What, White asked, was the parallel in a religion department to this "total involvement of the physics professor"? Complete involvement of a professor in one of the world's religions was the parallel. While not disputing the similarities, White asked, "If we are unwilling, as many are not, to teach the undergraduate religion in this way, because it is not our proper function, can we justify teaching what might seem like the religious counterpart to courses in the history and methodology of science?" His answer was a definitive yes.

According to White, other subjects could be taught as the corollary of scientific history, such as "the history of religion, a course in the philosophy of religion." Such courses would not teach the student to become religious any more than a history of science course would teach a student to become a scientist: "He may come to feel something of what the scientific life is like, but if he has not had serious contact with some one science and lived in it for even a short time, no amount of methodological tourism will make him a scientist." If the student becomes more religious after having taken a course *about* religion, this, for White, was acceptable and understandable: "If, in absorbing this knowledge students develop deep religious feelings, it will happen *per accidens*, as it were, and not as a result of the concerted efforts of the professors."[40] Examining one final analogy, that of political science in general and the study of communism, White addressed the primary difference between studying *about* a subject and studying to practice a subject. The former aims at understanding, while the latter aims at initiation into a way of life: "Teaching *about* religion, or communicating moral feeling and esthetic appreciation while one is teaching philosophy, literature, and history, no more constitutes teaching people to *be* religious in any ordinary sense of that word, than teaching *about* Communism amounts to propagating it. To teach people to be religious, I repeat we must do something which is beyond the function of an undergraduate college simply because it involves inculcating a total appreciation of and belief in historical religions treated as the vast, all embracing structures that they are."[41]

White's primary concern was that colleges, having survived the crises of midcentury, would erroneously change what he understood to be their function—namely, to understand subjects, not to assess the moral or spiritual value of such subjects: "We must remember that the colleges and the universities have lived through crises before, and that some of the severest blows at their greatness and their usefulness as social institutions have come when it seemed necessary to change their function under the influence of religious or political passion."[42]

According to White, to accept and implement the religious arguments of Reinhold Niebuhr, James A. Pike, Nathan Pusey, George Thomas, and Edwin Aubrey would mean sacrificing the "central function" and integrity of the college. At a time when few contrarian voices were heard clearly, White joined Sidney Hook, John Dewey, and several young religion professors like John Dillenberger, Van Harvey, and Huston Smith in arguing for religion's power as a subject, but one that should not be exploited for its conversion potential. White's own rationale appeared somewhat muddled, however, as he gave little justification for his claim that the mission of colleges excluded encouraging a religious life through religion classes.

He also clung to outdated definitions of *religion* at a time when those definitions were very much in flux, shifting in response to the tenets of existentialist philosophy, the new findings of anthropologists in the field, and revolutionary linguistic theories about the relationship between language and reality. White was, however, vigilant in his scrutiny of Protestant educators who used the expanding definitions of religion to their advantage in the hope that they might teach religion generally while examining Christian approaches particularly. White's battle against the rising interest in teaching the benefits of a religious way of life would not be an easy one. It was not only Protestant and Catholic educators who saw benefit in teaching religion to undergraduates.

CHAPTER EIGHT

Turn toward Religion Drives Columbia University, the University of Pennsylvania, and Stanford University

A few months after Columbia's James A. Pike announced his university's bold new religion department, Will Herberg, American Judaism's closest equivalent to neoorthodox thinker Reinhold Niebuhr, visited Cornell University with his ears attuned to the undergraduate clamor for instruction in religion. Herberg, professor at Drew University and author of the most widely cited analysis of American religious life to appear in the 1950s, *Protestant Catholic Jew*, visited Cornell University under the auspices of the Cornell United Religious Work, a university agency. The response to his lectures included an editorial in the *Cornell Daily Sun* noting "the inadequacy of instruction in religion at Cornell" and demanding more opportunities to study religion within the curriculum. Herberg's description of his visit to Cornell was typical of the confident rhetoric of religious scholars and intellectuals who traveled across America to college campuses seeking to engage students and faculty on important spiritual and political issues.

Herberg was surprised by the students' level of interest in his lectures and reflected on his visit, giving special attention to the ambiguous definition of "religion," the subject about which he was regularly asked to lecture on campuses: "It is variously understood, or misunderstood, as an institutional vested interest, a metaphysical system, a 'rewarding' emotional experience, an impressive ritual, the preachment of high ideals, a code of laws and observances—and against all these students usually have their immunizing prejudices. But once it was discovered that I was talking about something else—about the meaning of existence and the nature of one's ultimate loyalties—the initial resistance was overcome."[1]

Many accounts echo Herberg's in describing theologians speaking to packed lecture halls on campuses, from Charles Gilkey and Paul Tillich to Reinhold Niebuhr. It is difficult to determine whether such gatherings represented a new enthusiasm, as lecturers often described it, or an increased awareness by the lecturers of a postwar college generation experiencing the "pervasive insecurity of contemporary life." Herberg concluded that many of the students he met in his seminars were not "returning to religion" so much as they were "struggling to make the primordial decision of faith *anew.*" Lecturing in various departments on communism, democracy, the labor movement, religion and law, and faith, Herberg was given free rein to spread his religion, most authentically "the Judeo-Christian" religion. He recognized among the students what he considered their great need to understand the "ultimate" issues of life in a religious way: "What the young men and women wanted was not merely help in solving a series of isolated problems but also light on how religious faith could give the insight and power to deal with the crucial situations of life."[2]

The interests and needs that Herberg identified at Cornell were those identified as worthy of response by founders of religion departments throughout higher education: the response was to teach Christian history, thought, and ethics. This renewed interest in all things religious was not limited, however, to twenty-year-old college students or the surge in piety of returning servicemen or the bulging churches experiencing growth in numbers and buildings. The "new turn toward religion" was also turning heads—and some stomachs—around New York City's intellectual scene. Several of the self-described intellectuals who either applauded or derided these changes in attitude were considered leading influences on religion department founders; among their number were Jacques Maritain, Hannah Arendt, Paul Tillich, Sidney Hook, and John Dewey.

Religion and the Intellectuals

The journal whose articles and subscribers were most easily identifiable as the movers and shakers within this intellectual scene was the *Partisan Review.* Their series in 1950 entitled "Religion and the Intellectuals" was a lengthy collection of essays by leading writers, theologians, self-described thinkers, artists, and political commentators addressing the recent "turn toward religion" among intellectuals.

In opening the series of reflections by leading thinkers on the nature of the religious revival among literary types and intellectuals, Sidney Hook summarized changes from 1943 to the 1950s as follows: "Seven years ago, in opening the series of articles on 'The New Failure of Nerve,' in PR [*Partisan Review*], I offered an explanation of the revival of religion in terms of the decline of capitalism, the rise of totalitarianism, the outbreak of war, and the simultaneous decay of socialist belief. What then seemed to be a strong current, has now become a tidal wave."[3] Political and social philosopher Hannah Arendt spoke out directly against the primary arguments made by religion department founders who claimed teaching religion could help the nation fight totalitarianism and reintegrate human civilization when she wrote,

The idea of somebody making up his mind to believe in God, follow His Commandments, praying to Him and going regularly to Church, so that poets again may have some inspiration and culture be "integrated," is simply exhilarating. The Catholicisme cerebral which you mention is one of the surest ways to kill religion—as the Church, by the way, knew well enough. . . . The same is true, of course, with respect to the use of religion as a weapon against totalitarianism or "a safeguard for civilized tradition." Moreover, it seems that all such attempts would be doomed to failure, particularly in the struggle against totalitarianism; recent history has demonstrated how weak and helpless organized religion is when confronted with the new totalitarian form of government.[4]

Arendt continued her critique of this use of religion, bringing the discussion to a consideration of the role of truth vis-à-vis the pragmatic God presented so often by elite Protestant educators during the 1940s and 1950s: "The trouble here, as in all discussions of religion, is that one really cannot escape the question of truth and therefore cannot treat the whole matter as though God had been the notion of some especially clever pragmatist who knew what it is good for . . . and what it is good against. It just is not so. Either God exists and people believe in Him . . . or He does not exist and people do not believe in Him—and no literary or other imagination is likely to change this situation for the benefit of culture."[5]

Renowned theologian Paul Tillich (Union Seminary NYC, Harvard, Chicago), arguing against Arendt's interpretation, echoed the analysis of religion department founders, many of whom considered Tillich an inspiration for their work. Tillich proclaimed that a turn toward religion was taking place among not just intellectuals but a wide array of individuals: "It is difficult to find in the outstanding recent philosophers, novelists, poets, playwrights, educators, psychologists, physicists, anybody who would stand for the shallow atheism or optimistic secularism of two or three generations ago."[6] For Tillich, this turn toward religion was not a turn toward Christianity so much as it was a realization that "ultimate" questions were important, especially in the face of the misguided optimism of early twentieth-century liberals. After two world wars, now it was understood in a profoundly different way that humans were capable of unimaginable horror.

Responding to the familiar refrains of neoorthodox theologians' generally low view of human nature, Sidney Hook offered the following: "Some have become so obsessed with the animality of man that they can see no grandeur at all in human life; so fearful of the possibilities of human cruelty, that they are blind to still existing possibilities of human intelligence and courage; so resigned to the betrayal of all ideals, that they can no longer make distinctions and regard all social philosophies which are not theocentric as different roads to the culture of *1984*."[7]

Hook regarded this new appreciation of religion by intellectuals as foolish, remarking that those whom "Hitler and Stalin have caused to flee to the arms of God" had never taken seriously all the historical monographs detailing the great crimes of religious people down through the centuries in western Europe.[8] To further bolster his assertions, he attacked the type of religion to which respectable and respected intellectuals were returning. Such theologians made spurious arguments, according to Hook, about how the nonexistence of God was not logically falsifiable and thus belief in God was on the same footing: "If we are unjustified in disbelieving an assertion save only when its contradictory is demonstrated to be impossible, we should have to believe that the universe is populated with the wildest fancies. Many things may exist for which we can give no adequate evidence, but the burden of proof always rests upon the individual who asserts existence."[9]

What the intellectuals were seeking was not theology properly understood, according to Hook; it was, rather, theodicy. They were not seeking truth so much as they were seeking comfort. If humans were evil as a consequence of having turned away from God, this would help to make sense of twentieth-century horrors: "It is not that the believer lacks the tough-mindedness to recognize the existence of evil, but that, if he is not to choke to death on it like Ivan Karamazov, he must blunt its sharp edge and learn to believe on no rational grounds that it fulfils a 'higher' purpose he does not see."[10]

Naturalism was not able to provide this comfort and thus left a gap that many "tender-minded" individuals needed filled. Personal religious belief and expression did not in themselves frustrate Hook any more than a private love affair with an individual, idea, or object. It was religion's institutionalization of authoritarian forms that disturbed him:

> So long as [religion's] overbeliefs are a source of innocent joy, a way of overcoming cosmic loneliness, a discipline of living with pain and evil, otherwise unendurable and irremediable, so long as what functions as a vital illusion or poetic myth is not represented as a public truth to whose existence the once-born are blind, so long as religion does not paralyze the desire and the will to struggle against unnecessary cruelties of experience, it seems to me to fall in an area of choice in which rational criticism may be suspended. In this sense, a man's personal religion justifies itself to him in the way his love does. Why should he want to make a public cult of it? And why should we want

him to prove that the object of his love is the most lovely creature in the world? Nonetheless, it still remains true that as a set of cognitive beliefs, religion is a speculative hypothesis of an extremely low order of probability.[11]

Intellectuals from a variety of fields and professions waxed eloquent about the various benefits and maladies associated with a turn toward religion, from Paul Tillich's welcome of such developments to Sidney Hook's predictable harangues. What was becoming clear, if not undisputed, however, was that whatever one's definition or appreciation of religious belief and behavior, its return was not a mirage.

This widely acknowledged turn toward religion among intellectuals and other leading personalities on the national scene was in part what gave religion department founders the necessary encouragement and legitimacy to boldly proclaim the importance and efficacy of their programs. But not everyone was pleased about the particular incarnations of the turn toward religion, given that there were as many religious attitudes toward which one could return as there were individuals.

God and Man and Religion Teaching at Yale

Yale student William F. Buckley Jr. provided just such a dissenting voice to the celebration of religion's strong return, pointing to the acids of modernity washing across his beloved Yale. While many Protestant educators were singing the praises of the new turn toward religion among academics, intellectuals, and college curricula, Buckley offered contrarian observations about the nature of Christianity on campus.

Buckley's *God and Man at Yale*, published in 1951, caused such a stir on campus and among alumni that Yale Corporation members Henry Sloane Coffin and Irving Olds were asked to lead an eight-member committee to investigate Buckley's claims about life on campus. Yale's leadership wanted desperately to be able to refute the claims that anticapitalism and atheism were the academic philosophies du jour on campus. Although Buckley never revealed in the book that he was a Catholic, few who reviewed it failed to use this distinction to explain away his criticism of the undergraduate experience, an experience that Buckley described as practically devoid of real religion.

Buckley paid special attention to philosophy professor Theodore M. Greene, close ally of George Thomas at Princeton: "While Mr. Greene is a Christian by a great many definitions (he replies ambiguously when asked if he believes in the divinity of Christ), his course is largely a completely nondogmatic examination of the philosophies of religion. Mr. Greene is unflinching in his respect for Christian ethics, but it is, after all, assumed that most people are. . . . There is a widespread opinion that what he teaches is ethics, not religion."[12] Greene's response in the *Yale Daily News* was also unequivocal: "What is required is more, not less tolerance—not the tolerance of indifference, but the tolerance of honest respect for divergent convictions and the determination of all that such divergent opinions be heard without administrative censorship. I try my best in the classroom to expound and defend my faith, when it is relevant, as honestly and persuasively as I can. But I can do so only because many of my colleagues are expounding and defending their contrasting faiths, or skepticisms, as openly and honestly as I am mine."[13] Buckley represented the other side of the conflict experienced by midcentury college teachers of religion. Not only were they too religious for their academic sparring partners who found religion to be at best only historically interesting, but they were not religiously aggressive enough to please students or alumni who wanted to hear a less-nuanced or less-tolerant view of non-Christian religious texts or movements.[14]

This latter point was not a problem for Stanford alumni, students, and professors who followed the career of Alexander Miller, founder of the religion program there. Professor Miller was very clear about his intentions to teach Christianity at Stanford—and not as a religion or as a way of saving Western civilization. His distinctive contribution to the history of college religion programs was his insistence that Christianity should not be taught as a religion properly understood.

Stanford's Two Aims

In 1950, Christian theologian Alexander Miller,[15] a New Zealand national with experience primarily leading Christian youth movements, was invited to help create a program at Stanford while serving as the new Stanford chaplain for Memorial Church. His graduate work in theology was completed at Union Seminary and Columbia University, heavily under the influence of Reinhold Niebuhr.

The religious studies program at Stanford was created in 1951, "partly in response to the concern of students themselves," according to the program's own brochure. Its goal was to ensure that students could "secure some understanding of the religious tradition of the Western world, to relate it to other religious traditions, and to discuss its relevance to individual and contemporary social life." Of note was the mention of the importance of individuals and the fact that the curriculum was designed "primarily to communicate the elements of Hebrew-Christian faith in their richness and variety." In much the same way that Carolina founder Arnold Nash had dreamed not of a department of religion but of a center at the university that would influence all departments, the Stanford program aimed to show the relevance of Christianity to "every area of intellectual interest." The curriculum was divided into three areas: biblical studies, Christian doctrine and ethics, and one course every year in comparative religions, which could include courses in "American Religious Communities and Christian Classics."[16]

In an official description of the program in 1952, it was clarified that "the purpose of the program is to introduce students to the world view of Biblical Religion as it has been developed and interpreted in the Western tradition . . . with a double intention: to enable students critically to appraise the religious tradition in which they stand, and to supply them with the intellectual basis for a personal judgment."[17] The strategic goals of the religion program were identified as twofold: (1) add additional staff to the "department" and (2) bring "Christian scholars of high repute who would serve as teachers in the department of their specialty, and be available as preachers in Memorial Church." The promotional materials describing the religion program included the hope that in forming such a program, Stanford might be able to influence other schools "by way of direct influence upon successive student generations . . . and by stimulating further experiments of the same fruitful sort."[18]

By 1953, donations from individuals and foundations made possible an expansion of the religion program. The expansion added a second professor to the faculty and doubled the courses offered, with student enrollment increasing to over five hundred annually. Before 1953, the university funded the religion program itself, but additional funds were aggressively solicited by the mid-1950s.[19]

The original impetus to create the program came from the office of the chaplain, D. Elton Trueblood, who served Stanford from 1936 to 1946. Trueblood was also supported by activist graduates of Stanford who desired that a more formal program of courses should be added to the chaplain's program. When Alexander Miller was found as the replacement for Chaplain Trueblood, Miller's academic background combined with his experience in the Christian youth movement made him a natural choice for creating the new program. Later in the 1950s, Miller's vision for a religion program that functioned far beyond a departmental model was welcomed at Stanford and criticized by those who wanted religious studies to become separate from religious activities on campus (similar to the Princeton innovation of the 1940s). Miller saw no distinction, and neither did many of the academic communities founding departments across the country.

Edwin Aubrey and a Shift in Emphasis at Penn

Joining the many elite institutions creating undergraduate religion departments in the early 1950s was the University of Pennsylvania. Although Penn chose a department founder with a pedigree similar to Miller's on paper, Edwin Aubrey's vision was not theologically neoorthodox.

The board of trustees voted to establish a Department of Religious Thought, and its creation, enacted during the 1950 school year, was recommended by the College Curriculum Committee as part of the postwar reconfiguration of the college curriculum. The committee's study revealed "the need for unification and expansion of the University's opportunities for instruction in religion."[20] Edwin Aubrey began his tenure as founding professor during the 1950 academic year but died unexpectedly in 1956. During his short time there, he taught theology and history courses such as "Theology of Christian Mysticism" (using Harvard philosophy professor William Ernest Hocking's[21] *The Meaning of God in Human Experience*), "The Christian Conception of Man," "Church and State in Contemporary Thought," and "Christianity and Democracy."

Aubrey was an attractive candidate for the position at Penn[22] for several reasons, not least of which was that he was chair of Princeton's Religion Department Advisory Board, where he had worked closely with George Thomas on the creation of the largest department in the country (until Columbia combined its program with Barnard to create an even larger one in 1950). Aubrey embodied the tensions inherent in creating a religion department in a university's college after the war. He wanted to bring academic credibility to the teaching of Christianity for the benefit of students' well-being, but he regularly spoke out against Protestant churches that too easily assumed colleges were long-lost secular enterprises. He had hopes for the renewal of both church and college through the examination of Christian theology and ethics. Aubrey was also an important Protestant educational figure nationally, consulting with numerous colleges and universities and participating in the influential conferences and foundations of the day. The tensions created by the dual role of the religion department manifested themselves in professors such as Aubrey, who was too academic and secular for many in the churches and too pious and sectarian for other academic departments.

Edwin Aubrey[23] was a churchman who realized how easily the rhetoric of despair about the university becoming "secular" degenerated into poor thinking about curricular matters.[24] Religion still had much to offer the student who was seeking valid worldviews, with Christianity being the most desirable for study in the classroom, according to Aubrey. He believed that in the search for scientific truth about religion, the practical virtues of Christianity would win the day. As the founder of the University of Pennsylvania's religion program, Aubrey was convinced that the prevalent vocational aim of higher education itself needed modification. He believed it needed to be supplemented by the effort to enrich the life of the student as a person, and he thought it should set the vocational task in the broader context of social life and human destiny. The teaching of religion, he was convinced, could help the university attain this goal. Aubrey believed that "if we are to talk of religion as an integrating force in human life, we must know what religion is. There is need, therefore, for systematic courses in the field of religion: its history, its basic concepts, its psychological processes, its great literary products and expressions, its role in social change, its demands on conduct."[25] Aubrey is important to the history of college religion programs not only because he founded Penn's department but also because he represented a shift in the philosophy of such departments.

By the early 1950s, the rationale for creating religion programs was no longer focused solely on what they might do for the curriculum, as the benefits of such programs had become better established or accepted. Now, it was thought, such programs might play an important role in saving the churches from themselves, particularly from their success.

Aubrey argued that the teaching of religion to undergraduates was as important for its potential positive influence on the Protestant church as it was for the curriculum. Churches needed the university's approach to understanding religion—a theological approach but one that withstood the rigors of academic inquiry. According to Aubrey, the mid-century existentialist theologians had understood religion best. They related intuition to an existential moment, during which God confronts the individual at the point of that person's "moral extremity." Aubrey argued that such an understanding of religion was needed in the classroom. He and other founders of departments or programs believed that religion was important to a curriculum because teaching religion showed that "it all hangs together, and this is the source of any hope that men may have for the unification of knowledge and for the integration of meanings which are the obverse and reverse of the human quest in education."[26] The unity of knowledge was what made a university a university; otherwise, it was merely a collection of departments.

Aubrey was a theologian who focused much of his professional effort on encouraging other theologians to consider how all religious language might be employed to explain the meaning of life and ensure the proper adjustment to such a life by the future generation. He stood within the Christian tradition while pointing to the ways in which all religious language, belief, and behavior attempted to address the same human issues. In *Living the Christian Faith* (1939), he continued his attack on any part of the theological renaissance that "handed out musty traditional language meant to warm hearts in place of addressing serious issues that the non-theologian layperson faced."[27]

In 1953, Aubrey gave the Ayer lectures at Colgate Rochester Divinity School; he titled his lectures, *Secularism, a Myth*. "Secularism" had become a rallying cry, a call to action pitting one group against another at midcentury. From Monsignor Fulton J. Sheen's claim that secularism would compete with Christianity to dominate in the postwar era to H. Richard Niebuhr's observation that secularists were in opposition to "Christ's people," the battle cry against secularism only increased suspicions among competing religious communities.[28] In addition to their concerns about the differences among themselves, Protestants, Catholics, and Jews now began to concern themselves more seriously with a fourth category: philosophies whose adherents did not view their beliefs to be contained by or originating from Christianity or Judaism.

Aubrey was an exemplar of the dual role played by religion professors, but he was less concerned for the soul of the university than for that of the Protestant churches that spurned the so-called secular university. He wanted to expose the use of secularism as an epithet by pointing to the real issues that lay behind its use. Christianity was indebted to secular forces because it had always developed alongside such influences. In fact, secular movements had produced spiritual values that could not be attributed to Christianity. Only through such honesty and humility did Aubrey believe that the truth about secularism could be determined.

Aubrey traced the history of the attack on secularism to the statements made at the Protestant ecumenical gatherings of 1937 (the second Universal Christian Conference on Life and Work at Oxford and the second World Conference on Faith and Order at Edinburgh) and 1948 (the first Assembly of the World Council of Churches at Amsterdam). *Secularism* became the catchphrase for many of the churches' problems (nihilism, communism, nationalism, scientific humanism, a morally bankrupt society). Much to Aubrey's surprise, higher education was seldom mentioned in the debates about secularism, save in incidental references about the necessity of education for freedom and responsibility and the prevalence of agnostic philosophy in colleges. *Secularism* had become a catchall code word for that with which Christian leaders disagreed. These exaggerated characterizations were for Aubrey the result of the failure to make distinctions between the "realities of the situation and a spurious sense of crusading." He wondered aloud if these attacks on secularism were not just a "pathological phase of ecclesiastical psychology."[29]

Aubrey's book *Secularism, a Myth* was written as an apologetic for a humanistic Christian faith and as a viable alternative to the neoortho- dox revival at midcentury. He defined Renaissance humanism as an adulation of ancient cultures, a discovery of a "fresh sense of the pur- pose of knowledge, a sense of 'the civilizing and refining influence of polite letters and of the liberal arts.'"[30] He contended that knowledge should not become an end in itself; rather, it "should serve the ends of human improvement."[31] Aubrey's description of knowledge was a glowing one. He treasured the seventeenth-century Christian human- ists because they were balanced. Aubrey insisted on avoiding the polar opposites of rationalism and naturalism, dogmatism and supernatu- ralism. He was a centrist, a reconciler, seeking to create and then to embrace a middle way. In making his arguments against the easy attack on secularism, Aubrey stood out against many of his colleagues.

The rationale given for the existence of religion departments through- out much of the late 1930s and early 1940s was that scientific naturalism, materialism, and modernism had failed, and Protestant Christianity ("religion") could become a corrective, bringing meaning and unity to a fragmented curriculum and world. Although Aubrey himself was part of the group of Protestant educators who made such claims during that time, his focus had changed by the late 1940s. For Aubrey, religion as an academic subject was meant to make an alliance with modern scientific knowledge in the interests of promoting the good life, eschewing theo- logical speculations, and concentrating on the moral enterprise. Reli- gion helped humans "stand over against the natural world in the pursuit of blessedness."[32] In Aubrey's vision, science had come to play a strong role in the university, and now religion could become its faithful partner in creating a better life for all citizens.

As universities became more focused on basic research through gov- ernment and private funding, the research emphasis of the dual role for religion departments increased in its intensity. The other role—the emphasis on character formation—did not wither, however.[33]

Aubrey criticized Christian ethicists for focusing on theoretical problems, while the practical matters of life were solved by secular movements. He wanted secularism to get its due, which Christian crit- ics did not give it, according to his evaluation. Aubrey insisted that the Christian community should not exaggerate the difference between secular and religious thinking. According to Aubrey, the mission of the church was to dwell with the secular mind, to understand it while not becoming identified with it, and finally to "tell it about what it ought to become."[34] How then were Christians to get into the secular mind? Education. Aubrey was resoundingly clear, moreover, about who was able to deliver such an education on university campuses: the church was ill-prepared for such a task, so it fell to academics.

Aubrey cited three reasons for his frustration with the attention churches had given to secularism in higher education. First, he found the church lacking in mastery of the art of education, thereby disqualifying itself as a legitimate critic. Second, he believed the church's discomfort with the "critical study of religious ideas in classrooms" was driving the campaign of "concern for Christian values" on campuses. Aubrey assumed that a critical study of religion was nothing to fear and was not in opposition to Christian values. Third, Aubrey did not believe church leaders had learned enough about what colleges and universities were already doing to "correct abuses in the pursuit of truth."[35] He did not disagree that such abuses occurred, but he believed that these were the necessary evils of an institution dedicated to pursuing truth unshackled except by reason.

Obviously, the new religion departments shared overlapping social roles with the church, and in some cases the state, which encourages a solid citizenry. If the church wanted to criticize the university, it must first understand what higher education was doing about its own problems. Aubrey's plea for understanding was that of a thoughtful individual standing firmly within two often contentious communities. He was a bridge builder when most optimistic and a surveyor of the chasm when not as confident in the church. Clearly, he kept his strongest criticism for the religious community. Aubrey's dream for the church, the university, and the country was for cooperation. Ideally the church would welcome the sociologists' words of wisdom regarding the health of institutions, while the sociologist would be drawn to the church's prophetic words of redemption. The country as a whole could not help but profit from these cooperative moves toward a firmer faith: "If the church approaches society in this constructive spirit, with a humbler heart and a clearer head, it may yet save men through its loving cooperation and lead them to a larger life not only in the beyond but in this world as well."[36]

This exhortation was meant for the church, but it was delivered from the perspective of a university professor who had discovered that the secret of a healthier society was a cooperative effort among church, academy, and community. The religious community could make individuals better believers when, at its best, the university could make individuals better thinkers; however, by working together, each fully open to the other's critiques, they could make better citizens. For Aubrey, the crucible for this task was the religion department that he founded at the University of Pennsylvania.

An additional rationale given for religion departments in the 1930s and '40s was that religious thought could present a worldview that would unify the fragmentation of the knowledge that university research produced. In 1951, Amos N. Wilder's much-cited *Liberal Learning and Religion* included Aubrey's essay "Scientia, Scientific Method and Religion."[37] Here, Aubrey addressed the place of science and religion in higher education, with special attention paid to their relationship to vocational and general education.[38] In this essay, he asked, What is the proper aim of liberal education? If it is knowledge, how can we teach such a fragmented *scientia*? An unintended consequence of modernity was that knowledge was now fragmented because of our having discovered that putting too much faith in science was no better than putting too much faith in the Bible or dogmatic theology. Now a balance of each could help bridge the gap between science and religion. Science and religion needed each other, and a particular brand of theology offered resources that were particularly helpful in bringing them together.

Aubrey placed himself tangentially in the camp of midcentury existentialists.[39] He claimed that existence and reflection upon it brought one to appreciate the fact that culture transcended science because it included morality and religion.[40] He was convinced that more was at work in the world than that which could be seen and scientifically verified, but that Christian doctrine was not always the best description of that deeper reality. Only cultured persons have a "deep and critical knowledge . . . [a] philosophy of life that looks beyond the present historical situation to the meanings of human existence."[41] Liberal education was to bring culture to the country.

Clearly, Aubrey was not satisfied with traditional Christian (liberal or conservative) doctrine, and he was convinced that science was fallible, incomplete, and open to interpretation: "Science and religion did not need to be brought together in harmony as much as science needed to be exposed to the 'depth of human experience.'"[42] Religion could save science, but not in the way Fundamentalists of the early twentieth century might have imagined.[43] Science could also provide a grounding for religion, which is why the university was a proper place for the teaching of religion.

One of the most difficult problems for the study of religion as Aubrey saw it was how it compared with science's aim of objectivity. Aubrey believed that the study of religion "demands personal involvement if the situation is to be understood. . . . The man who has never made a personal commitment in the area of religion cannot know what religious experience is. In this respect religion is closer to art than to science."[44] The core of religion was, for him, the realization by humans that final decisions and actions must be made with limited and incomplete knowledge. Humans either rebelled against acting and deciding (but in doing so did act and decide) or rebelled against complete understanding by making decisions and acting as if they had no reason whatsoever to be tentative. This was a universal condition, according to Aubrey, and the decisions one made seemed to denote what kind of religion one had. Education should strive to reveal this dynamic, thus clarifying human thought, action, and struggle for the individual. He believed this clarity was facilitated in part by teaching religious thought.

In pointing out that those who have not made a commitment to religion cannot understand religious experience, Aubrey was claiming not that one must be religious in order to study religions but rather that one cannot know deeply that which one has not experienced. Aubrey's theological position changed from the 1930s to the 1950s, and we can see this by observing his criticisms of various authors or religious leaders. Early on, during the religiously triumphalist years between the wars, he attacked the "sectarian and neo-orthodox" approach. In the 1940s, he suspected the turn toward religion of being superficial and wrong, but he found it understandable and interpretable. In the 1950s, Aubrey wondered why morals, values, and religious insights were not welcome in the university, pointing out that astronomy was not removed from the curriculum because a large number of people believe in astrology.[45] To those individuals who wanted Christianity to be in charge once again, Aubrey seemed an antidogmatist, and he was far too religious, superstitious, or moralistic for those who refused the supernatural realm any foothold in the university.

As for broader academic issues such as "general education," Aubrey echoed the University of Chicago's Robert Hutchins: "The major issue in education today is whether science, knowledge, and wisdom are identical terms. Here lies a fundamental problem in the relation between vocational and general education."[46] For Aubrey, unity in education, a must for him as for Hutchins, depended on wisdom, which was in jeopardy because scholars from different fields no longer communicated with one another: "In the face of such attitudes [specialization] all talk of education as a process of developing an integrated personality has been all but futile, and the student has been victimized by a process that leads to more confusion than wisdom."[47]

Religion had something to offer the curriculum, however. Religion could help keep scientific exuberance in its proper place. Aubrey appreciated scientific discovery when it was kept humble, but students needed to realize there existed a realm that transcended their understanding. Religion was the realm that keeps us from too much certainty. Scientific knowledge was not intrinsically good (atomic energy and the bomb were cited): "What we need is a recovery of perspective. And this is the meaning of wisdom."[48] Perspective was what religion had to offer the science-laden curriculum of general education. Aubrey did share Stanford professor Alexander Miller's and Arnold Nash's views regarding the Nazi university and the supposed neutrality such a model offered: "When scientists refuse to recognize [false neutrality] they have no protection against sinister forces in society which, as in Nazi Germany, prostitute science to the cause of oppression, deception, and false propaganda. The uneasy conscience of nuclear physicists about the atom bomb is a hopeful sign. . . . Man now finds himself in a position to bring human history to an end, and he is not only frightened by the prospect but confused about its meaning."[49] Again, when students understood what religion brought to the discussion, to the cultural critique, they found the deeper meaning that science simply could not give.

Like other Protestant educators of the 1950s, Aubrey believed that religion courses were only a beginning. He believed that he would not be doing his full duty if he were merely to encourage "instituting courses in religion, valuable as these are in clarifying the nature of the religious moment we have discussed. The religious perspective must be brought to bear on the determination of the function, the methods and the content of education." Aubrey wanted all who were thinking about education to be subject to intelligent thinking from the religious perspective. Though skeptical of calls to end "secularism" in education, Aubrey did want the "chief ends of human life" to guide the "distribution of subjects" in a curriculum. In full agreement with Hutchins's complaints about the increasingly professionalized curriculum across the country, he wrote, "The purely vocational aim must be modified and supplemented by the effort to enrich the life of the student as a person and to set the vocational task in the broader context of social life and human destiny." Aubrey wanted students to see their "own special vocation[s] in the larger perspective."[50]

Aubrey did not differ greatly from George Thomas at Princeton in expressing why he thought religion should be part of the curriculum. If religion was a significant facet of human culture, clearly it should be studied as carefully as other factors. If we are to talk of religion as an integrating force in human life, we must know what religion is. The need existed, therefore, for systematic courses in the field of religion: its history, basic concepts, psychological processes, great literary products and expressions, role in social change, and demands on conduct. Such studies must be carried on with exacting scholarship, with appreciative understanding, and with a sense of religion's crucial importance comparable to the best in scientific and humanistic study.

Only against such a background could any useful appraisal be made of the so-called spiritual aspects of our experience. At the same time, such courses provided an opportunity for studied consideration of other aspects of our common life in the light of religion. They dealt with convictions about the nature of humans in relation to their responsibilities, about the extent of their knowledge of the world, and about the meaning of history seen in reference to the universe of which it was a part.[51]

Religion found its home in the colleges somewhere between the humanities, as Aubrey placed it, and the social sciences, as many historians and sociologists imagined it. So then, could the study of religion be objective, according to Aubrey? Sometimes yes and sometimes no, but in any case, a negative verdict could not be used to exclude religion from the college's curriculum, as art and literary appreciation would have to be jettisoned by this criterion. Aubrey did not consider religion objective in the sense of being "completely detached," but no one can make that claim about any subject, he argued. Religion was objective if it recognized "personal bias in the reporting of experience and in the forming of conclusions based on experience. . . . As the theologians would say, there are limitations of both sin and finitude which restrict us in the endeavor. It is to the credit of religion that it freely recognizes these limitations. This is in itself a corrective. This corrective is part of the discipline of religious studies."[52] Thus for Aubrey, the religious person and the scientist were on common ground. Naturally, universities should have religion departments that stand alongside biology departments. Both were necessary to aid the other. Aubrey did not see clearly the tensions that would be inherent in a Protestant minister teaching Christianity as the best option among many at an institution such as the University of Pennsylvania, and he found little resistance there. However, at Yale, the tension evident in the prewar arguments for teaching religion continued to manifest itself.

Benjamin E. Mays as Schoolmaster

Edwin Aubrey's additional contribution to the creation of religion programs in the United States included his earlier mentorship of the great African American scholar Benjamin Elijah Mays. Aubrey was Mays's dissertation advisor at the University of Chicago, and Mays went on to establish the new School of Religion at Howard University under the leadership of the first Black president of Howard, Mordecai W. Johnson. While the school's purpose was distinguished from college religion departments in that it was to serve graduate students preparing for the ministry, the teaching of religion at Howard to college students was within the purview of Mays, and he became known as the "Schoolmaster of the Movement."

Mays's project at Howard was simultaneously to shut down the bachelor of theology degree and elevate the status of the study of Christianity on campus as he focused his efforts on the graduate and professional study of theology in the divinity school. Chicago professor

H. N. Wieman, noted previously, was also a great influence on Benjamin Mays, who himself was recruited to Fisk University (alma mater of, later Chicago professor, John Hope Franklin) before heading directly to Howard after having been made an offer that was more enticing to him than Fisk's.

Between Morehouse, Fisk, Virginia Union, and Howard, historically Black college and university religion departments were bolstered or created in the 1930s and '40s with distinctive concerns related to the limited opportunities and plight of African American students in the Jim Crow United States of America, placing race restrictions on scholars at the very height of their scholarship.[53]

CHAPTER NINE

Yale Tensions Reveal Divinity School Model Problems

At Yale, proponents of the importance of Christian advocacy in teaching religion were still being opposed by advocates of a more scholarly investigation of religion. The Reverend John Schroeder chaired the new Department of Religion from 1946 to 1954.[1] Religion department faculty members were caught between divinity school partisans who joined with students wanting more Christian faith–based courses and their own intentions to be "more objective," which Erwin R. Goodenough supported vigorously. The development of the department during this period was filled with instance upon instance in which such issues were played out.[2]

While Princeton's innovation was to separate the practice (chapel, counseling, campus ministry) and classroom teaching of religion de jure if not de facto, Schroeder explained to Yale's new president A. Whitney Griswold the possible costs of a corollary separation at Yale: "Were we to attempt to separate the work of the Department of Religion from the Divinity School, not only would it prove to be a most expensive operation, but it would also tend to create an unfortunate division among faculty who are committed to the same end. We had this situation before the Department of Religion was formed in 1946 and there were many unhappy conflicts." The creation of the new department at Yale in

1946 ensured that the divinity school was at least as integral as it had been before World War II, and possibly even more so.[3]

In bringing the subject of religion to college students in the 1940s and 1950s, Yale professors and administrators hoped not to convert students to Protestant Christianity per se but to give them a philosophical framework for life. Objectivity versus advocacy or, more precisely, scholarly research versus teaching traditions was the contested ground upon which college faculty, divinity school professors, corporation members, and presidents fought about this incarnation of taught religion. The rationale given for teaching religion at Yale also clarified one of the more important dynamics of midcentury higher education and one that is still with us: the college becoming university or the inculcation of tradition becoming the creation of new forms of knowledge through original research. As Schroeder described the tension, while some Yale college professors were focused more on investigating religion as a phenomenon, others felt the pull of student needs, which to them seemed paramount:

> The major complaint against the department is that the courses do not convert men to Christianity (Actually some men have joined the church as a result of an interest development in a course in religion). This is a variation of THE GOD and MAN at YALE[4] theme. But if this is the acid test of what we are seeking to do, the Department of Religion is in no worse case than that of liberal education as a whole.[5]

Conversion to Christianity was not the primary focus of teaching religion for most Yale professors, but a disinterested investigation of the "facts of religion" (à la Goodenough) was of little use also. Too much was at stake in the formation of the country's future leading citizens.

Innovation at Princeton

Highly varied college religion departments were scattered throughout the landscape of American higher education in the 1940s. The National Association of Biblical Instructors (NABI) counted among their members many teachers from these departments. Most were seminary-trained teachers of courses focused primarily on biblical texts and

Christian history. And though some may have been innovators in this college or that, we find every indication, even from NABI leaders themselves as expressed in presidential addresses from 1945–47, that the academic quality and scholarly content of such courses were generally not comparable to similar courses and professors in other disciplines.[6]

The department at Princeton did embark on a radically different path from those of other schools in at least two aspects. Their initial innovation was the attempt to separate religious studies from the chapel and campus ministry programs and to insist that faculty be trained in more rigorous PhD-granting institutions. The second aspect that made this department interesting and exemplary involved the arguments educators made for teaching religion and the circumstances under which religion was taught and the religion department was created. The goal of the department was to serve students, religious institutions, Princeton, and the country while mirroring other academic departments in their standards for research and teaching.

The courses offered at Princeton in 1950 by Thomas and his colleagues were focused primarily upon basic introductions to the biblical texts and modern religious thought, from Immanuel Kant to Reinhold Niebuhr. Courses of the latter category were concerned mainly with strands of religious thought that brought into question theism as a viable religious belief. Examination questions encouraged students to explain the threat to theism and how Schleiermacher, Kierkegaard, and others might have answered such critiques. William Adams Brown, W. E. Garrison, B. H. Streeter, Henry P. Van Dusen, and Reinhold Niebuhr were used as secondary sources. These authors were the epitome of mainstream liberal Protestantism at midcentury. When religions were divided up in the curriculum, the three categories were Judaism, Catholicism, and Protestantism. Oddly enough, the latter was divided again into six denominations and sects, including Mormonism, Christian Science, and the Oxford movement.

George Thomas was not the Princeton equivalent of the globetrotting lecturers who visited three campuses per week with uplifting religious reflections or political exhortations. He did, however, lecture several times per year at campuses across the country on topics such as ethics, philosophy of religion, and the need for the study of religion in higher education. Between 1943 and 1956, Thomas gave addresses at

Jewish Theological Seminary, Virginia Theological Seminary, Princeton Theological Seminary; Virginia Polytechnic Institute (Virginia Tech); Berkeley Divinity School; Sweet Briar, Hollins, Harvard, and Oberlin Colleges; and the University of Pennsylvania. In addition to campus visits, he participated in the Kent Fellows Week of Work, lectured at church conferences and congregational gatherings, and participated in various seminars, including Hazen Foundation conferences and the science, philosophy, and religion conferences.[7]

Thomas became an important consultant for more than forty schools interested in investigating the creation or revitalization of a department of religion. In addition to his correspondence with Huston Smith (Washington University / Syracuse[8]), Arnold Nash (University of North Carolina), William Christian (Yale), Glenn Morrow (University of Pennsylvania), and students at Harvard, Thomas also regularly corresponded with numerous other colleges and universities, many of which were church-affiliated. He encouraged their attempts to create departments and find a home for religion in the curriculum.[9]

In several surveys of student opinions, which Thomas acknowledged he did not take too seriously,[10] the religion courses, and Professor Thomas in particular, were rated highly by students. Thomas kept the *Daily Princetonian*'s survey articles regarding the religion courses in a personal file which became part of his papers in the Princeton archives concerning the department. Whether the religion courses were rated highly because they were enjoyable, fascinating, rigorous, graded more easily, or all of the above is not easy to determine. But we can fairly say that there were no protests about the creation or continual activity of the department during its early years of existence—that is, until the "Catholic Controversy" of 1954 marked the end of any real or imagined honeymoon period for Thomas and the department.

In summary, analysis reveals several tensions common to many attempts to teach religion in colleges during the period:

1. self-imposed boundaries of religious belief versus the freedoms of academic exploration at a budding research university;
2. advocacy versus chastened objectivity;
3. religion as a special sui generis force versus religion as reducible, describable phenomenon;

4. religious knowledge as accessible to reason versus the inaccessibility of such a special knowledge, which disallows academic investigation;
5. secularism (via naturalism and materialism) versus a religion that is the basis of democracy, freedom, and unity of meaning;
6. professional seminary training versus liberal arts training;
7. religion as a new descriptive category embracing a force underlying all particular religions versus the study of specific religious traditions; and
8. the practice of religion versus teaching about religion.[11]

In the 1930s and '40s, Princeton joined many schools in their attempt to bring religion back into the curriculum, this time as an academic subject equal to other disciplines. The arguments made by the institution as a whole and by individual presidents, deans, and professors were filled with earnest attempts to treat religion, usually Protestant Christianity and its interpretation of the Hebrew tradition, as a subject more than a method or practical classroom goal.[12] For the most part, however, religion returned to the classroom with a less sectarian image, more educated teachers, and an appreciative glance toward non-Western religions. As the departments developed, they faced questions about how inclusive their definition of religion was going to be. Were Catholics and Jews welcome to teach Catholicism and Judaism or even Protestant thought and practice? Other questions arose about the way in which Christianity was or was not best categorized as a religion itself. Further debate about religion's place in the curriculum brought to light the question of whether a department was necessary to better teach about religion.

The importance of religion in the classroom was not foreign to Christian Gauss.[13] At the end of his career as college dean at Princeton University and only a few years before he died, Gauss edited *The Teaching of Religion in American Higher Education*. This group of essays, developed from consultations with a committee including George Thomas and Theodore M. Greene, restated the goals of introducing college students to religion. Gauss explained succinctly the origins of the rethinking of religion's place in the college curriculum:

The appearance of new ideologies in Hitler's Germany and in Soviet Russia, and systems of education hostile to our democracy, has shocked us out of our earlier complacency. Most of the curricular revisions made since the outbreak of World War II are an attempt to face these new situations and are, for the most part, concerned with providing some sort of core to American education. . . . Some of our tougher minded educators have occasionally used the phrase "the escape into religion." When they use this phrase they usually overlook the fact that for better or worse this is a new development in American education.[14]

Gauss also joined the growing number of Christian scholars who pointed to the religious foundations of colleges, and to religion's former place of prominence in these institutions, in order to explain, if not justify, the renewal of interest in religion. Regarding the attempt to keep religion out of state schools, Gauss interjected that communists and Nazis "are opposed to religion as such and exclude it from their system of education."[15] In defending religion as a college subject Gauss used the familiar analogy of political science. Teaching political science was no more dangerous than teaching religion. The way in which one taught a subject, not that subject itself, could present problems. Gauss did not, however, entertain the idea that political science professors would not have been allowed to teach communism with the same sympathetic tone as Thomas would be when teaching Christianity. Such liberties could be taken with teaching religion because it offered so much that was considered good for students.

According to Gauss, the purpose of teaching religion was not to convert atheists but rather to train the "whole man in the unity of knowledge." This was especially important, since naturalistic humanism missed the point that humans transcend these elements of human existence. Without religion, there was no reason to believe in the dignity of "man," and democracy depended on such a view. Gauss also reminded readers that freedom of inquiry was paramount and that scholars must take the subject where they will. He was, however, confident that religion (by which he meant liberal Protestantism) could not or would not be proven false when put to the test.[16] In short, professors such as Gauss saw no dual role for religion departments, no tension between practical and theoretical knowledge per se, because the practical study and application of Christianity would prove to be empirically verifiable truth.

The preface to *Religious Perspectives in College Teaching*, a celebrated book among Christian academics during the 1950s, identified several issues that Thomas, one of the authors, addressed regularly from his position at Princeton University's department of religion:

> Religion is not nature worship, or man worship, or science worship. It is not the totality of human value. Although it is metaphysical, ethical and humanitarian, it cannot be equated with metaphysics, or ethics or humanitarianism. Religion is a quest for communion with an ultimate spiritual reality completely independent of human desires and imaginings. Religion apprehends this Absolute Reality and Value in faith, and seeks to give concrete embodiment to the ineffable in creed, cult, and conduct. The creative power of the universe is not an intellectual abstraction but an objective entity, a Divine Being. Although God infinitely transcends our human nature and understanding, He most potently reveals Himself to those who conceive of Him in personal terms. Thus symbolized, He becomes for us not merely Cosmic Mind, but Creator, Judge, and Redeemer of mankind.[17]

Thomas focused on the fundamental reasons that professors should teach a religious outlook when teaching religion. He began by establishing that a process of moral breakdown in Western civilization had been occurring since the First World War, citing Germany's high intellectual development and base ideology and the use of the atomic bomb as prime examples of how such changes threaten our very existence. He described a spiritual and cultural crisis marked by the disappearance of a common view of man and the world—a view that manifested itself in traditional beliefs, habits, and sentiments underlying the convictions of citizens. Thomas proclaimed that higher education had both been affected by and helped create the crisis.

Colleges, according to him, had as institutions left behind their own ideals for those of the university, moving away from the classics of Western religious culture toward specialization and vocationalism. These developments aided the general process of secularization, which for Thomas meant a preoccupation with interests and values of the material world. Thomas wrote that religion had been virtually excluded from the curricula of liberal colleges, but the last ten years had seen a change for the better. A move against the evils of specialization and fragmentation and in favor of instruction in religion had swept through higher education.[18] These signs of good news were desperately needed in light of Thomas's and his colleagues' forebodings about the future of the nation.

The early 1950s was a period of relative calm before the storm regarding the rationale for the teaching of undergraduate religion: this was a time of unabashed advocacy for Protestant history and thought, a time when its advocates wasted few words arguing about its importance but instead simply stated it as if its relevance were understood and merely needed to be articulated and organized. There was little handwringing or self-doubt. The time for that was over and not yet begun. At the end of World War II, professors turned toward teaching new curricula that were no longer focused on wartime training. Courses were renovated to address postwar needs, and dramatic curricular reform continued throughout the late 1930s.

If the wartime crises of Western civilization and cultures helped open windows to the Protestant educators' dreams for teaching religion, the postwar turn toward religion only helped further. In the view of these educators, if religion was needed before the end of the war by a society that appeared to be crumbling, religion would certainly be needed in colleges during the rebuilding period. Those professors who argued in favor of departments were motivated by dreams for a stronger Christian influence on campus and by a need to articulate the new department's mission as academic, rigorous, and nonsectarian, if not objective.

Such a foundation for any given religion program was both helpful and problematic. It was helpful in that it covered both constituencies (church and school) and addressed the needs of the day. It was problematic because it created difficulty for the founders and their colleagues in clarifying their true mission in the university. Those who made the arguments for religion's resurgence in the curriculum were situated in the most elite institutions in the country at that time. These schools were watched closely by smaller, less prestigious schools, who looked to these postwar curricular changes in remaking their own schools.

Many administrators relied upon the development of religion programs as a force for good on campus. The creation of the University of Pennsylvania's religion department was an example of the continued goodwill toward religion in general on campus in the late 1940s. The 1950s, however, brought about conflict at both Yale and Princeton directly related to the dual role of the religion departments on those campuses. This change was indicated by the increased awareness of students about the Protestant focus of religion departments while universities were themselves moving away from their religious roots. Religion departments created in the 1940s came to face critical questions in the 1950s about their sectarian nature, and consequently, educators developed various rationales for the importance of teaching religion that moved away from advocacy and the enhancement of student life.

Most of the educators who argued for religion's place in a college curriculum were deeply certain that religion would hold up to the best scholarship. Their assurance came in part from their belief that religion opened a special door to a different kind of knowledge, thereby exempting them from having their religious assumptions subjected to the scrutiny of other modes of analysis. Religion, as part of the humanities, held the ultimate trump card in such a case. This protection against the ruling scrutiny of rationalism was also the basis for religion's entry into the humanities. It offered a different kind of knowledge, nonscientific but valuable based on its appreciation of and ability to further the flourishing of humanity. This humanizing feature of the study of religion would become an important rationale given by Protestant educators who sought to develop new religion departments in the late 1950s and early 1960s (the subject of the next chapter).

During the late 1950s, college religion programs primarily modeled on Protestant divinity schools faced a number of challenges to their curricula, but they were chiefly challenged by students and faculty who suspected that religion departments were less interested in understanding religion and humanity and more interested in promoting a particular brand of religiosity in order to mold humanity. The ideals upheld in the religion departments' creation during this period were a specific Protestant set of values in education that were no longer viable for the most part across entire institutions. So for a time, until the late 1960s brought a new focus, the religion departments held out hope that these values and beliefs might one day once again be viable beyond those teaching the theological and sacred texts to students. While that never happened on a large scale (save for a few narrowly religious colleges and universities), the humanities themselves, ever struggling with their own crises of faith, did, along with some biblical studies or theology departments under the developing concept of religious studies, begin to rebuild on the fractured foundations of these earlier departments. By the late 1970s onward, several major departments shifted from the one-to-two-person faculty model (with the Bible taught as literature and theology as philosophy) to a five-to-twenty-person multifaith study of religion as the Iowa model began to slowly win out over others for the teaching of religion.

The postfounding decade of 1954–64 signaled the beginning of a slow change away from unabashed advocacy teaching in elite college religion programs.[19] The model emerging from these controversies, and the hope of new faculty members, was that of studying and teaching religion in order better to understand humanity and thereby possibly understand how better to humanize the curriculum and students. What the programs shared in common, even in the 1950s, was the continuing assumption that the religion department's mission was both academic (to study and understand) and practical (to humanize and improve). Each of these roles was changing, but the dual role of the religion department remained an acknowledged goal throughout this period.

Here one finds the manifestations of the tension inherent in this dual role of religion departments at Princeton, Columbia, and Yale in the mid-1950s and, by way of comparison, at Stanford and Washington University. Stanford's Alexander Miller tried to eliminate the dual role by removing Christianity from the category of religion altogether. Washington University's Huston Smith tried to avoid the tensions inherent in the dual role by arguing against creating a religion department in the first place, preferring instead to allow religion scholars in other departments to do the research and teaching. These developments showed clearly the changes in the nature of the arguments advanced for the teaching of religion in colleges. Now no longer arguing for teaching Protestant Christianity on the basis of its efficacy in the religious lives of students or its salutary effects on Western civilization, religion educators were instead busy defending their faculties (composed primarily of Protestants), determining whether Christianity was a religion itself, and debating whether departments best served the topic of religion in the first place. The most active department founder at midcentury was not immune to the changes that came with this next stage in the development of college religion programs.

Protestant Departments of Religion?

George Thomas had defended the structure and purpose of the all-Protestant department at Princeton by arguing that surely one did not need to be a Buddhist or Catholic in order to teach these religions. But in the autumn of 1954, the director of the campus Aquinas Foundation, the Reverend Doctor Hugh Halton, publicly called into question the entire department of religion. Father Halton's earliest complaints were that a philosophy professor, W. T. Stace, was an atheist and that his system of morals was not compatible with Christian belief. Stace declined to comment, but religion professor Paul Ramsey answered these charges against Stace, refuting the claims by quoting from Stace's own writings.

Halton then turned his guns toward the religion department. Why were no Catholics on the faculty? How could Catholic students expect to get good training in religion from such a department? The editors of the *Daily Princetonian* reported this attack and added in an editorial, "We must concur, though perhaps from motives different from his, with Father Halton's recent reiterated criticism of the Department of Religion here." The student editors agreed that a group of committed Protestant professors would probably not be able to give a fair view of Roman Catholicism: "We are immediately faced, of course, with the problem of objectivity in teaching. . . . The University Catalog outlines a three-fold structure by which Princeton, though non-sectarian, remains religious: compulsory chapel [first two years], the Student Christian Association, and the Department of Religion." The editors also noted the catalog's comment that "the members of the Faculty of the Department of Religion regularly preach in the Chapel. This certainly sounds suspiciously as if Princeton is strongly promoting Protestantism over all other major religions."[20]

They leveled their most direct criticism in pointing out the Protestant advocacy focus of the department: "Although other faculty members may be considered biased in one direction or another, whole groups from one department do not have to be committed to one line as in religion: in other departments the professors are teachers, not preachers. To say that the religion department, as set up at Princeton inevitably fits into the liberal arts program therefore becomes ludicrous and Father Halton has reason to complain. . . . It seems strange to us that a religion department such as the one at Princeton should receive status as a full-fledged liberal arts department."[21] The religion faculty did not respond directly. Instead, E. Harris Harbison of the History Department replied in a letter to the newspaper. Though he agreed that it would be good to have a Roman Catholic on the faculty, he explained that it was not practical, because few laymen had received the education that Princeton would require in order to be a faculty member, while priests would be subject to church discipline, thus disqualifying them from true university research.[22]

Harbison's comments bring into focus one recurring dynamic with which new religion departments had to contend around the country. Namely, that when looking for faculty members to staff a department of religion, Princeton and other schools would only have been able to find seminary-trained individuals. There were no other options for the mass training of scholars of religion. Those who were interested in such an education were likely to be Protestants, usually members of liberal or mainline denominations. The economy of an academic discipline relies on the resources of the graduate education available. Charles Foster Kent understood this when he founded the National Council on Religion in Higher Education. What other options would Princeton have, had it wanted anything other than Protestant Christians teaching religion to its undergraduates? Such was the question posed by Thomas and other Protestant educators.

By 1959, the religion department at Princeton had nine members, the largest in the country at that time for a single institution.[23] Though courses on Judaism and two Eastern religions were offered, these subjects were taught by divinity school or seminary-trained Protestants, some of whom were ordained ministers. The controversy surrounding their ability to be objective did not go away quickly, and it served as a helpful clarifying moment for the department. During the 1960s, the department did diversify its faculty from the standpoint of the religious affiliation of its professors and the topics they taught. The seminary curricular model consisting of Old Testament, New Testament, church history, and theology began to expand to include ethics and world religions. Among recently renovated religion programs around the country, Princeton's was regarded as the consummate department's department: it was large, it included faculty dedicated to emerging subfields within the study of religion, and it viewed itself less as an influencer of other departments and more as a viable department structure that should be valued as such. This was a strategy entirely the opposite of Stanford University's new religion program, which was designed to permeate the entire faculty and each department with a deeper understanding of Christianity.

A Nondepartment to Address the Entire University

Alexander Miller was less concerned with saving Western civilization in the late 1950s than with saving Christianity from religion departments that treated it as just another religion. As a "Christian student activist from New Zealand," Miller took to task Columbia's John Dillenberger for conflating Christianity and religion. Miller took issue with Dillenberger's claim that "religion is a subject matter, but it is also a total outlook on life." This claim seemed to comport poorly with Dillenberger's demand that religion not be privileged. Miller wondered, rhetorically, if any other subject matter in the curriculum was a "total outlook on life." To answer his own question, Miller recommended the following three ways in which to approach religion in the classroom: (1) as a social-cultural-historical construct of endless variety, (2) as a dimension of particular academic disciplines, and (3) as Christianity, which cannot be subsumed under religion as one element within a category.[24] The first approach belonged in a religion department, the second should be handled by professors in their respective disciplines, and the third, Christianity, was of more use to students as theology taught outside any kind of religion department, which would merely point to it as one option among many.

Christianity had special privileges within the university system, according to Miller, because "the Western university is inexplicable without the Church of the Apostles." This argument found a corollary in the writings of Princeton's George Thomas and others. Thomas believed that university curricula and most areas of thought within the humanities were tied irreversibly to Christianity or the Western religious tradition in such a way as to require homage. In fact, according to Thomas and Miller, such institutions and areas of study (Western philosophy, for instance) owed their very foundations to Christianity, and therefore it deserved more than respect: Christianity deserved preference.[25] For Miller, the university needed to answer the question of its relation to the "Community of Faith" before it could answer the question of its own self-understanding.[26]

Harvard's situation (having a divinity school on campus) was one helpful way to think through a university's identity, Miller believed. The divinity school at Harvard was so lacking in influence that the philosophy department exerted more sway over the teaching of religion to undergraduates.[27] But Miller lamented that at Stanford, the chapel and curriculum did not play more important roles in determining the way in which the "Communities of Faith and Learning" related.[28] He spent the remaining years of his life (he lived only until 1961) creating a religion program that would address the issues surrounding the church's relationship with the university.

Miller did not want religion to become a separate department, nor did he understand Christianity to fit properly within the category of religion, at least not in the same way that Hinduism or Buddhism might be taught in such a department. Miller showed disdain for bringing together the practice of Christianity and the study of religion, not because he feared "the practice" would contaminate the objective study of religion, but the reverse: the study of religion subordinated Christianity and was therefore dangerous.

His book *Faith and Learning*, written in 1959, put Alexander Miller on the map as the American heir apparent to Sir Walter Moberly, a British scholar accorded an honored place by many Christian educators. Miller's death at a young age was a blow to many who saw him as the "American Moberly," a champion for theology and the church within higher education. Miller was geographically far removed from the coterie of "religion and education" scholars of the East Coast, but Stanford University provided for him a bully pulpit from which to preach the reunification of theology and the church. The professor of religion who jump-started the department in 1956 became just as well known as such Stanford chaplains as B. Davie Napier, D. Elton Trueblood, and Robert MacAfee Brown. Reinhold Niebuhr's written introduction to Alexander Miller's *The Renewal of Man* placed Miller alongside George Thomas, who fought vigorously against an interpretation of human existence that reduced individuals to biological mechanisms devoid of a spirit.[29] All three believed that the traumas of the first half of the twentieth century proved non-Christian schemes of salvation to be devoid of true redemption, whether material or spiritual.

Miller summed up the most common tension between religious practice and university practice when he wrote that "Christianity cannot be true to itself without claiming in some sense *to be the truth* about life, and education cannot be true to itself without cherishing the utmost freedom in the undogmatic *quest for the truth* about life."[30] Not only did Miller reveal something about life at Stanford in suggesting that "the Christian enterprise in the university may have things too easily its own way,"[31] but also telling was the date of his proclamation: 1959. The turbulent 1960s had not yet left their mark on campuses, and the Cold War concerns of national moral decay from within remained strong.

The university, in Miller's estimation, had found its freedom from any church authority and now lacked any ordering principle. Although the church had not been able to offer any help before the war, now a more unified and stronger "Community of Faith" had something to offer the "Community of Learning": "This does not at all mean that the university is in any mood to put itself under theological tutelage again; but it does mean that it is less self-confident and more ready to pick up clues where it can. The effect is that the university's interior debate about its own nature and function can readily be widened to take in the contribution of the theologian, provided . . . he has no personal or professional axe to grind."[32] The organizing principle for this university was to be Christian theology.

Eighteen months after his arrival at Stanford as the "first person to receive a special teaching appointment in the field of religion," Miller was interviewed about his work by the alumni magazine, the *Stanford Review*. He described his passion for the opportunity to "teach the Christian faith and tradition, with complete Christian and scholarly freedom, to the student body of one of the most influential universities in America."[33] Huston Smith's program at Washington University involved having a religion specialist in each major department, though not a department unto itself.[34] Miller argued vigorously for—and then created a program at Stanford that included—both a study of "religions" and an examination of Christianity as a viable worldview within the humanities.

Miller was confident that Christian theology would be welcomed into colleges because the "intellectual atmosphere" on campuses had changed. Comparing 1930 with 1952, Miller described the situation:

> The prevailing mood was dominated by an evolutionary theory offering itself as an optimistic life philosophy, and by a mechanistic science. . . . As for historic Christianity—"Christianity," said a young spokesman for the triumphant mood, "is dead. The problem is how to get rid of the body before it smells too much." . . . Now, the naturalist-mechanist in the classroom may be vocal and terrible there, but he is actually an anachronism, his stuff a little musty and around him the aura of a forgotten man. . . . It is a very curious anomaly that just about the time when we have naturalistic presuppositions structured into our academic disciplines—especially in the social sciences—the most influential intellectual workers of our day are preoccupied again with the issues of faith, and many of them are explicitly Christian—like Berdyaev, Maritain, Niebuhr, Toynbee and the later Eliot.[35]

Christianity was intellectually acceptable on campus again, and Miller believed it deserved respect and thoughtful discussion more than a spiritless examination by the specialized social scientists. In commenting on Huston Smith's departmentally based specialists, Miller noted that there was "something invidious in the notion of specialists in religion, as if any cultural materials could be adequately studied by anyone without reference to that dimension of depth which is implicit everywhere, whether or not it finds explicit expression in religious phenomena."[36] Miller feared the religion specialist who saw no deep meaning in religious behavior and practicing religious communities. His concern mirrored that of those Protestant educators in the 1930s who were concerned not with the absence of scholarship and writing on religious matters at colleges and universities but with the particular kind of attention that was paid to religious data. Miller and other program founders had in mind a Christian perspective that needed to be inserted into curricula regardless of the general coverage that "religion" might be receiving in history, literature, sociology, anthropology, art, and other departments.

Miller used the new "turn toward religion" during the early 1950s to create a program that he felt addressed the needs of the times. He also noted the tension inherent in the call to religion for a university such as Stanford. When the new mood of the post–World War II period presented universities not only with the need but also with the responsibility for "doing something about religion," they were faced with a twofold problem: on the one hand, to be substantially faithful to the intention of the founders of the university and to the developing character of the university and, on the other hand, to do justice to the religious and theological facts of life.[37] Miller found this dual role for the religion department problematic.

Critics of religion departments have argued that the model of departments failed because it immediately relieved other departments from the responsibility of teaching religion. According to Miller, such a department also tends to "subsume Christianity under religion-in-general, and therefore does not properly discriminate and properly use the unique starting point and method of Christian theology."[38] Miller wanted every department to study religion so that Christianity could do the work of changing the campus one student at a time. In this way, his argument was like that of the University of North Carolina's Arnold Nash.

Miller was adamant in arguing that Christian faith and theology should not be set apart from business and politics, as would be the case if Christianity were classified as just one more manifestation of "religion-in-general." He was concerned that Christianity would lose its power and force in the practical world if it were categorized in such a way. Miller was deeply interested in how Christian reflection could improve the everyday lives of individuals, and he concluded that "Whatever be the authentic relation of Christian faith to the university curriculum, it is not 'departmental.'"[39]

In attempting to reunite the "Community of Faith" with the "Community of Learning," the department of religion was of little use. Miller

set out to present another option—"theology for the undergraduate."
Fewer than ten years later, such a plan for Stanford would seem outdated
to many younger scholars, but Miller was riding the wave of renewed
interest in postwar piety, and he received all the necessary support from
the Stanford administration. In a parenthetical remark, Miller admitted that "the word *religious* is no doubt a concession to habitual usage;
it is actually an undergraduate curriculum in theology . . . housed in a
Special Program in Humanities." The courses in the program focused
on "the biblical and Christian heritage."[40] Miller stated outright what
most Protestant educators were hesitant to admit: namely, that when
they said religion, they meant Protestant Christian theology. Many
Protestant educators, however, felt that "theology" as a word and concept carried partisan overtones when used in the context of curricular
developments.

When confronted with the plurality of religious communities within
a university context, Miller explained his approach to pluralism in this
way: "Though some of us may be committed to the truth of Protestant
Christian faith, the university is not so committed, so that our right to
a place in its curricular life must be grounded on the relevance (not
the truth) of biblical faith to the university debate."[41] "Relevance" was
a theme that had not yet had its new day in universities, as it would in
the mid-to-late 1960s. Miller reclaimed what early religion department
founders argued during World War II: that religion was relevant to the
task at hand, whether that task was conceived of as saving Western civilization through democracy (Thomas, Shedd, Nash) or reuniting the
wrongly divorced segments of university and church (Aubrey, Miller).
Miller's rationale was just the kind of reasoning that Huston Smith
wanted to avoid in creating his nondepartmental program of religion at
Washington University. Smith wanted to move beyond pushing Protestantism per se and lean toward an appreciation of both religions in
specific and religion in general—a move that Miller feared would do a
disservice to the church.

Studying Religion within Other Departments

The first significant attempt during the 1950s to avoid the tension of the
dual responsibilities of the religion department was made by Smith, a

University of Chicago PhD in the history of religions. Smith became the director of the religion program in the college at Washington University during the early 1950s after completing his doctoral studies in philosophy at Chicago in 1945. Over the next fifty years, he taught at several institutions and made popular his own view of the world's "major religions," most notably in his book *Man and His Religions* (later retitled *The World's Religions*), which has sold nearly two million copies. He clarified his position in his 1955 *The Purposes of Higher Education*: "In one sense the problem of religion's place in the curriculum is so simple that it affords the most obvious plot on which both secular and religious can stand; in another it is so difficult that it utterly precludes concerted solution in our time."[42] Smith argued that a religion department would not be as effective as having one religion scholar on each of the relevant departments, such as philosophy, sociology, history, and literature. Religion should be studied throughout the curriculum, not cordoned off in a department of its own.

Smith was confident that every educator agreed religion should be part of the curriculum, but no one could agree on exactly how it should be taught. Smith disagreed with many of his Protestant educator colleagues, stating that this question was not easily answered. He identified four pieces of the problem: (1) how to teach factual information concerning religion, (2) how to evaluate religion's worth, (3) how to delineate desirable life qualities, and (4) how to estimate the validity of the opposing worldviews.

The first piece of the problem was most easily resolved by clarifying common ground among educators, according to Smith. A vast majority of educators would agree, he stated, that religion is a valid field of scholarship, that it is not possible to understand our own cultural heritage without exposure to the facts of our religious traditions, and finally, that religion could be taught with objectivity: "Religion can be taught with an objectivity equal to what education expects in other fields. Obviously no subject, least of all one with a heavy value component, can be taught without a point of view. But . . . objectivity does not require complete detachment; it requires fairness with regard to evidence, respect for reasonable differences in point of view, and avoidance of all intent to proselytize among the institutions of one's culture. In this sense it has been widely demonstrated that religion can be easily

taught as objectively, say, as economics."[43] Departmental budget limitations aside, there was little argument that teaching factual information
about as many religious movements as possible would be desirable. It
was the evaluation of religion's worth where difficulties began.

Evaluating the worth of a religion while teaching it was at the heart
of the disagreement between what Smith referred to as the "secularist"
and "religionist" positions. Here Smith sought to show that the well-
known extreme positions were untenable by hypothesizing the following: "It is equally untrue that religion is always or is never (a) an escape
mechanism, (b) opposed to truth, or (c) socially reactionary."[44] Certainly, many given religions had become escape mechanisms for some
individuals, but not all religions are escape mechanisms. Likewise, not
all religions are opposed to truth, but neither are all religions always
concerned primarily with finding the truth, and the same holds for religion and reactionary tendencies. One can often find religions "sounding
a retreat from reality that is caused by timidity, personal inadequacy, or
neurosis. Millions have used religion as a curtain to draw across aspects
of reality they could not stand." Smith's departure from the traditional
religion department founders' defense of "high religion" or Protestant
Christianity was one characteristic that set him apart from so many
religion professors gone before. Smith struck a new chord of balance,
noting that "religion has fostered some of man's most sentimental illu-
sions and most craven wishful thinking, but it has also inspired some of
his clearest realism."[45] Religions can harm and religions can help—their
followers are capable of both, their texts include possibilities for interpreting both as inspired, their effects include good and ill. For Smith, it
was no longer only Christianity properly practiced that was most desirable, but an appreciation of all things negative, destructive, futile, and
dangerous about a religion, in addition to all the positive, constructive,
life-giving, fruitful, and good within a religion that made studying it
important.

Smith still had to fight the assumption he found among intellectuals and academics that theology was "in principle out of date." He had
observed that this assumption was widespread: "There is considerable
opinion among educators, particularly on the college and graduate lev-
els, that intellectually speaking religion represents the childhood mind
of the human race—fanciful, beautiful, even effective in its day but an

anachronism by the findings of twentieth-century science. . . . The truth of the matter is that college thinking about religion has remained too much dominated by the old Comtean view, which interpreted theology as primitive and largely misguided science standing in relation to our developed scientific world view as astrology does to astronomy or alchemy to chemistry."[46] This "negative evaluation" of religion troubled Smith, as it had elite Protestant educators for the previous forty years; however, Smith emphasized a concern not that students' religious lives would therefore be impoverished but that common ground between educators would be jeopardized. He claimed, above all, to be seeking the avoidance of "blanket evaluations that indiscriminately extol or deprecate religion as a whole."[47]

Smith's curricular agenda was made clear as he explained that, at times, religion "fully supports Marx's view of being the opiate of the people, both deadening the pain that arises from economic misery and dulling the drive to action that might otherwise remove its real course. But religion does not always function in this way."[48] Smith's goal was to show the college faculty and students alike that religion was not simply humanity's highest good, as had been argued by Protestant educators in the past, but that it was complicated and potentially harmful as well as personally and socially beneficial.

Smith's arguments for the importance of religion within the curriculum did not represent an entirely new stage in the development of teaching religion in college. The dual role of departments had not been entirely collapsed or separated in his program or thoughts. First, he affirmed the dual role of the old-style religion department when he argued that "secular and religious can agree that education should further certain life qualities that are often associated with religion but are honored by secularists also."[49] Educators should use religion (1) to quicken the student's aspiration; (2) to produce men and women capable of loving their neighbors, becoming good beyond matters of duty, and being kind, merciful, and compassionate; (3) to increase the student's sensitivity to the vast reaches of the world (to believe there are "more things in heaven and earth than our philosophy has dreamed of"); and (4) to deepen a student's faith, "not in the technical Thomistic sense of belief in the truth of propositions that reason cannot demonstrate, but in the commonsense meaning of the word, which is CONFIDENCE."[50]

Then Smith argued that religion departments were less useful than having religion specialists spread throughout the faculty. Professors in a religion department would not be able to influence the work of the entire faculty as much as specialists in each department. It was also problematic to have a religion department when the very definition of religion had been brought under scrutiny in recent years.

According to Smith, precise descriptions of religion were never pure. Rather, they reflected the metaphysical perspectives from which, consciously or not, they proceeded. A given description of religion could be understood only insofar as the perspective from which it viewed its subject was grasped. The validity of a given description of religion was contingent in large part on the relative adequacy of the metaphysical perspective from which it viewed its subject.[51] Smith asserted that in seeking to perfect our understanding of religion, attending to the perspectives from which religion was approached was just as important as improving descriptions of religions.[52] Better descriptions were contingent on improved perspectives. That is, when one taught religion in the classroom, one was about the business of helping students and colleagues examine their perspectives and how to improve them. Unfortunately, Smith never adequately clarified the criteria by which to judge these "improved" perspectives.

Huston Smith and Alexander Miller were founders of religion programs at a comparatively tranquil time in higher education's history. The turbulence of the early to mid-1960s would transform campuses, and the wartime fears of the 1940s had given way to Cold War concerns and space race fears of Russian dominance. Each, however, was fully convinced that a better understanding of Christianity (for Miller) and world religions (for Smith) would help students better navigate their experience of life. Smith represented an early departure from the dual tensions inherent in college teaching of religion at Princeton, Yale, Columbia, Stanford, the University of North Carolina, Penn, Harvard, and even Chicago. Miller also broke down the dual role of the department by moving toward the pole of theological advocacy for Christianity. Smith's model of a nondepartmental collection of religion professors did not win the day, but his attempt to move toward the pole of "teaching religion to understand humanity" did win out over Miller's approach.

Huston Smith, along with John Dillenberger and Van Harvey, represented a group of midcentury religion professors who were more interested in making the study of religion palatable to the new research university culture than in helping Protestant churches gain a foothold in colleges again.[53] For them, the teaching of religion was less of a cover for Protestant hopes and dreams and more of an attempt to find a way out of the Protestant hegemony of midcentury toward a general appreciation for the ambiguity of the term and of religion itself's meaning for societies. It was this general trend that Oberlin College's Clyde Holbrook hoped to propel when he researched and wrote his description of the field of religion as it stood in the early 1960s.[54]

Examples of the new curricular models can be seen in Alexander Miller's and Huston Smith's work, but theologians and philosophers who were not working on the implementation of such curricular ideas were also influential. Upon reading numerous volumes of the *Review of Religion* or the *Journal of Bible and Religion*, it becomes clear that these professors of biblical literature, theology, religious studies, and even world religions were not interested primarily in converting their students or even advocating for a particular theological position so much as they were using their academic positions to research, write, address, and work through answers to the most pressing theological problems in their own religious communities. Their discourse and the writings and teachings they produced thereby were not an attempt to persuade so much as they were an attempt to determine how to go forward. It was an exceedingly internal conversation that today would be found more likely in seminaries, some divinity schools, and only a few colleges (many of them denominational or even sectarian in nature).

Influencing the Founders

Underlying much of the Protestant rationale for the teaching of religion in colleges was the influence of Reinhold Niebuhr. Niebuhr not only contributed directly and indirectly to many of the arguments made for the teaching of religion in colleges, but he also spent time encouraging and training several of the department founders, and he served as advisor to several elite universities as they were creating departments.

For instance, he played an important role in the decision of Harvard University to create a religion curriculum that would especially reach undergraduates with Christian theology. He also was a leading force in the creation of Columbia University's large religion program and was colleague to founders at Penn, Princeton, and Stanford. Alexander Miller at Stanford had served as Reinhold Niebuhr's research assistant and protégé in many ways. Niebuhr rarely wrote directly about the issues of religion and higher education; his concerns were more deeply rooted in the tensions evident from the 1930s through the late 1950s. Niebuhr's article in Henry Kissinger's Harvard journal, *Confluence*, clarified his own understanding of how to move forward with the teaching of religious perspectives. Niebuhr, who had earlier championed the inculcation of particularly Protestant theology at Harvard and Columbia's colleges, took a step toward "critical detachment" in 1957 because he was deeply disturbed by what he regarded as the dangerous runaway American devotion to its own way of life.[55]

Reflecting upon why neither antireligious nor antisecular forces had taken over the college scene, Niebuhr noted that there was no religious instruction in the lower schools and it was forbidden by law in the state universities:

> Privately endowed universities of the East . . . often have departments of religion in which the student may come in contact with both the scriptural and historic roots of his faith, and almost all have rather vital extra-curricular religious activities. We do not, therefore, give a consistently secular education, though the rigorous separation of Church and state has certainly affected our culture in many respects. Chiefly it has reduced the religious tradition to a quasi-secular affirmation of those parts of the Christian tradition in which the religious and the secular part of the culture agree. The chief agreement is found in the emphasis on the "dignity of man." . . . This virtual agreement between the religious and secular traditions in a common humanism and humanitarianism has prevented the generation of fiercely antireligious and anti-secular movements.[56]

Thus according to Niebuhr, the old models did not work because they were not Christian enough.

Meanwhile, Niebuhr's common critic at Harvard, Morton White, continued to argue that Niebuhr was right in at least one regard—namely, that one cannot teach religions generally, only specific religions. White proposed a new model that was designed mainly to remove religion from the undergraduate curriculum and keep the teaching of religions in divinity schools or schools of theology only. White, then chair of Harvard's philosophy department, directly addressed Niebuhr's arguments in his *Confluence* retort three months later. He asked, Can a teacher give instruction—excellent instruction—about a given religion without being committed to that religion? Can a scholar successfully study a given religion without being committed to that religion? He concluded that the questions may be answered simply by appealing to the history of education and scholarship,[57] and he referred to George Foot Moore's studies of Judaism. The answer was resounding: "It is hard to know what is meant by those who maintain that one must be committed to a given religion in order to study it and to teach about it fully. Their error is just the reverse of those who say that an objective study of a religion can only be made by those who reject it."[58]

In an uncanny foretelling of a 1963 Supreme Court decision, White proclaimed that "in matters of scholarship and teaching *about* religion, literature, politics, philosophy, sociology or morals, the doctrine *Credo ut intellegam* [Augustine via Anselm] has no standing. . . . A scholar and teacher must insist that it is possible to understand a statement without accepting it."[59] Teaching about religion was acceptable to White, but since one cannot teach about religion in general, and there were too many specific religions about which the teacher would need to educate students, religion should be examined in graduate schools only. White's suggestion was never taken seriously, because those professors who had the greatest stake in teaching religion to undergraduates would not entertain such a seemingly outrageous idea. Religion would be taught more and more in undergraduate curricula throughout the country. White would have applauded several important developments in the early sixties, each of which played a significant role in the collapse of the dual role of religion departments from the 1960s to the beginning of the twenty-first century.

The historical trajectory of this book does not extend much beyond 1963 for several reasons. First, although the story of the dual role of the religion department (involving both pious examination and investigative teaching) certainly continued into the 1960s and well beyond, the handwriting was on the wall by the early 1960s that significant shifts in such models were arriving quickly. Confessionally trained and focused college professors of religion were on notice that their teaching, research, and writing would continue to be called into question in the public arena, whether by growing religious and academic pluralism on campuses, concerns of church-state separation, or widening definitions of religion among scholars and practitioners. Second, the responses of professional societies and Protestant elites to these changes comprise an entirely different story in the history of religious studies, and that story has been detailed in important books by D. G. Hart and Donald Wiebe.[60] Third, this book has specifically intended to contribute to the conversation by highlighting archival resources and historically significant college religion department-focused activities, the analysis of which might assist in a more balanced view of the thirty years leading up to this period of dramatic change and even turmoil. That having been clarified, the story would not be complete without a thumbnail sketch of the transition to a new day in religious studies.

Conclusion

College Model Shift Signals Religious Studies Start

In 1963, there were several events that significantly influenced or altered the landscape of the newly formed college religion departments and the nascent field of religious studies in such profound ways that their occurrences mark a transition away from midcentury debates, though not from their underlying tensions. These events particular to the teaching of religion do not include very important national events such as the killing of President John F. Kennedy Jr. and student movement protests and campus activity across the country over the next five years.

First, the National Association of Biblical Instructors (NABI, Hebrew for "prophet") issued a report stating that it should change its name to the American Academy of Religion (AAR) and the name of its journal to the *Journal of the American Academy of Religion* from the *Journal of Bible and Religion* beginning in the year 1964.[1] Second, the Supreme Court of the United States of America delivered a majority opinion in the case of *Abington v. Schempp* that was interpreted by religion department founders and professors (technically incorrectly) as confirming that state higher education institutions were allowed to teach "about" religion, though they could not teach it religiously. Third, Clyde Holbrook's *Religion, a Humanistic Field* was published as a part of Princeton's landmark series on the humanities, and John F. Wilson's response made clear the divisions founders had experienced for decades. Fourth, after the 1962 summer break at Yale University, several divinity school professors such as B. Davie Napier[2] returned to discover they were to be primarily located up the hill on the divinity campus, while others were assigned mainly to graduate students "down the hill" on the main university campus, with the college. That divide made more formal some of the fault lines revealed in earlier chapters regarding the teaching of religion at Yale. Finally, the Higher Education Facilities Act—along with other steps toward professionalization, including versions of the American Association of University Professors' academic freedom statements—pushed religion departments and professors toward the university model and one of the dual roles of religion discussed previously.

Furthermore, college campuses across America and throughout the world were beginning to come alive with student activism, protest, and concern about issues ranging from Vietnam, free speech, and government propaganda, to academic exploration of Eastern religions and pacifism. *Relevance* became a byword as leaders of ethnic factions began to make curricular demands on college administrations. Each of these four cultural, academic, and social changes shifted the debate in ways that did not exactly resemble those fault lines evident in debates from the 1930s through the 1950s.

Religion as a Humanistic Field, or as a Field within the Humanities

When Oberlin professor of religion Clyde Holbrook wrote one of the two commissioned "religion" books in the Princeton University series that assessed the progress of the humanities in the academy, he met with criticism from Princeton professor John F. Wilson (George Thomas's successor). Wilson was frustrated that once again Holbrook was promoting the idea that religion departments were meant to humanize students and better humankind. Wilson was ready to move to a fifth stage in the study of religion, where professors approached the material as critical scholars, working with the students to understand rather than to humanize or better.

Holbrook showed some appreciation for the problem when he wrote the following: "It seems crystal clear that the religion scholar must accept the ground rules of university education at its best, and not seek special privilege among the humanities for his field of competence.

He enters the scene . . . dedicated as his colleagues to the elimination of ignorance and superstition, arrant dogmatism and provincialism." Holbrook went on to add that the religion professor joins the other humanities professors in "showing wherein the hope of man may lie."[3] This attitude struck Wilson and others as a step backward. Ironically, however, from George Thomas to George Marsden to the present day, there exists a phenomenon that many religion professors face from their first session in the classroom: some students will find a particular religion professor alarmingly scientific, to the point of doing harm to religious belief, while others in the same room will find the same professor's content and style entirely too pious.

Holbrook's vision of the place that teaching religion should hold is the other bookend in the study of this period. Holbrook, the last president of NABI (before it became the AAR), represented the last of a generation that imagined the teaching of religion as a humanizing if not unifying force within the humanities or a college curriculum in general. He ultimately chose to reject this model in favor of a new sort that was being born. Holbrook understood that courses in a religion department could provide students ways of understanding the world, even improving the world, but by 1963, he had begun to emphasize "what might be called disinterested scholarship." His observations about the field of religion were the foundation upon which many early AAR leaders began to build: "The three biases which seem to me to have warped the presentation of studies of religion are these: courses in western religions, especially Christianity, heavily outweigh those offered in non-western religions; secondly, biblical courses make up more of the curriculum than do courses in phenomenology, and thirdly, a Protestant orientation of curricular content is more common than that of other religious traditions."[4] At midcentury, the interest in teaching religion in colleges grew ostensibly from the need of a burgeoning modern university to create coherence in the curriculum of its undergraduate program, and from the discovery of a means by which Protestant Christianity could make its way back into the institutions that its followers had nurtured. Holbrook acknowledged that he was historically nourished by the activities of these midcentury Protestant educators, but he was planning for a new day, in which regardless of how religion departments arrived at their own existence, they might become a place where members of an academic academy could share research and wisdom about religion and religions.

William Adams Brown's lament in 1936 that the modern university "has no unifying principle to give definiteness and consistency to its policy"[5] was not the first nor would it be the last complaint along these lines. Clyde Holbrook's call for a new appreciation for religious scholarship and teaching was rejected by some critics in the academy as too parochial for the early 1960s. The contentiousness of both Brown's and Holbrook's rationales for the study of religion became increasingly clear at schools whose formation of a religion department strained the attempt to both teach about religion and encourage its practice.

In February 1963, the Supreme Court of the United States heard and ruled on a First Amendment case that echoed the way in which many religious studies professors and college administrators came to view the right to teach religious studies to college students in state schools. Although it is an exaggeration to claim that the decision in *Abington v. Schempp* inspired the beginning or renewal of religion departments in state schools[6] (many state colleges actually pioneered in the creation of departments in the early twentieth century), it did send a positive signal to state-sponsored college educators that teaching "about" religions was perfectly acceptable as a state-sponsored activity.

Abington v. Schempp was itself a review of the Pennsylvania state law established in 1949 that provided for mandatory devotional Bible reading in public schools statewide. Through the appeals process, this Pennsylvania case was consolidated with a similar Maryland case, brought to court by Madalyn Murray, the renowned atheist who was later murdered in Texas in the mid-1990s. The court's decision, that school-sponsored readings and prayer are not constitutionally acceptable, but instruction "about" religion is acceptable and even desirable, was interpreted as both blessing and bane for the teaching of religions to college students. On one interpretation, state colleges were given a confirmation of their long-since-established religion departments, which ostensibly were teaching "about" religion, not preaching religious doctrine (itself debatable depending on the school and professor). The other interpretation, however, concluded that pious theological teachings on Christianity might no longer be acceptable, whether at state or private colleges, as most private colleges accepted federal funding.

In its majority opinion the court proclaimed the following:

> As we said in Engel v. Vitale . . . , "The history of man is inseparable
> from the history of religion. And . . . since the beginning of that history
> many people have devoutly believed that more things are wrought by
> prayer than this world dreams of and we are a religious people whose
> institutions presuppose a Supreme Being." . . . In addition, it might be
> well said that one's education is not complete without a study of com-
> parative religion or the history of religion and its relationship to the
> advancement of civilization. This is not to say, however, that religion
> has been so identified with our history and government that religious
> freedom is not likewise as strongly embedded in our public and private
> [lives]. . . . The government at all levels, as required by the Constitu-
> tion, must remain neutral in matters of religion "while protecting all,
> prefer[ring] none, and disparag[ing] none."[7]

Rather than serving as a catalyst for either founding religion departments or shutting down the departments of pious Protestant educators,
ultimately the court's ruling was seen as an affirmation of the current
practice of religion departments. That is, most college religion professors proclaimed the difficulty if not impossibility of achieving objectivity or equality in the teaching of all religious perspectives, but they
affirmed the desirability of teaching various religious beliefs, however
focused on Christianity most courses would have been. The Schempp
case has become more important as a historical marker than it was as a
historic moment, at least regarding the teaching of religion in colleges.

During the early 1960s, a new generation of religion scholars spe-
cializing in non-Western religious traditions faced a generation of students who demanded relevance. Unlike Protestant religious educators'
particular call for moral relevance in religion courses in the 1930s, this
student call for relevance was focused on examining moral authority
more than establishing it. However, both the basic courses taught in
many colleges in the 1960s and the texts employed in those courses still
reflected the interests and concerns of an earlier generation of religion
teachers. Teachers who took advantage of their own interests in Christian theology and colleges' needs to answer perennial questions about
what is worth teaching, created departments and programs designed

with the inherent tension of teaching about religion and how better to be religious.

Fault Lines Revealed

A previous iteration of the website of the AAR contained a section entitled "A Brief History," in which the narrative moved abruptly from 1937 to the "dramatic changes" that took place in 1963. As I have tried to show, the messiness of this period might explain why the casual historian would leap over these years. Whether or not this period was overlooked purposefully by the AAR web editor or administrative historian, these years are viewed by some members as troubling, given the association's primary goal of maintaining itself as a legitimate cohort of scholars within academe. However troubling this period may be, studying these years can produce a helpful understanding of the struggles, fault lines, and influences of this loosely knit field of religious studies.

The efforts to bring religion courses back into the college curriculum with renewed force in the 1930s, '40s, and '50s were fraught with a basic tension: how to advocate for the moral and civic value of teaching religion while creating an academic program consistent with critical scholarship and departmental credibility addressing that very subject matter. This basic tension at the denominationally founded colleges in which it existed was what made the teaching of religion in colleges important then and what makes it interesting now. The fact that this happened while the college ideal was being abandoned or morphed into the university model, meant that religion departments were a temporary location for what college had meant to an earlier generation.

Lawrence P. DeBoer, the executive director of the Society for Religion in Higher Education at Yale (successor to Charles Foster Kent's organization of Protestant educators), made clear a policy shift in his organization's understanding of its role in 1964:

After World War II the new interest in religion and higher education was prompted by a concern over the "moral and spiritual crisis" in our society, and it was widely believed that the introduction of religion in the curriculum might help stem the tide of that crisis. In other words, one reason given for including religion in the university curriculum was to do a job appropriate to the work of the Church, to reach the young people with the Christian message. Although we ought to realize by now that the religion department is not an arm of the Church, there are still considerable numbers of colleges and universities as well as theologians and churchmen who are operating under the illusion that the study of religion does and should produce Christian character or commitment. This is not to say that the Church should not address the university. Indeed, higher education is rapidly becoming a major influence in Western culture, and the Church must find ways of speaking prophetically to this institution as it has in the case of economic and political institutions. But it ought not speak its message by using—or misusing—the department of religion.[8]

DeBoer's understanding of the changing role of his own organization is representative of the many watershed moments in the shift from Christian advocacy teaching to another type of advocacy during the early 1960s. The new advocacy involved showing that learning about religion could have great relevance for an undergraduate wanting to be an educated citizen and professional. It should not escape the attention of any good historian that both higher education and church writ large have achieved both staying power and cultural power over so many centuries that each would naturally consider itself worthy of separate or combined attempts to shape and influence civilization, culture and individuals. How they do it and in what context are important to observe, analyze and critique.

Today it is almost unthinkable to suggest that religious studies should be only considered objective and descriptive, while theological or seminary training should be only considered subjective and normative. Such a neat division defies both reality and any ideal or reasonable goal. Although the tension between these two ideals was at the very heart of the matter for many educators in the early and mid-twentieth century, such a tidy dichotomy is now revealed to be just one more way of establishing oneself politically. That is, distinguishing strictly between teaching about religion and practicing religion is itself a normative stance that must be examined. Such a strict division is made more difficult by the diffuse nature of recent definitions of religion (e.g., if Marxism, economics, and other isms are religious themselves, one is supposedly always prescribing, preaching, or inculcating something). The extremes represented by religious instruction at Bob Jones University on the one hand and graduate work in the sociology of religion at Reed College or the University of Wisconsin, Madison, on the other are apparently easily categorized as prescriptive and descriptive. But as University of Chicago professor Jonathan Z. Smith argued, in many ways, the difference between religious studies and religion is really "no difference at all."[9] Religion as a category is perhaps best understood as a construction of scholars whose very attempts at defining, describing, and researching it are of a religious nature themselves.

The place of religion department founders in this story of religion's reentrance into the curriculum at midcentury is a curious one. They were not the creators of religious studies (though forerunners to be sure), nor did they provide critical methods for teaching religion for the most part. They did appropriate liberal Protestant theological ideals in the context of wartime teaching and Cold War rhetoric in creating departments that fulfilled the needs of the university, citizenship and their own ideals of general education and Protestant renewal. They did this by offering students a way of discovering the meaning that was all around them in the form of religion (most often Protestantism of one kind or another), and they used the available curricular model of the day—the divinity school model (Old Testament, New Testament, theology and ethics, church history, world religions). In most cases, their commitment to the separation of the practice and teaching of practiced religion was rigorous for their day, though not when compared to the antiproselytizing standards of today's elite college undergraduate religion departments.

Whether they recognized it or not, religion department founders and religion teachers in this era were struggling with fundamental issues that separated what many consider the academic study of religion from the teaching of religion constituted by theological advocacy. Each of their departments or programs was founded with the dual assumption that research about religions would be advanced and that the teaching of religion would offer something to students, and therefore the country, by way of spiritual or moral insight.[10] This dual role of the department created a tension for some professors and was a hurdle that others avoided by favoring dramatically one role over the other. Ultimately, this dual role created rifts that are still evident today in some college departments, especially those with religious missions, such as self-identified Christian colleges (Liberty University, Pensacola Christian College, Messiah College, Calvin University, and Wheaton College—notably, five very different such Christian schools).

Confusion, ignorance, or dismissal of the tensions arising from this dual role for departments further complicated the status of such programs. Early attempts to create religion departments or to argue for a favored place for religious studies were successful in part because they seemed to address the crises of Western civilization and the old priorities of colleges just as these institutions were becoming full-fledged universities. A better understanding of this history can illuminate later and current fractures within religious studies departments at smaller colleges that have attempted to model themselves after early programs at Princeton, Yale, Columbia, Stanford, the University of North Carolina, and Penn. It is important to reemphasize that, contrary to the claims made by many advocates for Christian theology, there was no absence of scholarly attention to religion and religions in universities at midcentury. Rather, the ways in which religions were studied did not promote the kind of attention to practical Christianity that these Protestant educators desired. American history professors studying Puritanism, art history professors studying medieval art, and English literature professors studying and teaching biblical literature were not necessarily pressing Christianity as a college subject that could help students fight and survive a devastating war or more easily survive personal crises.[11] This was the kind of teaching and research in religion that these founders believed was needed; after all, every other area of study appeared to have a way in which to help the war effort; why should "religion" be any different?

When religion department pioneers began their work, one of the primary models for teaching religion involved pastor-teachers filling Bible chairs in state schools where half credit was given for courses, such as could be found in at the University of Virginia as early as the 1890s. Today, an American Academy of Religion meeting with seven thousand participants and fifty subgroups for the study of religion represents a different mode of scholarly engagement with the complex nature of religion and religions. The road from the former model to the latter was filled with many theoretical and theological shifts, but the arguments made for the teaching of religion in colleges were an important part of how departments were and are structured today. The debate concerning the importance and viability of teaching about religion in colleges continued in various forms throughout the later part of the twentieth century.

In the 1990s, arguments were made by the University of Notre Dame's professor of American religious history George Marsden in *The Soul of the American University* and by D. G. Hart in *The University Gets Religion* in which each took slightly different approaches to the question of how religion itself, especially evangelical Christianity, can flourish in an academic context. On the opposite end of an imaginary spectrum are Donald Wiebe's *The Politics of Religious Studies* and a book by his student Russell McCutcheon entitled *Manufacturing Religion*—which is, in several ways, a response to the first three of these books. Marsden believes the soul of the university was lost during the twentieth century, and I have shown that this happened not because of an inevitable path of secularization but in part because those who were at the perfect place to counter such a loss of soul were busy fighting and surviving other battles. Hart believes religious studies has failed, and he is correct that it has failed his own religious community and possibly radical empiricists like Wiebe. However, more hopeful signs are actually on the horizon for the study of religion, especially if we understand how struggles with the dual role of the department have shaped its "failure" while appreciating the ways in which the pious, skeptic, and reconciler roles can often create a more vibrant college department of religion when balanced well.

Marsden writes the history of religion's decline in universities from the perspective of evangelical Christians, for whom universities became too liberal—and unwelcoming—a project. Marsden contends that academics at midcentury were basically asked to check their religion at the door of research universities. Wiebe, on the other hand, is deeply troubled that religion departments are, according to him, filled with pious advocates, that the American Academy of Religion is filled with religious believers, and that the history of religious studies is the history of Christian theology morphing its way into religion, all the while shackled by "religious and theological determinism." Wiebe has something very particular in mind when he imagines the study of religion. If he applied his standards to most of what happens in the humanities and social sciences disciplines, many professors would be ousted from the academy on the basis of his strict analysis. I agree with Wiebe's call to focus religious studies more on "scientifically" acquired knowledge than on theological musings, but he fails to appreciate the rich and complicated diversity of education in North America. For instance, religious studies positions are increasingly filled with practitioner-scholars of religions beyond the traditional Christians against whom Wiebe was arguing. The rich observations of a Black Church scholar who is from and participates in that incarnation of religious community might not make it through Wiebe's filter; likewise the mujerista theologian, the Korean Presbyterian scholar and so forth.

Wiebe uses the history of religious studies to critique severely its present and its future. He misses the important fact, however, that the teaching of religion in colleges is not now, nor will it ever become, "one thing." Rather, it is a mixture of the Calvin University religious historian who wants to better understand Mormonism so that she can help students avoid its pull and the Ivy League radical empiricist religion professor who might scoff at the pious follower of the Nation of Islam. American higher education consists of both research universities and fundamentalist Christian colleges. To hope for a day when the study and teaching of religion are "one" is to dream with the utopian, not the historian. Wiebe's conclusions are most intelligible if read as a call to arms in a prescriptive rather than a descriptive work of historical analysis, but that kind of prescriptive move is ironically what he appears to have been trying to remove from the academy.

Hart may be correct in his assessment that the history of religious studies shows that religion departments have been neither entirely successful academic ventures nor religiously helpful to churches. Hart is an evangelical Christian who notes the problems with religious studies as an academic discipline because religious studies has failed his own religious community. Religious studies does indeed consist of most of the things he says it does, and it came to be in most of the ways he says it came to be, but it is also a work in progress, as are history departments and literature departments, gender studies and departments focused upon the culture, history, and writings of specific ethnic groups.

Religious studies departments are moving, one could argue, further and further from their Protestant roots as they become less apologetic for Christianity and Western religious thought. They also, however, are moving closer to their roots by focusing on the questions of religion's relevance, civic importance, and importance for understanding culture.

When a field of study, area of study, or discipline is in its infancy, there will be messy decades of wandering around the minefields of methodology, professionalization, credentialing, and renewing or changing purposes of various subdisciplines. Even during the middle-aged, maturing years of a field of study, there will be more than enough methodological and scholarly messiness to survive. As Hart suggests, evangelical Christians (as well as orthodox Jews and traditionalist Muslims, among others) should indeed be wary of the secular research university as the primary model for truth-seeking by their religious communities. Liberal religious adherents, on the other hand, have little to fear (though much to learn) from the content and conclusions of university research investigations into religion. In short, for better or worse, a research university model and academic department produce a distinct form of inquiry that may not suit all religious communities, not even all colleges.

There are many questions left unanswered by this discussion of tensions inherent in the dual role of religion departments, their role in retaining the college ideal and in the formation of what is either a field of study or discipline. Where exactly does the study and teaching of religion fit within the disciplines of the humanities and social sciences, especially given their own concerning crisis-cycles? What are the appropriate and defensible reasons for religion's place in the college classroom? How important is it that a deep appreciation of religious belief or living religious communities be included in or kept out of the classroom? Is religion a subject, method, field, or a category unto itself, given arguments about its centrality to human culture or nation-formation, essentially different from all other categories of knowledge, thought, or experience? Also, what qualifies as *religion* or *religions*, and which of those categorized as such are worthy of the valuable resources that must be thoughtfully allocated within the university? The University of Vermont's attempt to eliminate their religion department was not the first and will not be the last such action. These questions occupied the minds of religion department founders and their critics in the 1950s, and many remain to be answered.

Until at least the 1970s, most college religion departments were filled with what Bruce Lincoln describes as "caregivers" and "voyeurs." This is similar to the skeptic and pious believer, or questioner and supporter characterizations I have detailed. Bruce Lincoln was himself easily cat-egorizable as a skeptic in my model, where Lincoln the skeptic and Paul Griffiths the pious true believer were translated by reconcilers Martin Marty and Wendy Doniger on the religion faculty during my graduate school days. One can easily argue against this very categorization, as Griffiths often played the skeptic, Doniger the pious (for the historians of religion at least), Lincoln the reconciler, even, and so forth.

Many history, English, anthropology, and economics classrooms were and are filled with similarly directed teachers. The tension between the caregivers and the voyeurs in religious studies departments need not be detrimental in some colleges and should not ostensibly exist in the case of research universities. It is antithetical to the mission of the research university scholar, as defined by modern research, to press ahead with one religious perspective in spite of new data. In the case, however, of professional schools attached to universities, and of smaller church-related colleges who can afford it, having both the academic study of religions and practicing religious adherents certainly would be more interesting, just as a political science department would be a more interesting place to do scholarly work were partisan politicians in residence, as is the case in some schools.[12] This has in fact become the very useful and intriguing model that many Catholic institutions have instituted and developed.

The creative tension between moral formation and the unhindered search for truth (as an ideal, if not practically feasible) is one of the odd blessings of university teaching and research. If many of the Protestant educators of the 1940s had survived to see the state of mainline Protes-tant churches and universities in 2021, they too might have appreciated Hart's critique and celebrated Wiebe's conclusion that religion depart-ments are still filled with advocates of religiosity.

Scholars of religion can benefit from better understanding the ten-sions created by the dual role of a religion department at midcentury. A greater appreciation of this dynamic and others can help us point to ways in which current debates within academe might be approached and furthered, whether regarding religion, ethnicity studies gender and sexual identity studies, or any other nascent area of study. The question of relevance surfaced again as literature departments were taken to task by conservative cultural critics in the 1980s for eschewing literature as an object to be loved and understood and instead embracing deconstruction as method and style. When the commonweal or public square is looking for resources with which to replenish itself, when lovers of democracy seek institutions to support it yet again, they turn to the college as a "seminary," as the word was understood in its earliest usage—a place to nurture students and citizens. Colleges find that their new professors were trained in a research university environment, yet many college leaders vaguely hope that something more than research comes through when a teacher presents a subject. Religion departments faced this conflict head-on from the beginning. To some extent, every academic department has a dual role. Gender, environmental, health sciences, business and ethnicity studies, for instance, experience obligations to be both activist departments and departments that seek truths about their subjects. What does one do when one's research data, pedagogical models, and university structure do not match the activist ideal of one's department or its students? This is the story of religious studies in the 1960s and quite possibly will be the story of other departments in the decades to come.

Most likely, few religion department professors in the early twenty-first century would find foreign the tension inherent in the dual role of their departments (viz., advancing knowledge about religion and advancing religion itself). To this day, many biologists, economists, and literature professors wonder what exactly the purpose of the religion department is or should be in a research university or nonreligiously based college. Understanding how the tension of this dual role played out in this critical period from the early 1930s to the early 1960s can be an enlivening and enlightening process that may assist in making progress in this field of study.[13]

The skeptics question teaching religion (as faith) in a particular way, inadvertently improving its practice. The pious protect it, seeing it as life-giving, but by studying it begin to nuance it if not relativize it, thus perhaps weakening faith practices. Reconcilers address each while translating from pious to skeptic and back to pious. To study skeptically among practitioners can keep one more honest and may transform one into an appreciative inquirer. Types blend too, over time, over academic years and careers. Sometimes the skeptics chair the religion department and become inadvertent part-time reconcilers, and occasionally, the pious encounter those so pious that they themselves begin to function more like the skeptic among the pious. Many founders during this period may have landed on their own version of the Krister Stendahl rules of studying religious people comparatively (the faithful should get to tell their own stories as opposed to merely their enemies; you don't get to compare their worst with your best practices and stories; leave room for holy envy—meaning it's OK to fall prey to some appreciation of the other).[14]

The formation, structure, and rationale for college religion departments and courses have always been situated in a particular location and time period, whether World War II, the Cold War and the Great Depression or the attacks of September 11, which for some necessitated more in-depth learning about Islam, whether one considered the attackers to be true members of their faith or not. Colleges were founded ostensibly as a public good, though exclusionary practices have plagued each institution. Many became as aspirational local or national treasures even, and felt the need to respond in service to the local schools' constituents and the needs of the nation. In the 1940s, many college campuses and academic departments responded to help their students (soldiers or not) and their country as they saw fit. Science departments found their place among its research, armaments, or the intelligence needs of the nation. The formation of religion departments was in part as a repository for the values of the college ideal while also as a response to what was presumed to be the needs of students serving a country wherein having Protestant Christian values was a good that could be delivered by the study and teaching of those values for many schools.

What was assumed good for the students and country would have been seen by the pious as good for the Christian faith and thus for the university still seeking that college ideal itself. Religion departments earlier in the twentieth century trained both practitioners and theorists, like a business school and economics department, respectively.

What happened in colleges at midcentury, then, was the beginning of Protestant educators' attempts to supersede, however unsuccessfully, the tensions I am illuminating here. The new religion departments were conceived of as departments the university could be proud of, that would be accepted by nonreligious academic colleagues in other departments who had high standards in mind. Such colleagues were in many cases studying religious texts, communities, ideas, and movements themselves, only not with the same intention of showing the forces of those people, texts, and movements to be of specific practical concern or use to the republic. As was the case in several academic disciplines, by the 1940s, those religion professors who were *not* able to show a practical use for their subject were on the outside looking in. Unlike the specialist in medieval art, literature, or history, who did not study religious artifacts, texts, or movements for their relevance to "today," founders of religion programs had to show that their subject *was* practical in the face of national crises. The uses of Protestant religion on campus were many and not limited to the often-opposing poles of, say, campus ministry and critical analysis of religions. From this tension, this middle ground at midcentury, came new religion departments to schools which bolstered the college ideal in a university model, with all their baggage and blessing. The ends of a college education have naturally at their center the characteristics of the college ideal. The end of college as the university model took hold, was partly housed by newly formed religion department for a time. Today the college ideal has shifted and moved on (alumni/ae relations, student and residential life, honors colleges *inter alia*?). But for a while the end of college was delayed on the way to the university ideal which ultimately the field of religion followed with enthusiasm.

Appendix of Typologies

In telling this story I have followed six layers of activity:

1. The national mood, external economic factors, and other movements and influences from the 1930s to the 1960s.
2. Higher education trends, including graduate training, curricula more generally, and the Carnegie Corporation's movements to codify and bureaucratize the college credit system and faculty pensions, removing religion restrictions as they did so.
3. Alumni/ae, donors, and student life. If there is one area to which the college ideal has migrated in higher education in recent years, it is student life professionals. Namely, they are a newly professionalized cadre of administrative professionals who focus on student morality (differently understood both for each generation and region/subculture in America), residence-hall living, and various other important elements of the traditional college impulse. Teaching those things in the official curriculum would be difficult or out of place in a university curricular model on the whole, but the college impulse, which shifted in part into the religion department (where we discuss the important foci of life), has now found other places in which to thrive.
4. What educators believed should be taught, studied, and emphasized.

5. Financial interests and capabilities that drive or influence many of
   the above decisions; in short, following the money, philanthropic or
   otherwise.
6. Deep-seated values, religious traditions, and academic cultures
   that shaped disciplines, and colleges and universities operating
   like small communities attempting to withstand changes from
   "outside."

Ways that the study of "religion" was viewed in religion department formation

1. Teaching about religion as a sociologist-anthropologist, purposefully or inadvertently debunking it as a cultural artifact or mere
   social construction by less developed cultures.
2. Teaching about religion as a category to contest, given its social
   construction.
3. Teaching religion to understand it.
4. Teaching religion in the context of other disciplines/phenomena—so
   not a separate or sui generis force or revelation.
5. Teaching religion because it is good, period (and one's own is func-
   tionally the best).
6. Avoiding studying religion because, whatever you examine, you
   may be causing harm by spreading it, reinforcing it when it's not
   based in reality, or weakening it because teaching relativizes it.

Stages of the teaching of religion in departments

1. Religious belief is so integral to the school it doesn't need special
   mention, as it is all about that in practice and theory.
2. Religion is so central that it is constantly noted, but now needs to be
   enforced.
3. Christianity is important enough to be present throughout curricula, but staff do not need to be steeped in religion, as faculty
   must be.
4. Protestantism needs special emphasis in chaplaincy and required
   courses, but some faculty need not be religious.

5. Faith is appreciated generally, and there are courses to take and the faculty for those courses need to be religious.
6. Religion needs a department with dedicated scholars, as faith is needed for students in times of crisis, but religion professors must be credentialed, as other faculty, in their specialized field.
7. Religion is an important subject that needs to be studied but merely one among many subjects.
8. Specialized courses in any number of religions are possible within curricula but need regular rationalizing, and now must be practical in some form beyond ministry profession, while professors must themselves be experts in narrower fields.
9. Religion/religions must be understood in order to interpret what is happening to society outside college.
10. The diversified nature of higher education means that at this point, the teaching of religion is highly differentiated in each context. Though all such teaching is gathered together conceptually under the auspices as a discipline of the American Academy of Religion, what each professor, school, and student body understands as the teaching and study of religion (at, e.g., Brigham Young University, Northern Virginia Community College, University of Notre Dame, Hillsdale College, Reed College, University of North Carolina, Liberty University, Pensacola Christian College, inter alia) is highly varied.

Movement from the college ideal to the university ideal

1. Aim: from subjectivity to objectivity.
2. Formation: from moral to research/scientific/practical/useful.
3. Content: from received to created.
4. Outcomes: from cultured citizens to professional producers.
5. Method: from listen/receive to speak/engage (small classes to lecture halls, TA sections, or seminars)
6. Supporters: from church/private to government/industry/private.
7. Constituency: from elite to democratized.
8. Residency: from small houses or homes to large dorms.
9. Structure: from one school to many, including graduate.
10. Geographical context: from rural to suburban, urban, or exurban.

11. Sociopolitical context: from appreciative trust of institutions to skeptical questioning of institutions between the 1940s and 1960s.

12. Economic context: as US national economic power rose, universities became more important to and integrated with the economy.

13. Professors: from generalists to specialists, church-trained to research university–trained.

14. Understood: from a shared moral commitment to a commitment to a process of inquiry (e.g., the principle of noncontradiction).

The college ideal was an attempt to gain coherence for a narrow selection of young citizens by teaching the truth, while the university ideal became an attempt to seek truth through specialized knowledge and research to serve the country, and corporations or at least a corporate-centered business standard. Student life writ large (the current primary holders of the college ideal) knows the truth it has to share with its students (about vocation and later job searching, morality, civic responsibility, living together in community, social justice, mental and physical health, and being open to all humanity-enhancing change within students and society, ranging from LGBTQ progress to racial justice) so that professors need not tend to those topics from a truth perspective, per se. Religion departments as they were created at midcentury held a good deal of the college ideal, while the university ideal was being held up as the better model for higher education. The dual role of religion in schools was no longer needed in the same way, but for a time, that was religion's way into the university, as a department.

Teaching of religion

We teach/study religion to inculcate explicitly.

We teach/study religion to inculcate implicitly.

We teach/study religion because it's vital for our future survival as a country and/or species.

We teach/study religion because certain people (and philanthropic dollars) want us to.

We teach/study religion because religion helps define us as human (humanities rationale).

We teach/study religion because it exists, and we are a professional class of researchers.

We wonder why we teach/study religion if the pious don't want to be relativized, the skeptics consider it like astrology, and the reconcilers who stand between the two seem unnecessary as we move toward the university ideal.

Individuals (Schools)

Edwin E. Aubrey (University of Pennsylvania)

Frank W. Aydelotte (Swarthmore)

Fred Berthold (Dartmouth)

William Adams Brown (Yale)

Dwight Marion Beck (Syracuse)

Bernard Iddings Bell (Bard)

Edward Blakeman (Michigan)

Charles Bond (Bucknell)

Robert McAfee Brown (Stanford, Union Theological Seminary)

William Clayton Bower (Chicago)

Charles Braden (Northwestern)

William F. Buckley Jr. (Yale)

Victor Butterfield (Wesleyan)

Robert C. Calhoun (Yale)

James Bryant Conant (Harvard)

Virginia Corwin (Smith)

Merrimon Cuninggim (Pomona, Southern Methodist University)

John Dewey (Chicago, UM, Columbia)

John Dillenberger (Columbia)

Harold Dodds (Princeton)

Harry Emerson Fosdick (Union Theological Seminary–NYC)

Charles Foster Kent (Yale)

Horace L. Friess (Columbia)

William Foxwell Albright (Johns Hopkins)

John Hope Franklin (Chicago, Madison)

Christian Gauss (Princeton)

Harry Gideonse (Columbia, Chicago)

Charles W. Gilkey (Chicago)

Robert Goheen (Princeton)

Erwin Goodenough (Yale)

Theodore M. Greene (Yale)

Alfred Whitney Griswold (Yale)

E. Harris Harbison (Princeton)

Georgia Harkness (Garrett Theological Seminary, Northwestern)

Cyril Harris (Brown)

Julian Hartt (Yale, University of Virginia)

Van Harvey (Stanford, Princeton, University of Pennsylvania)

Eustace Haydon (Chicago)

Theodore Hesburgh (Notre Dame)

Ernest Hocking (Harvard)

Clyde Holbrook (Oberlin)

Jessie Holmes (Swarthmore)

Sidney Hook (New York
University)

Mildred McAfee Horton
(Wellesley)

Robert Maynard Hutchins
(Chicago)

John Hutchison (Williams)

Rufus Jones (Haverford)

Charles Foster Kent (Yale)

Albert Knudson (Boston)

M. Willard Lampe (Iowa)

Franklin Littell (SMU)

Charles Long (Chicago, University
of Virginia)

Benjamin E. Mays (Howard
University)

S. Vernon McCasland (University
of Virginia)

Robert S. Michaelson (Iowa, UCSB)

Alexander Miller (Stanford)

J. Hillis Miller (Florida)

Charles Clayton Morrison
(Chicago, CC)

B. David Napier (Stanford, Yale)

Arnold Nash (University of North
Carolina)

John W. Nason (Swarthmore)

Reinhold Niebuhr (Union)

Richard Niebuhr (Harvard)

Ursula Niebuhr (Barnard)

Albert Outler (Southern Methodist
University)

Edmund Perry (Northwestern)

James A. Pike (Columbia)

Nathan Marsh Pusey (Harvard)

Paul Ramsey (Princeton)

I. A. Richards (Harvard)

Kenneth Scott Latourette (Yale)

John Schroeder (Yale)

Charles Seymour (Yale)

Clarence Shedd (Yale)

William Sloane Coffin (Yale)

Ninian Smart (UCSB)

Huston Smith (Washington
University, Syracuse)

Seymour A. Smith (Yale)

Wilfred Cantwell Smith (Harvard)

Willard Sperry (Harvard)

Paul Tillich (Harvard, Chicago
UTS)

George Finger Thomas (Princeton)

Howard Thurman (Boston)

D. Elton Trueblood (Stanford,
Earlham)

Henry Pitt Van Dusen (Union
Theological Seminary,
Princeton)

Gregory Vlastos (Cornell)

John Paul Williams (Mount
Holyoke)

Morton White (Columbia)

John F. Wilson (Princeton)

Amos N. Wilder (Chicago)

Harvey Wooster (Oberlin)

Henry Wriston (Macalester)

Each individual and institution has a religion department/program history that can be told either during the time period covered here or in the period just after 1964. See in particular the following schools, whose histories are likely to reveal additional important stories of how college religion departments were founded in the twentieth century: American, Amherst, Barnard, Boston, Bowdoin, Brandeis, Brigham Young University, Brown, Cal Tech, Colby, Colgate, Cornell, Dartmouth, Duke/Trinity, Emory, Fisk, Florida State, Georgetown, Haverford, Howard, Iowa, Johns Hopkins, Lafayette, Lehigh, Michigan, Middlebury, MIT, Morehouse, Northwestern, Notre Dame, Oberlin, Pepperdine, Pomona, Rice, Smith, Spellman, Swarthmore, Sweet Briar, Syracuse, UC Berkeley, University of Florida, University of Miami, USC, Vanderbilt, Vassar, Virginia Union, Wellesley, Wesleyan, and Williams, inter alia.

Selected Works

Archives

Columbia University Archives

Harvard University Archives

Princeton University Archives, George F. Thomas Papers

Princeton University, Mudd Library

Stanford University Archives

Stanford University Archives, (Miller, Alexander Papers)

University of Chicago Special Collections, Robert Maynard Hutchins
   Presidential Papers

University of Iowa Archives, School of Religion Collection

University of North Carolina Archives, Presidential Papers

University of Pennsylvania Archives

Yale University Archives, Charles Seymour Papers

Yale University Archives, Alfred Whitney Griswold Papers

Yale Divinity School Archives, Clarence P. Shedd Papers

Published Works

Abbott, Andrew Delano. *The System of Professions: An Essay on the
   Division of Expert Labor*. Chicago: University of Chicago Press,
   1988.

Altick, Richard. "The War of Nerves." *Journal of Higher Education* 14, no. 9 (December 1943): 477–482.

"Announcement of Courses, 1932–33, College of Arts and Sciences." *Bulletin of Oberlin College.* 1932.

Arendt, Hannah. "Religion and the Intellectuals." *Partisan Review* 41 (1950): 115.

Ashmore, Harry S. *Unreasonable Truths*. Boston: Little, Brown, 1989.

Aubrey, Edwin Ewart. *Humanistic Teaching and the Place of Ethical and Religious Values in Higher Education*. Philadelphia: University of Pennsylvania Press, 1959.

———. "Pro and Con: The Democratic Value of the Conference on Science, Philosophy and Religion." *Humanist* 3 (Spring 1943): 24–25.

———. *The Religious Element in Higher Education*. New Haven, CT: Ronald Press / Edward R. Hazen Foundation, 1952.

———. *Secularism, a Myth: An Examination of the Current Attack on Secularism*. New York: Harper, 1954.

Beuttler, Fred W. "Organizing an American Conscience: The Conference on Science, Philosophy and Religion 1940–1968." PhD diss., University of Chicago, 1995.

Bixler, Julius Seeyle. *The Resources of Religion and the Aims of Higher Education*. New Haven, CT: Ronald Press / Edward R. Hazen Foundation, 1942.

Blakeman, Edward W. *The Administration of Religion in Universities and Colleges: Personnel*. Ann Arbor: University of Michigan Press, 1942.

———. "Realistic View of Religion." *Religious Education* 7 (1944): 355.

Braisted, Paul J. *Religion in Higher Education*. New Haven, CT: Ronald Press / Edward R. Hazen Foundation, 1942.

Brown, William Adams. *The Case for Theology in the University*. Chicago: University of Chicago Press, 1938.

Buckley, William F., Jr. *God and Man at Yale*. New York: Regnery, 1951.

Burtchaell, James Tunstead. *The Dying of the Light: The Disengagement of Colleges & Universities from Their Christian Churches*. Grand Rapids, MI: William B. Eerdmans, 1998.

Calhoun, Robert L. "Comments on the Proposals for Strengthening Religious Life and Instruction in Yale University." Yale Divinity School Archives, Clarence P. Shedd Papers, box 13, file 6.

———. *Place of Religion in Higher Education*. New Haven, CT: Ronald Press / Edward R. Hazen Foundation, 1949.

———. *Religion and the Modern World*. Philadelphia: University of Pennsylvania Press, 1941.

———. *What Is Man?* New York: Association Press / Edward W. Hazen Foundation, 1939.

Cherry, Conrad. *Hurrying toward Zion: Universities, Divinity Schools, and American Protestantism*. Bloomington: Indiana University Press, 1995.

Chomsky, Noam. *The Cold War & the University*. New York: New Press, 1997.

Cohen, Shaye J. D., and Edward L. Greenstein, eds. *The State of Jewish Studies*. Detroit: Wayne State University Press, 1990.

Cuninggim, Merrimon. *The College Seeks Religion*. New Haven, CT: Yale University Press, 1947.

DeBoer, Lawrence P. "Seminary and University: Two Approaches to Theology and Religion." *Journal of Bible and Religion* 32, no. 4 (October 1964): 346.

Dewey, John. "Anti-naturalism in Extremis." *Partisan Review* 10, no. 1 (1943): 31.

———. "Commentary." *Humanist* (Autumn 1945): 105.

———. *A Common Faith*. New Haven, CT: Yale University Press, 1934.

———. Untitled essay in "Religion and the Intellectuals." *Partisan Review* 43 (1950): 129–130.

Dillenberger, John. *Contours of Faith*. Nashville: Abingdon, 1969.

———. "Teaching Religion: Problems and Requirements." *Review of Religion* (November 1956): 9.

Dzuback, Mary Ann. *Robert M. Hutchins: Portrait of an Educator*. Chicago: University of Chicago Press, 1991.

Eccles, Robert S. *Erwin Ramsdell Goodenough: A Personal Pilgrimage*. Chico, CA: Scholars Press, 1985.

Eckardt, Roy A. *The Surge of Piety in America*. New York: Association Press, 1958.

Editorial. *Christian Century*, November 17, 1943, 1327.

Elderkin, George. *The Roman Catholic Controversy*. Princeton, NJ: Princeton University Press, 1955.

Fairchild, Hoxie N. *Religious Perspectives in College Teaching*. New Haven, CT: Ronald Press / Edward R. Hazen Foundation, 1952.

Ferré, Nels F. S. *Christian Faith and Higher Education*. New York: Harper & Brothers, 1954.

Fisher, Galen M., ed. *Religion in the Colleges*. New York: Association Press, 1928.

"Forty-Sixth Annual Register, 1936–37." *Bulletin of Stanford University*. 1936. Available at https://exhibits.stanford.edu/stanford-pubs/catalog/mv791vf3738.

Freidson, Eliot. *Professional Powers: A Study of the Institutionalization of Formal Knowledge*. Paperback ed. Chicago: University of Chicago Press, 1993.

Friess, Horace. "Religion at Columbia." Departmental report, 1950. Columbia University Archives, series 1, Central Files. https://findingaids.library.columbia.edu/ead/nnc-ua/ldpd_4080177/dsc/1.

———. "The Study of Religion at Columbia." *Review of Religion* 19 (1954): 36.

Gauss, Christian, ed. *The Teaching of Religion in American Higher Education*. New York: Ronald Press, 1951.

Gideonse, Harry D. *The Higher Learning in a Democracy: A Reply to President Hutchins' Critique of the American University*. New York: Farrar and Rinehart, 1937.

Gilpin, W. Clark. *A Preface to Theology*. Chicago: University of Chicago Press, 1996.

Goheen, Robert F. *The Human Nature of a University*. Princeton, NJ: Princeton University Press, 1969.

Goodenough, Erwin. "The Inspiration of New Testament Research." *Journal of Biblical Literature* 71 (1952): 2.

———. "Needed: Scientific Study of Religion: How Long Will Free Inquiry Neglect This Basic Field?" *Commentary* 5 (1948): 272.

———. "Scientific Living." *Humanist* 2 (1942): 9–10.

———. *Toward a Mature Faith*. New York: Prentice-Hall, 1955.

Graff, Gerald. *Professing Literature: An Institutional History*. Chicago: University of Chicago Press, 1989.

Greene, Theodore, ed. *Liberal Education Re-examined: Its Role in a Democracy.* New York: Harper & Brothers, 1943.

———, ed. *The Meaning of the Humanities: Five Essays.* With an introduction by T. H. Greene. Princeton, NJ: Princeton University Press, 1938.

———. "The Seminaries and the Future of Liberal Education." *American Association of Theological Schools*, no. 16 (June 1944): 53.

Griswold, Alfred Whitney. *In the University Tradition.* New Haven, CT: Yale University Press, 1957.

Harkness, Georgia. *Religious Living.* New York: Association Press / Edward W. Hazen Foundation, 1937.

Hart, D. G. *The University Gets Religion.* Baltimore: Johns Hopkins University Press, 1999.

Hartt, Julian N. *Toward a Theology of Evangelism.* New York: Abingdon, 1955.

Harvard University Committee. *General Education in a Free Society.* Cambridge, MA: Harvard University Press, 1945.

Harvey, Van A. *The Historian and the Believer.* New York: Macmillan, 1966.

Hauerwas, Stanley. *The State of the University: Academic Knowledges and the Knowledge of God.* Oxford: Blackwell, 2007.

Herberg, Will. *Four Existentialist Theologians.* Garden City, NJ: Doubleday, 1958.

———. *Protestant-Catholic-Jew.* Garden City, NJ: Doubleday, 1956.

———. "The Religious Stirring on the Campus: A Student Generation 'Accessible to Good.'" *Commentary* 5 (1952): 242.

Hook, Sidney. "A Challenge to the Liberal Arts College." *Journal of Higher Education* 10, no. 1 (1936): 21, 23.

———. "The New Failure of Nerve." *Partisan Review* 10 (1943): 2.

———. *Out of Step.* New York: Carroll & Graf, 1988.

———. "Religion and the Intellectuals." *Partisan Review* 42 (1950): 225.

———. "Theological Tom-Tom and Metaphysical Bagpipe." *Humanist* 2, no. 3 (Autumn 1942): 96.

Hutchins, Robert Maynard. *Education for Freedom.* Baton Rouge: Louisiana State University Press, 1943.

————. *The Higher Learning in America*. New Haven, CT: Yale University Press, 1936.

————. *Morals, Religion and Higher Education*. Chicago: University of Chicago Press, 1950.

————. *No Friendly Voice*. Chicago: University of Chicago Press, 1936.

Hutchinson, William R., ed. *Between the Times*. Cambridge: Cambridge University Press, 1989.

————. *The Modernist Impulse in American Protestantism*. Cambridge, MA: Harvard University Press, 1976.

Jackson, Katherine Gauss, and Hiram Haydn, eds. *The Papers of Christian Gauss*. New York: Random House, 1957.

Jelks, Randall Maurice. *Benjamin Elijah Mays: Schoolmaster of the Movement*. Chapel Hill: University of North Carolina Press, 2012.

Karabel, Jerome. *The Chosen*. Boston: Houghton Mifflin Company, 2005.

Kemeny, P. C. *Princeton in the Nation's Service*. New York: Oxford University Press, 1998.

Kent, Charles Foster. "Filling the Gap in Modern Education." *Bulletin of the Council of Schools of Religion* 2, no. 3 (February 1927): 5. https://digitalcommons.wku.edu/svhe_pubs/3.

Knudson, Albert C. "Humanism and Barthianism." *Religion in Life* 4 (Winter 1935): 22–31.

Lacey, Michael J. *Religion & Twentieth Century American Intellectual Life*. Cambridge: Cambridge University Press, 1989.

LeFevre, Perry D. *The Christian Teacher*. New York: Abingdon, 1958.

Malin, Patrick M. *Teaching Economics with a Sense of the Infinite and the Urgent*. New Haven, CT: Ronald Press / Edward R. Hazen Foundation, 1942.

Malkiel, Nancy Weiss. *"Keep the Damned Women Out": The Struggle for Coeducation*. Princeton, NJ: Princeton University Press, 2018.

Maritain, Jacques. *The Education of Man*. Edited by Donald Gallagher and Idella Gallagher. New York: Doubleday, 1962.

Marsden, George M. *The Soul of the American University: From Protestant Establishment to Established Nonbelief*. New York: Oxford University Press, 1994.

Marsden, George M., and Bradley J. Longfield, eds. *The Secularization of the Academy*. Religion in America. New York: Oxford University Press, 1992.

Marty, Martin E. *Modern American Religion*. Vol. 3. Chicago: University of Chicago Press, 1996.

McCutcheon, Russell T. *The Discipline of Religion: Structure, Meaning, Rhetoric*. London: Routledge, 2003.

———. *Manufacturing Religion: The Discourse on Sui Generis Religion and the Politics of Nostalgia*. New York: Oxford University Press, 1997.

Meyer, Donald. *The Protestant Search for Political Realism*. Middletown, CT: Wesleyan University Press, 1961.

Miller, Alexander. *Faith and Learning*. New York: Association Press, 1960.

———. "Religion in the Curriculum." *Stanford Review* 53 (July 1952): 8.

———. *The Renewal of Man*. Garden City, NJ: Doubleday, 1959.

———. "Teaching Religion and Teaching the Christian Faith." *Review of Religion* (January 1957): 9.

Miller, Randolph Crump. *Education for Christian Living*. Englewood Cliffs, NJ: Prentice Hall, Inc., 1956.

Nash, Arnold S., ed. *Protestant Thought in the Twentieth Century: Whence and Whither?* New York: Macmillan, 1951.

———. "The Totalitarian University and Christian Higher Education." *Theology Today* 6, no. 3 (October 1949): 336–347.

———. *The University and the Modern World*. New York: Macmillan, 1948.

Nason, John W. "The Program of Faculty Consultations on Religion in Higher Education." *Educational Record* (October 1946), 3.

Newfield, Christopher. *Ivy and Industry: Business and the Making of the American University*. Durham, NC: Duke University Press, 2003.

Newman, John Henry. *The Idea of a University*. New Haven, CT: Yale University Press, 1996.

Niebuhr, Reinhold. "Higher Education in America." *Confluence* 6 (Spring 1957): 9.

Novick, Peter. *That Noble Dream*. Cambridge: Cambridge University Press, 1988.

Pike, James A. "Annual Report of the Chaplain." 1950. Columbia University Archives, series 1, Central Files 1880–1984.

Princeton University Report of the Special Committee of the Faculty on Religious Education. April 11, 1935. Princeton University Archives, George Finger Thomas Papers, box 13, file 5, n.p.

"Proceedings of the Stanford Conference on Religion in Higher Education." *School and Society* 55, no. 1432 (June 6, 1942): 647.

Ramsey, Paul. "Religion at Princeton." *Religious Education* (March–April 1947): 67–69.

Ratner-Rosenhagen, Jennifer. *The Ideas That Made America: A Brief History.* New York: Oxford University Press, 2019.

Reuben, Julie. *The Making of the Modern University.* Chicago: University of Chicago Press, 1996.

Richards, I. A. "The Two Rings: A Communication." *Partisan Review* 10, no. 4 (1943): 381.

Root, Robert. "Princeton's New Curriculum." *Journal of Higher Education* 18, no. 1 (1947): 16.

Rorty, Richard, Julie A. Reuben, and George Marsden. "The Moral Purposes of the University: An Exchange." *Hedgehog Review* 2, no. 3 (Fall 2000): 106–119.

Ross, Dorothy, ed. *Modernist Impulses in the Human Sciences.* Baltimore: Johns Hopkins University Press, 1994.

Rudolph, Frederick. *The American College & University.* Athens: University of Georgia Press, 1962.

Russell, Bertrand. "A Dilemma of Education." *Journal of Higher Education* 4, no. 3 (1936): 164.

Schilbrack, Kevin. *Philosophy and the Study of Religions: A Manifesto.* Wiley-Blackwell Manifestos. Oxford: Wiley-Blackwell, 2014.

Schlatter, Richard, ed. *Humanistic Scholarship in America.* Hoboken, NJ: Prentice Hall, 1965.

Schmalzbauer, John Arnold, and Kathleen A. Mahoney. *The Resilience of Religion in American Higher Education.* Waco, TX: Baylor University Press, 2018.

Shedd, Clarence P. "Education, but Not as Usual." *Intercollegian* (November 1942): 1.

———. *Proposal for Religion in Postwar Higher Education*. New Haven, CT: Ronald Press / Edward R. Hazen Foundation, 1945.

Shepard, Robert. *God's People in the Ivory Tower*. New York: Carlson, 1991.

Shuster, George N. *Education and Religion*. New Haven, CT: Ronald Press / Edward R. Hazen Foundation, 1945.

Sloan, Douglas. *Faith and Knowledge*. Philadelphia: WJKP, 1991.

Smith, Huston. *The Purposes of Higher Education*. New York: Harper, 1955.

Smith, Jonathan Z. "'Religion' and 'Religious Studies': No Difference at All." In "The Santa Barbara Colloquy: Religion within the Limits of Reason Alone," special issue. *Soundings* 71, nos. 2–3 (Summer/Fall 1988): 231–244.

Smith, Richard Norton. *The Making of a University to a Nation*. Cambridge, MA: Harvard University Press, 1986.

Smith, Wilfred Cantwell. *The Meaning and End of Religion*. Minneapolis: Fortress, 1991.

Stringfellow, William, and Anthony Towne. *The Bishop Pike Affair*. New York: Harper & Row, 1967.

Tead, Ordway. *The Relation of Religion to Education—with Special Reference to Citizenship: A Layman's View*. New Haven, CT: Ronald Press / Edward R. Hazen Foundation, 1944.

Thomas, George Finger. *Religion in an Age of Secularism*. Princeton, NJ: Princeton University Press, 1940.

———. "Religion in the American College." *Religious Education* 53 (1944): 102–107.

Tillich, Paul. "Religion and the Intellectuals." *Partisan Review* 43 (1950): 255.

Towner, Milton C., ed. *Religion in Higher Education*. Chicago: University of Chicago Press, 1931.

Toynbee, Arnold. *An Historian's Approach to Religion*. 2nd ed. Oxford: Oxford University Press, 1979.

Trueblood, Elton. *Alternative to Futility*. New York: Harper & Brothers, 1948.

Van Dusen, Henry P. "The Faith of John Dewey." *Religion in Life* (Winter 1935): 123.

———, ed. *The Christian Answer.* New York: Charles Scribner's Sons, 1948.

Walters, Raymond. "Facts and Figures of Colleges at War." *Annals of the American Academy of Political and Social Science* 231 (January 1944): 8–13.

Ward, F. Champion, ed. *The Idea and Practice of General Education: An Account of the College of the University of Chicago.* Chicago: University of Chicago Press, 1992.

White, Morton. *A Philosopher's Story.* University Park: Pennsylvania State University Press: 1999.

———. "Religion in the University." *Context* (1949): 402.

———. "Religion, Politics, and the Higher Learning." *Confluence* 6 (Autumn 1950): 402.

———. "Religious Commitment and Higher Education." *Confluence* 9 (Summer 1957): 138.

Wiebe, Donald. *The Politics of Religious Studies: The Continuing Conflict with Theology in the Academy.* 1st Palgrave ed. New York: Palgrave, 2000.

Wieman, Henry Nelson. "Wanted: A Structure of Religious Thought for Higher Education." *Religious Education* 35 (1940): 26–27.

Wilder, Amos, ed. *Liberal Learning and Religion.* New York: Harper, 1951.

Williams, George. "Religion at Harvard." Unpublished manuscript, 1999.

Williams, J. Paul. "The Present Status of Research in Religion (Presidential Address—National Association of Biblical Instructors)." *Journal of Bible and Religion* 15, no. 1 (January 1947): 3–9.

Wooster, Harvey A. "To Unify the Liberal-Arts Curriculum." *Journal of Higher Education* 3, no. 7 (1932): 377.

Zook, George F. "How the Colleges Went to War." *Annals of the American Academy of Political and Social Science* 231 (January 1944): 1–7.

Notes

Preface

1 Longtime vice president of Duke University Robert Shepard helps to highlight this difference between the study of religion more broadly in the university and the formation of religion departments in specific colleges in the middle of the twentieth century. Shepard, *God's People in the Ivory Tower* (New York: Carlson, 1991).

2 College had been for decades, if not two centuries, understood as predominantly a (1) small, (2) residential (3) knowledge transference experience (4) for the few, (5) taught by generalists, (6) supported by mostly private sources or local towns in order to create leading citizens likely to reinforce the norms encouraged by the school (7) with its prospective students and recent graduates practicing nearby, and (8) Protestant Christian influenced or supported. During the early and middle part of the twentieth century in American higher education, such a description of college was coming undone, as has been well documented by scholars, popular writers, and confirmed by government statistics. While the collegiate model continued in some form within universities—and in many ways was taken up by religion departments in their formation—the university model was shifting toward (1) larger, (2) less strictly residential (3) knowledge expansion / research experiences (4) for the many, (5) taught by professionally trained specialists, (6) supported by tuition and government loans primarily, with (7) alumni practicing around the globe. Those were, succinctly, both the desired ends and the end of college as the primary model. Scholars have more recently highlighted many additional

features of higher education that were exclusionary, namely, restrictions regarding race, gender, and religion. See Nancy Weiss Malkiel's *"Keep the Damned Women Out"* (Princeton, NJ: Princeton University Press, 2018), Jerome Karabel's *The Chosen* (Boston: Houghton Mifflin, 2005), and Craig Wilder's *Ebony & Ivy* (New York: Bloomsbury, 2013).

3 My professor Jonathan Z. Smith, having casually noted the role German theologian Paul Tillich played in the formation of religion departments, returned to the idea more systematically in his article on the matter. Jonathan Z. Smith, "Tillich['s] Remains . . . ," *Journal of the American Academy of Religion* 78, no. 4 (2010): 1139–70. As I discovered in the Harvard University archives' sealed dean's report on curricular programs in religion (it appeared I was the first, or one of the first researchers, to read it unsealed after fifty years), he was indeed invoked and utilized in that effort. However, most religion department founders were fairly adept at utilizing any reinforcing ideas or leading thinkers to help them move from an explicit Protestant theology to a more implicit use of teaching "religion" as culture, morality, and values but without the questionable intellectual baggage so far as university scientists were concerned. Having been the research assistant to Tillich's research assistant, Dean Jerald C. Brauer, I became aware early on of how central Tillich's understanding of religion as the substance of culture, and culture as the form of religion, was within the academy. During my interview with Iowa School veteran Robert S. Michaelson in 1998, he highlighted the importance of Tillich in the formation of the University of California, Santa Barbara, religion department.

4 Donald Meyer, *The Protestant Search for Political Realism* (Middletown, CT: Wesleyan University Press, 1960), 223.

5 Shaye J. D. Cohen and Edward L. Greenstein, eds., *The State of Jewish Studies* (Detroit: Wayne State University Press, 1990).

6 "Untimely death" is perhaps a feature of any institution, movement, or academic discipline that exists for very long. Stanford professor Lex Miller's early death was only one of four such departures I have followed in this research, ranging from Princeton University trustee and union seminary president Henry P. Van Dusen's (double marital) suicide to Columbia University bishop Pike's death in the Jordanian desert. It also includes my own experience with such a story, having met my religious history department head, Ioan Culianu, during admitted students' day April 1991 and, one month later, while trying to interview evangelical dictator Efrain Rios Montt in Guatemala, learning Culianu had been murdered in the university's Swift Hall's third-floor bathroom, ostensibly because he had been an outspoken critic of Romanian strongman politics, whose control of the Iron Guard had

deadly consequences. Ted Anton, *Eros, Magic and the Murder of Professor Culianu* (Evanston, IL: Northwestern University Press, 1996).

7 "Many American intellectuals regard theology also as something akin to astrology. Moreover, they believe it to be divisive as well as obscurantist and therefore a threat to the common presuppositions on which civic discourse in a democracy must necessarily rest." Van Harvey, Lacey, ed., "On the Intellectual Marginality of American Theology," in *Religion and Twentieth Century Intellectual Life*, ed. Michael Lacey (Cambridge: Cambridge University Press, 1989), 172. See also Sydney Ahlstrom's "Theology and the Present-Day Religious Revival," *Annals of the American Academy of Political and Social Science*, no. 332 (November 1960): 20–36.

8 Condoleezza Rice, interviewing Van Harvey, Stanford University, 2018.

9 Edmund Perry, interview by author, Northwestern University, 1997. Charles Braden himself was the religion department head at Northwestern until 1954, when Edmund Perry began teaching. President J. Roscoe "Rocky" Miller wanted the religion department shut down from 1949.

10 Noteworthy in making this case would be Christopher Seiple's work across several institutes, institutions, and foundations regarding religious freedom and also Brian Grim's leadership regarding religious freedom and business (food, car, airline, and technology companies, among many others, have religion employee resource groups (ERGs), departments or chaplains in the United States, to attend to religion as a measure of diversity and needs for religious understanding across a diverse range of employees).

11 Robert Sullivan elaborates,

> Not until the 1960s did the Church officially recognize that it "goes forward together with humanity and experiences the same earthly lot which the world does." Then sponsorship of cultural medievalism ended, and a predictably indiscriminate antimedievalism ensued, notably on America's Catholic campuses. But the long Catholic deprecation of the modern world seemed to vindicate the secular cliché that Catholicism has little to contribute to present-day civilization. . . . American Catholic Colleges Trying to Become Universities . . . During the twentieth century American Catholic institutions tried to accommodate themselves to the dominant secular research universities. Like much of the rest of higher education in the United States, Catholic schools were entrepreneurial from their beginning, founded to serve specific communities, often immigrant or local. After World War II the Catholic colleges

and universities emulously faced the great American research universities, which had now become elite corporate units of society. Church-schooled to conformity while simultaneously hungry for American legitimacy, the Catholic academy was insecure about its status and insular in its outlook. It possessed, moreover, no model of a great research university that advanced scholarship, some of which was specifically Catholic but neither theological nor medieval. It came to seem self-evident on most Catholic campuses that modern knowledge, apart from theology, is essentially secular and that to modernize was inevitably to secularize.

Robert Sullivan (Department of History and Erasmus Institute) with the editorial assistance of Walton R. Collins (emeritus, Department of American Studies, University of Notre Dame), "The University of Notre Dame's Catholic and Catholic Future: Professors, Teaching, and Scholarship," white paper, 2008, https://provost.nd.edu/assets/60163/sullivan_white_paper_abridged.pdf.

12   It is unlikely that Stanford emeritus professor Van Harvey has an equal if one seeks a living individual who has worked, studied, and taught at so many of the institutions at the center of this story. He alone has taught at Princeton with George Thomas and Paul Ramsey, as well as at Penn in the department Edwin Aubrey created, and studied with Robert Calhoun at Yale, where the department and divinity school split, and taught at Southern Methodist University where Thomas studied and Kent Fellows originated, and finally at Stanford, in the department whose history he wrote and lived out as a professor and department leader there.

13   Important research has been conducted by those attending to the history of the college and university ideals (Julie Reuben, George Marsden, D. G. Hart), the manufacturing or formation of religious studies / religion studies (Kevin Schilbrack, Donald Wiebe, Russell McCutcheon), church work in higher education (Douglas Sloan), the divinity school model's evolution (Conrad Cherry), and the changing relationship of originally religiously oriented schools and their missions and the teaching of and practice of religion (James Burtchaell, Stephen Haynes, Rhonda and Douglas Jacobsen). Learning from their research and reflections on these areas related to my story of the founding of college religion departments during this four-decade period (1924–64) allowed me to focus on the archival work behind and public arguments for departments' shift away from chapel, church work, and the way religion research across many disciplines had been conducted in an understandably disparate manner before this new centralizing. Each of the stories they tell is important in highlighting what was happening

in the church and academy that made possible, necessary, or at least relevant the formation of religion departments at Princeton, Penn, Yale, Columbia, and Stanford and the related developments at Harvard, Chicago, and other universities.

Introduction

1 In 1929, the American Council of Learned Societies accepted the Society of Biblical Literature into its membership, founded in the late nineteenth century.

2 This court case was not, as some have suggested, the reason state college and universities launched religious studies programs, nor did the substance of the case have anything to do with college or university instruction about, in, or for religion. However, over the decades, it became for many a touchstone for arguments regarding teaching about religion and was easy to point to as justification for this or that effort. The case became something to which people referred, and citing it gave arguments a causal legitimacy they did not deserve.

3 "This act authorizes the grant or loan of Federal funds to assist public and other nonprofit institutions of higher education in financing the construction, rehabilitation, or improvement of academic and related facilities in undergraduate and graduate schools." 1926.12(b)(16) Higher Education Facilities Act of 1963, 20 U.S.C. 753. This and other professionalizing moves decades earlier, like the American Association of University Professors' "Statement on Principles of Academic Freedom" and its revisions, were considered in NABI's decision to recommend a name change to the American Academy of Religion (AAR).

4 Clyde Holbrook's book *Religion, a Humanistic Field* (Englewood Cliffs, NJ, Prentice-Hall, 1963) and the correspondence between him and George Thomas and Paul Ramsey's successor John F. Wilson, also served as a demarcation for those still hoping for something of an advocacy-based instruction in religion, however academically credentialed, and for those ready for a clean break, however difficult, from the divinity school–trained professors and curricula of appreciative inquiry still regnant in most elite universities. Stanford department architect Alexander Miller was dead, and the project begun by Thomas and others in the 1940s, however important for the next steps toward religious studies as we understand it today, was on life support after 1963–64.

Chapter One

Central to my claims in this book is the notion that what we mean by the teaching of religion in colleges (at most any time but certainly in the period focused upon here) is clearly not univocal, not consistent across presumed meanings, not at all the same at all schools and for all professors. Namely, when one professor says they are teaching religion at one school, they are not in fact descriptively doing the same thing (or even intending to do the same thing) as another professor at another school, in another decade or the same decade. For instance, when a strident atheist who is a self-proclaimed anti-Christian dogmatist teaches the Bible at a state school, they are ostensibly and practically doing something significantly different from what an observant Catholic priest is doing when teaching confessional theology at an Augustinian university. Both professors may have attended the University of Chicago and studied under theologian philosopher David Tracy, and both may have written books for Oxford Press and be teaching in a department of well-trained scholars teaching English-speaking highly vetted undergraduates who believe they are taking religion courses. But alas, the intention of the teachers' institution is different, the subject matter may be different, and the result will likely be different, though of that one can rarely speak authoritatively.

1 This newly formed Council of Schools of Religion included Riverside Church minister Harry Emerson Fosdick, seminary professor and Yale Corporation member William Adams Brown, former Harvard president Charles W. Eliot, leading proponent of modernism and University of Chicago professor Shailer Mathews, *Christian Century* editor Charles Clayton Morrison, Chicago biblical educator Herbert Willett, Yale Divinity School professor Luther Weigle, Chicago religious education professor William Clayton Bower, Yale historian Kenneth Scott Latourette, Harvard philosopher Ernest Hocking, and Chicago historian of religions A. Eustace Haydon. Also included on the council were numerous denominational education board administrators, college presidents, and Protestant ministers led by Charles Foster Kent of Yale University and inspired by University of Michigan president Marion Leroy Burton. Their original focus was on eliminating the barriers to teaching religion in state universities, but this quickly expanded to include private universities and liberal arts colleges.

Two years after its founding, it was renamed the National Council on Religion in Higher Education and became known for its Kent Fellows program, which trained and supported Protestant teachers and scholars of religion in the early twentieth century. Later, it was renamed the Society for Religion in Higher Education, and in 1975, it was again renamed the Society for Values in Higher Education. Useful in understanding its history is the document "Fifty Years: 1923–1973: A Brief History of the National Council on Religion in Higher Education and the Society for Religion in Higher Education, Martha H. Biehles, Editor." From their archives, then in Portland, Oregon, currently at the Western Kentucky University archives, "UA101/5 Society for Values in Higher Education Publications" (2019), WKU Archives Collection Inventories, paper 860, https://digitalcommons.wku.edu/dlsc_ua_fin_aid/860.

2   Charles Foster Kent, "Filling the Gap in Modern Education," *Bulletin of the Council of Schools of Religion* 2, no. 3 (February 1927): 5, https://digitalcommons.wku.edu/svhe_pubs/3.

3   Kent, 4–5.

4   The council often used *religion* and not *Christianity* partly to distinguish its members from their more conservative brethren, who emphasized the theological doctrines of fundamentalist Christianity, and partly to address legal concerns regarding the teaching of "religion" in state schools, which the council considered legitimate.

5   Kent, "Filling the Gap," 7.

6   Kent, 4.

7   Kent, 14.

8   Harvey A. Wooster, "To Unify the Liberal-Arts Curriculum," *Journal of Higher Education* 3, no. 7 (1932): 377.

9   Wooster, 374.

10 Wooster, 374.

11 Wooster, 374.

12 Richard Rorty, writing in the *Hedgehog Review*, revealed that scholars were having the same arguments in the 1990s as in the 1920s regarding purpose and meaning in college. Richard Rorty, Julie A. Reuben, and George Marsden, "The Moral Purposes of the University: An Exchange," *Hedgehog Review* 2, no. 3 (Fall 2000): 106–19. Enter Steven Pinker in the 2000s on the teaching of religion at Harvard (he believes teaching religion is like teaching astrology), and there remains continuity in this century-long debate. Sidney Hook hands the baton to Pinker, and Niebuhr to Cornel West, and so on. When Harvard president Derek Bok heard about professor Steven Pinker's comment that the school doesn't need astrology classes to balance astronomy classes and thus doesn't need a course attending to religion, Bok noted it wasn't Pinker's most helpful comment. Lisa Miller, "Why Harvard Students Should Study More Religion," *Newsweek*, February 10, 2010, https://www.newsweek.com/why-harvard-students-should-study-more-religion-75231. The pattern was for skeptics to confront pious

supporters of teaching a practical Christian theology to college students and for intermediary appreciative reconcilers on campus (or in a school's administration) to find a way to explain the importance of teaching religion in a way that was acceptable to both skeptic and pious true believer alike where possible. Without reconcilers, skeptics, and pious true believers, there may not be enough attention, energy, and understanding to create or maintain a religion department.

13 "Announcement of Courses, 1932–33, College of Arts and Sciences," *Bulletin of Oberlin College* (1932).

14 Wooster, "To Unify the Liberal-Arts," 373.

15 Kent, "Filling the Gap," 14.

16 Kent, 15.

17 The committee responsible for initiating the conference included presidents of the following institutions: Union Theological Seminary, Henry Sloane Coffin; Swarthmore, Frank W. Aydelotte; Cornell University, Livingston Farrand; Williams College, Harry A. Garfield; Princeton University, John Grier Hibben; and Dartmouth College, Ernest Hopkins. Deans of the following institutions were included as well: Columbia University, Herbert Hawkes; Yale University, Clarence Mendell; and Harvard University Divinity School, Willard Sperry. Also part of the committee were John R. Mott, general secretary of the National Council of the YMCA, and Henry P. Van Dusen, secretary to the committee and National Student Council of the YMCA.

18 Galen M. Fisher, ed., *Religion in the Colleges* (New York: Association Press, 1928), 66.

19 Delegates to the conference included presidents from the following schools (in addition to the conveners): American University, Amherst College, Clark University, Colgate University, College of CUNY, Franklin & Marshall College, Gettysburg College, Haverford College, Hobart College, Howard University, Lafayette College, Middlebury College, Muhlenberg College, Oberlin College, St. John's College (Annapolis), Temple University, Trinity College (CT), Tufts University, the University of Buffalo, the University of Delaware, the University of Maine, the University of Michigan, the University of West Virginia, Ursinus College, and Wesleyan University (CT). Also included were four of Princeton University's deans, including Christian Gauss; Clarence Shedd, Yale University Divinity School; Rufus M. Jones, Haverford; R. H. Edwards, National Council on Religion in Higher Education (formerly Council on Schools of Religion); Robert Kelly, Council of Church Boards of Education; James L. McConaughy, president of Wesleyan University; and numerous YMCA officers, theological school representatives, and members of denominational education boards.

20 Fisher, *Religion in the Colleges*, 65.

21 Fisher, 65.

22 The organizing committee narrowed the invitation list to college presidents and a few guests, purposefully, though not maliciously, to include "no women educators, only one undergraduate, and no Roman Catholics or Jews." They wanted to begin with as homogenous a group as possible in order to develop strong consensus. One observer noted that "even as it was, some participants felt the personnel was too varied, both religiously and academically, to make possible the most fruitful outcomes." Fisher, vii.

23 Dean Hawkes argued in favor of creating courses by starting with a consideration of the students' needs:

> When I was in college myself, the approach toward religion seemed to be a desire or a suggestion or a pressure that one accept some kind of religion, or some attitude. We were asked to accept something, and then afterward, if at all, to examine it in order to see what it was that we had accepted. I think today we should show young people what religion is and then let them accept it, or reject it. . . . A real difficulty in this entire matter of religion is the suspicion on the part of the students that something is going to be put over on them. The whole object, however, in getting data and pointing out facts about religion is to help young men settle their own problems.

> Fisher, 49. Bernard Iddings Bell, president of St. Stephen's (later Bard) College, expressed himself to be in full disagreement with that approach and added that "what the student wants is intelligent leadership; kindly compassionate leadership, but it must be leadership, and the only significance in asking the student what he thinks about religious problems, is to find where he is not getting his leadership. The central figure in this problem is the teacher, not the student." Bell, an Episcopal priest known for his conservative social and cultural views, emphasized the great weight that this placed on each faculty member in the college to understand religion and to exhibit leadership. The problem, he asserted, lay with the religion that is often taught to students: "[The student] is thrown almost entirely, in his religious attitude, upon a sort of sentimental application of what he hasn't got, through social service and all that kind of thing—humanitarianism. I have found that students are interested in theology more than in anything else. . . . Of course, if you quote dogma, they don't like the word; it is unfashionable. What we want is a special technique, a dogmatic synthesis or pragmata. Our students have no such technique." Fisher, 50.

24   Brown University professor Cyril Harris was less concerned with a particular technique than with his observation that "we have allowed it to seem that religion is easy and immediately feasible and decidedly practicable. . . . What has got to take place if ever religion shall mean anything to boys and girls, is for them to discover that it is 'darned hard!' and that Jesus was after things that can't be viewed with equanimity, and that it takes all a man has got and more." Harris was alarmed at the way religion was treated as just another "labor-saving device" that was helpful to the student. Continuing the argument, Swarthmore professor Jesse Holmes took up the arduous task of defining *religion* for the college student. The conference committee had hoped to steer the attendees away from this complex and time-consuming task, but Holmes made it clear that his definition was all inclusive: "Neither we nor the students know exactly what we mean by some religious words. When we say God, it means one thing to one group, and another thing to a different group. Religion, likewise. I would suggest that religion is an attitude of mind. It is as much in one subject as another. Geology is religion, politics is religion. Even the politics of the United States of America is religion. If it isn't, it ought to be. . . . What we need is to live and teach on the religious level whatever we are teaching." Fisher, 53.

25   Dr. William M. Irvine, the chaplain at Mercersburg Academy, explained his philosophy as trying to "make every Jew a good Jew. I ask them if they go to the synagogue, and then get in touch with their rabbi. I try to make every Roman Catholic a better Roman Catholic." This philosophy would not likely have been accepted by most of the conference participants, but it describes well the philosophy of many religion professors by the late 1950s. Fisher, 61.

26   Fisher, 48.

27   Fisher, 45.

28   Boston University professor of religion Albert C. Knudson's article "Humanism and Barthianism," *Religion in Life* 4 (Winter 1935): 22–31, addressed two "contemporary theological movements" that were "antithetical to one another," one being anthropocentric and the other theocentric. Knudson concluded that "a theology which feeds on philosophical skepticism will perish thereby" (26). For him, metaphysical skepticism always undermines both authoritarian and humanistic faiths and thus was a disease in the body of human faith. Rationally grounded theism was the only answer for Knudson.

29   The cracks that they identified as religious in nature or that religion could fill, were in part cracks created by larger forces and could not be filled by any such moves on their part. Contemporary examples from college might be a student life office's desire to address student sexual

NOTES 227

mores, but these have little to do with college structure, argument, or programs but rather much larger social and bioevolutionary forces.

30 Knudson, "Humanism and Barthianism," 30.

31 They saw it as irreverent behavior regarding religion, but moving from knowledge transference to knowledge creation (from rote learning to potentially confrontational, dynamic, creative learning) can produce this also.

32 The Edward W. Hazen Foundation was a Protestant organization, fashioned as a "think tank," that focused on higher education issues. Based in New Haven for much of its existence, it funded research, teaching, and studies of Christianity in higher education. From the 1920s to the 1960s, it worked with a variety of congenial groups such as the National Council on Religion and Education and the Danforth Foundation. In 2019, the Hazen Foundation announced it would "spend down" its endowed funds, effectively going out of business within five years (focusing their current giving on issues of racial and social equity).

33 The list of presenters included theologian Edwin Aubrey of the University of Chicago, divinity school professor Clarence Shedd of Yale University, Quaker philosophy professor Rufus Jones of Haverford College, chapel dean Robert Wicks of Princeton University, former Union Theological Seminary professor George Coe, chapel dean Charles W. Gilkey of the University of Chicago, Catholic campus minister Father J. Elliott Ross of the University of Illinois, Rabbi Lee J. Levinger of the University of Ohio, Professor M. Willard Lampe of the University of Iowa School of Religion, religious education professor William Clayton Bower of the University of Chicago Divinity School, and Religious Life director Richard H. Edwards of Cornell University (also director of the National Council on Religion and Higher Education). Also included were officials of the YMCA and YWCA, campus social service directors, and campus chaplains from the University of California to the University of Pennsylvania. In all, over three hundred professors, campus chaplains, and denominational leaders were in attendance.

34 Milton C. Towner, ed., *Religion in Higher Education* (Chicago: University of Chicago Press, 1931), 261.

35 Quoted in Towner, vii.

36 Inherent in this tension is that of the old college versus the developing university.

37 Edwin Ewart Aubrey was born in Glasgow, Scotland, in 1896. He came to the United States in 1913 and became a naturalized citizen in 1918. He served with the US Ambulance Service in France and Italy during World War I. Aubrey earned his bachelor of philosophy degree from Bucknell University in 1919 and his MA (1921), BD (1922), and

PhD (1926) from the University of Chicago. Aubrey taught at Car-
leton College (Northfield, MN, 1922–23), Miami University (Oxford,
OH, 1923–26), and Vassar College (1926–29). From 1929 to 1944, he
served as professor of Christian theology and ethics at the University
of Chicago and was the chairman of the theological field. He became
president of Crozer Theological Seminary (Chester, PA) in 1944. He
remained at Crozer until 1949, when he established the program of
religious thought at the University of Pennsylvania. He finished his
career at the university as professor and chairman of the program
until his death in 1956. From 1940 to 1953, Aubrey held positions as
visiting lecturer or professor at Vanderbilt University, California Institute of Technology, Union Theological Seminary of New York, Evangelical and Reformed Seminary (Lancaster, PA), Swarthmore College,
Harvard University, Beloit College, and Colgate-Rochester Divinity
School. Aubrey authored *Religion and the Next Generation*, *Present
Theological Tendencies*, *Living the Christian Faith*, and *Man's Search for
Himself, Secularism: A Myth*. A nationally known theologian, Aubrey
was secretary and vice president of the American Theological Society
from 1945 to 1956. In addition, he provided leadership in the following
capacities: president of the University of Chicago Settlement, 1941–44;
chairman of the Department of International Justice and Good Will
of the Federal Council of Churches, 1944–48; treasurer of the American Association of Theological Schools, 1946–48; and chairman of
the National Program Commission of Student YMCA and YWCA,
1950–55.

38 Towner, *Religion in Higher Education*, 287.
39 Towner, 288–89.
40 Towner, 87–91.
41 One voice of protest at the conference was that of Rabbi Lee Levinger,
Hillel Foundation director at Ohio State University, who questioned
the definition of *religion* as it was being used at the conference. "The
Jew employs the word 'religion' not to signify a creed or church primarily, but to connote his entire culture and group life, in its historic
development." Towner, 108. For Levinger, his Christian colleagues
were defining it far too narrowly.
42 Some historians assume that this attempt to bolster religion in the colleges was due to a concern over the fact that religion was no longer
being taught in many colleges or universities. But the principal concern was that quality religious *instruction* was lacking. Religion itself
was being examined, but not as an important force in the lives of students and institutions.
43 This question was articulated by Catholic educator Father J. Elliot Ross
from the University of Illinois Newman Center: By the very fact of a

college being secularized and religion relegated to a comparatively unimportant place, the program for Catholics ceased to be "complete" or "ideal.... We want to have religion permeate the whole institution. I should like to see men with a respect for religion occupying the various professorial chairs. There should be no slurring at religion. No professor should ever try to break down the beliefs of his students.... When he robs a student of Catholicism, he steals what does not enrich him, and leaves the Catholic poor indeed with the blankness of agnosticism or atheism." Father Elliot expressed the concerns not only of Catholic educators but of many of the conference attendees when he addressed the issue of dangerous professorial behavior amounting to malicious intent to harm the faith of students. Towner, *Religion in Higher Education*, 5–97.

44 Towner, 85.

45 To claim that "you have to be it to know it and teach it" is another symptom of the shift away from college: namely, you must mark your ground as a specialist, and you thereby protect your claim to relevance in the new regime.

46 Towner, 87.

47 Few conference attendees would have disagreed with Gilkey's assessment, but debate did ensue when Harry Thomas Stock, representing the Congregational Educational Society, contended that although the "secular college" may not have been the ideal institution from a religious perspective, there was no other viable option for American higher education: "Although logic supports the theory of the Catholic church, history has demonstrated that when religion controls the educational system, both religion and education may suffer. Religion has become stultified or ossified when it has not had to contend with a fearless and free educational system. And, frequently, when schools are dominated by ecclesiastical groups, education makes its exit. For education is not synonymous with the transmission of dogmas, prejudices, laws or ideas." The president of Coe College, Harry Gage, responded from "a Protestant approach" that "what we know as modern education is derived directly from Jesus and the teachers he sent out to carry his message into regions he could not reach with his own voice.... The process reaches its climax in Christian wholeness or fullness of life.... It cannot be monopolized by individuals or classes. Christianity is democratic, therefore education must be so." Having detailed the failings of the "Church of Rome," Gage asserted that it was in America that "Protestantism had its fairest chance for expression of its genius without hindering traditions." Towner, 137.

48 In the 1980s, at the end of a long and prolific career, Hook argued in favor of a curriculum based on the historical development of Western civilization, against those who espoused what had earlier been his own Marxist and leftist leanings. His longevity and contrarian sensibilities and the irony of historical shifts led to his supporting a curricular model similar to that he had earlier opposed when he wrote against Robert Hutchins's Great Books program at the University of Chicago.

49 Sidney Hook, "A Challenge to the Liberal Arts College," *Journal of Higher Education* 10, no. 1 (1936): 21, 23.

50 Hook, 21.

51 Hook, 22.

52 Hook did support Hutchins's practice of academic freedom. When pharmacy magnate Charles Walgreen removed his niece from the University of Chicago under suspicion that Marxist philosophy was being purveyed there, Hutchins stood firm against the subsequent threat of witch hunts. Walgreen later came to appreciate Hutchins's insistence on academic freedom, and they worked together to their mutual benefit on several projects.

53 Martin Gardner's quote about the University of Chicago is relevant here: "The University of Chicago is a Baptist school, where atheist professors teach Jewish students about St. Thomas Aquinas."

54 Hook, 23.

55 The debate over what the centerpiece should be was finished, and the end of college wasn't up for debate—just a question of what would replace it or to where the collegiate ideal or impulse would migrate.

56 Bertrand Russell, "A Dilemma of Education," *Journal of Higher Education* 4, no. 3 (1936): 164.

57 John Dewey, *A Common Faith* (New Haven, CT: Yale University Press, 1934), 33–34. The three essays that make up this work were originally given as the Terry Lectures at Yale University.

58 Dewey, 33.

59 Dewey, 34.

60 Dewey, 38.

Chapter Two

1 *Princeton University Report of the Special Committee of the Faculty on Religious Education*, April 11, 1935, Princeton University Archives, George F. Thomas Papers, box 13, file 5, n.p, hereinafter cited as *Princeton Report*.

2 Research that we would understand clearly as being about religion was being conducted separately throughout the faculty and among many disciplines at the university. The chair of the committee, A. M. Friend Jr., was a medieval art historian primarily responsible for making the university one of the most important centers for the study of Byzantine and medieval art. One of his greatest achievements while at Princeton was the creation of the *Princeton Index of Christian Art.* He specialized in the reconstruction of the origins of illustrations in early biblical manuscripts, including Greek Orthodox monasteries on Mount Athos in the Aegean Sea. Friend was the first scholar to offer proof that John of Damascus, eighth-century theologian of the Eastern Church, was both "the father of Byzantine music and the father of Byzantine art." But while he was involved with such an "academic" pursuit of religion, Friend recognized its inadequacy in affecting the personal lives of students. So too with the rest of the committee members. Thomas Jefferson Wertenbaker was the chairman of Princeton's history department in the 1930s and author of a book examining Puritan oligarchy in early America. Wertenbaker published what the *American Historian Review* noted as the first "rounded picture of the Bible in all its aspects. His synthesis carries weight. It cannot be disregarded by any future student of our colonial beginnings." Charles G. Osgood was an English Renaissance scholar who championed the humanities as an approach to a subject, literature in his case, which involved "man's passionate interest in the human individual, his passionate concern in the spiritual life of men, in the issue between failure and success, between perdition and salvation." In his Phi Beta Kappa address at Princeton, Osgood called upon teachers to "transcend their specialty with a constant sense of its final value in human terms; so that whatever they teach, whether science or humanities, their teaching is authenticated, not only by their expert knowledge, but by this transcendent sense of its real values." He also held a visiting lectureship at neighboring Princeton Theological Seminary in 1940. Robert M. Scoon was a philosophy professor who specialized in classical Greece and chaired the religion department from 1932 to 1956. He was not a research scholar and was remembered by a university chronicler as one who fought for revolution in philosophy at midcentury, bringing social problems to the fore within the discipline. He had also been a member of the board of trustees of the Princeton Student Christian Association. P. A. Chapman was a Molière scholar and died a tragic early death.

3 See, for example, Theodore H. Greene, ed., *The Meaning of the Humanities: Five Essays* (by Ralph Barton Perry, August Charles Krey, Erwin Panofsky, Robert Lowry Calhoun, and Gilbert Chinard), intro. T. H. Greene (Princeton, NJ: Princeton University Press, 1938); Theodore H. Greene, ed., *Liberal Education Re-examined: Its Role in a Democracy* (New York: Harper & Brothers, 1943).

4 In a letter dated December 20, 1948, to F. A. Brewster of the University of Wisconsin, Thomas wrote that the original committee report on

religion was "adopted with very little criticism by the faculty." Princeton University Archives, George F. Thomas Papers, box 6, file 2, n.p.

5 Institutions reassessing their curricula during this period included Columbia, Harvard, Yale, Stanford, Princeton, and the Universities of Pennsylvania, Michigan, and Virginia.

6 *Princeton Report.*

7 *Princeton Report.*

8 *Princeton Report.*

9 *Princeton Report.*

10 Note that committee members argued for religion's place in the curriculum within the humanities rather than advocating that it be taught from a social sciences perspective. The former is more interpretive, while the latter is more explanatory and thus potentially more dangerous. This theme appears throughout this work. These fault lines live on in current debates over the true disciplinary home of religious studies. See Charlotte Allen, "Is Nothing Sacred? Casting Out the Gods from Religious Studies," *Lingua Franca: The Review of Academic Life* 6 (November 1996): 30–40.

11 *Princeton Report.*

12 *Princeton Report.*

13 *Princeton Report.*

14 *Princeton Report.*

15 In his memoir, *Keeping Faith at Princeton: A Brief History of Religious Pluralism at Princeton and Other Universities*, Frederick Houk Borsch describes how Princeton navigated the landscape between chaplaincy and religious studies.

16 Bower, quoted in Towner, *Religion in Higher Education*, 135.

17 Towner.

18 The concerns of Protestant educators that colleges were unduly emphasizing a research-based scientific worldview were further deepened by the research of Bryn Mawr psychology professor James Leuba. From 1925 to 1935, Leuba examined the religious beliefs of American-educated scientists and determined they were "losing their faith in the 'God of the churches.'" William Adams Brown understood Leuba himself to be interested in the health of the church, but Brown disagreed with Leuba's recommendation that "if the churches wish to retain their hold upon the coming generation, they will be wise to imitate the example of the scientists and to throw overboard the God whom they have hitherto worshiped." Leuba, quoted in William Adams Brown, "A Psychologist Advises the Churches," *Religion in Life* 4, no. 1 (1935): 5–6. Brown and other leading Protestant educators had no such interest in throwing overboard their God or their particular brand of Protestantism.

19 Robert Maynard Hutchins, *The Higher Learning in America* (New Haven, CT: Yale University Press, 1936), 96.
20 Hutchins, 108–9.
21 Hutchins, 112; Hutchins added that

> the prospective clergyman would come to the end of his sophomore year with a good general education derived from the classics and the liberal arts. In the university he would spend the greater part of his time under the faculty of metaphysics. But he would also study ethics, politics, economics, and law. . . . Although he would acquire some familiarity with the leading ideas of natural science, he would not need much in this field beyond what is supplied by metaphysics itself. If it were desirable or necessary for him to learn certain ministerial habits before he could be trusted with a congregation, he might acquire them through a system of apprenticeship or in a technical institute established near the university for the purpose.

22 William Adams Brown, *The Case for Theology in the University* (Chicago: University of Chicago Press, 1938).
23 Hutchins, *Higher Learning in America*.
24 Hutchins, 111.
25 Hutchins, 111.
26 Brown, *Case for Theology*, 7.
27 Brown, 77.
28 William Adams Brown, a professor at Union Theological Seminary in New York City, was a member of the Yale Corporation from 1917 to 1934 and acting president from 1919 to 1920. Robert Maynard Hutchins was acting dean of Yale Law School from 1927 to 1928 and dean from 1928 to 1930, at which time he was appointed president of the University of Chicago.
29 Quoted in Brown, *Case for Theology*, vi.
30 Brown, vii.
31 Brown, viii.
32 Brown, 1–2.
33 Merrimon Cuninggim (acting chaplain), "On the Status of Religion on the Yale Campus," memo to A. W. Griswold (Yale president), Yale University Archives, Alfred Whitney Griswold Papers, box 11, folder 73, 1.
34 Cuninggim, 1.
35 Cuninggim, 2.
36 Cuninggim, 4.
37 Cuninggim, 5.
38 "Forty-Sixth Annual Register, 1936–37," *Bulletin of Stanford University* (1936), p. 378, Stanford University Archives.

39 Stanford University, while much younger as an institution (founded in
    the early 1890s, like Chicago), taught religion to undergraduates during
    this decade, though it did not form a department until the 1950s.

40 Much of the philosophical basis for the founding of departments of
    religion lay in arguments made in the 1930s, surrounding both new
    humanist and Barthian interpretations of Christianity. Professor
    Albert Knudson of Boston University was among the first to claim
    that setting a course between these two, avoiding what was perceived
    to be their extremist deviations from Christian philosophy, was the
    best measure for liberal Protestants to take, especially as it related
    to higher education. The new humanism became the major religious
    philosophy against which the founders of religion departments were
    to struggle, especially in regard to its naturalistic explanations for reli-
    gious experience and its disaffected stance toward the concept of God:
    "The distinctive characteristic of religious Humanism is its antithesis
    or at least indifference to the belief in God . . . a reaction against an
    unethical otherworldliness." The gist of Knudson's critique—which
    was often repeated, in one form or another, by other leading Protes-
    tant educators—was that no made-to-order religion, no "religion of
    reason," no "religion of science" would ever command the allegiance
    of men or fulfill the function that religion ought to fulfill in human
    life. The only religion that would avail among men is the religion that
    springs up spontaneously in the world, the religion that arises both
    as a divine revelation and as a normal and vigorous expression of the
    religious nature of man. Knudson, "Humanism and Barthianism," 24.
        Knudson's criticism focused on influential German Protestant
    theologian Karl Barth's understanding of revelation, which Knudson
    thought to be too closely associated with philosophical skepticism. The
    writings of Barth, many of which were translated into English only
    in the 1930s and influenced many Americans who understood them-
    selves as "neoorthodox," had been used by many Protestant educa-
    tors as justification for their positions on reason and religion. Barth's
    religious hermeneutic had allowed them to dismiss the numerous
    scholarly calls for religion to be either rational or removed from the
    college. Respected academic opinions from Europe were always help-
    ful in the fight for "religion's" legitimacy with American colleges.
    Knudson warned, however, that "[Barth] denies that there is any
    way of justifying the Christian religion by an appeal to experience,
    to reason, or to utility. The whole modern theological movement
    from Schleiermacher down to the present he denounces as leading
    to 'a manifest destruction of Protestant theology and the Protestant
    Church.' There is, he insists, no way of making the Christian faith
    or revelation rational. If you ask him why we should believe that the

Bible is God's Word he answers: 'The Bible is God's Word because it is.'" Barth's teaching was, in the end, "so one-sided and extreme as seriously to impair its own usefulness as a system of theology," according to Knudson. The nature of academic discourse was such that even the pious advocates of establishing religion departments would not tolerate arguments in favor of Christian thought simply because they were "said to be true." But while those advocates were busy picking their way between the new religious humanism and Barthianism, both of which partook of an unacceptable philosophical skepticism, an even greater threat had to be faced—the proscientific naturalism of American pragmatism.

Though Boston University's department did not form officially until 1967, Howard Thurman became the dean of Marsh Chapel and professor of Spiritual Resources and Disciplines in 1953. Courses in religion were taught outside of a religion department structure for many years before the official department formation.

41 Modes or eras in the formation of college religion departments followed the trajectory of typologies noted in the appendix of this book.

Chapter Three

1 Robert Ellwood described the decade as containing both the residue of the old Protestant regime's institutional power and the seeds of the diverse paths taken in the 1960s, given that ideology, technology, and progress were central to religionists across the country. Ellwood, *1950, Crossroads of American Religious Life / Robert S. Ellwood*, 1st ed. (Louisville, KY: Westminster John Knox, 2000).

2 George Thomas, unpublished lecture, Philadelphia, 1970, Princeton University Archives, George F. Thomas Papers, box 21, file 8, n.p.

3 Frank Porter Graham (October 14, 1886–February 16, 1972) was an American educator and professor of history. He was elected president of the University of North Carolina in 1930.

4 Greene, *Liberal Education Re-examined*, 59.

5 Greene, 68.

6 The lecture was later expanded on and published as a book. George F. Thomas, *Religion in an Age of Secularism* (Princeton, NJ: Princeton University Press, 1940).

7 His inaugural address was cited in numerous archival records of religion department founders and in books and articles during the 1940s and 1950s. Additionally, he answered many letters of appreciation, including one dated October 27, 1950, from Theodore Hesburgh of Notre Dame, later president there. Thomas wrote back,

I appreciate more than I can tell you your letter concerning my address, "Religion in an Age of Secularism." The address was received extremely well and I got a number of letters from all over the country after it was printed and distributed by the University.... Last week I developed the thought of the address further by relating secularism to the humanism of the modern period and by trying to show that Communism was simply an extreme expression of secularism and should be regarded as a judgment upon the West where it arose. It seems to me that it is very important at the present time for us to realize that Communism is not the only enemy or even the most fundamental one facing Christians today, but that it is the materialism and secularism which have sprung from modern humanism and which are present in a less extreme degree in the Western democracies also. (October 27, 1950, p. 1, Princeton University Archives, George F. Thomas Papers, box 12, file 3)

8 Thomas, *Religion*, 3.
9 Jacques Maritain wrote of President Harold Dodds at Princeton University in 1952,

I do not submit my remarks on the present crisis of our world for the sake of pessimism or melancholy. I submit them to stress the fact that the task of education and educators is all the greater and all the more necessary.... As to education, its final aim is to prepare men for wisdom. "The end of liberal education is wisdom," as President Harold Dodds of Princeton University insisted in a recent address. And as to the humanities, they are in jeopardy if they do not tend to wisdom, just as human wisdom is in jeopardy if it does not tend to a higher wisdom that God gives in love, and which alone can truly set man free. (Maritain, *The Education of Man*, ed. Donald Gallagher and Idella Gallagher [New York: Doubleday, 1962], 102)

10 P. C. Kemeny's book *Princeton in the Nation's Service* (New York: Oxford University Press, 1998) includes a helpful discussion of this change at Princeton.
11 Thomas, *Religion*, 3.
12 Thomas, 7–8.
13 Thomas, 9.
14 Douglas Sloan, *Faith and Knowledge* (Philadelphia: WJKP, 1991), xi.
15 It is not easy to place these scholars on the Protestant landscape. These spokesmen for the place of teaching religion in higher education and against the corrosive effects of secularism and materialism were not operating in the same geographic, social, or cultural circles as such

popular evangelicals of the day as Carl F. H. Henry or Jack Fuller—and certainly did not fit into the category of Fundamentalists such as Bob Jones Sr. and Mordecai Ham. They were mainline Protestants who were convinced that religion was absolutely necessary to Western democracy and for whom Protestant Christianity was the best expression of religious truth. Their language was similar to that later used by evangelicals from the mid-1970s to the present, as these latter-day evangelicals have assumed many of the same issues, tropes, and perspectives of the liberal Protestant elite during World War II and the early postwar period.

16 Thomas, *Religion*, 10.
17 Thomas, 11.
18 Thomas, 14.
19 Thomas, 15.
20 Thomas, 16.
21 Sidney Hook, "The New Failure of Nerve," *Partisan Review* 10 (1943): 2.
22 Hook, 3.
23 Hook declared that none of Niebuhr's political and social views were tied necessarily to his theology (Hook, 13). This assertion was countered by the generally like-minded Harvard philosophy professor Morton White, who in the 1950s argued that one must take Niebuhr's theology along with his political philosophy, as they were inextricably intertwined.
24 President Conant, a scientist, had been blamed by many for allowing the divinity school to reach its nadir in the late 1940s at Harvard. He did, however, try to acquire Reinhold Niebuhr, whom he liked, for the divinity school faculty. George Williams (former Harvard Divinity School Winn Professor and subsequently Hollis Chair), interview with author, March 12, 2000.
25 Hook, "New Failure of Nerve," 9.
26 Hook, 9.
27 Hook, 12.
28 Hook, 14.
29 Hook, 22.
30 Hook, 23.
31 Robert Calhoun, *Religion and the Modern World* (Philadelphia: University of Pennsylvania Press, 1941), 70.
32 Calhoun, 63.
33 Calhoun, 64.
34 Calhoun, 64.
35 Calhoun, 68.
36 Calhoun debated J. A. C. F. Auer at Antioch College in 1948 on the question "Is Humanism the Religion of the Future?" Calhoun argued

that humanism, while it might be believed in religiously, was not able to consider the complex nature of human behavior and desires that Christianity recognized and accounted for.

37 Calhoun, 70.

38 William F. Buckley Jr., *God and Man at Yale* (New York: Regnery, 1951), 15.

39 We can see how the college ideal, traditional Christian theology, or the weight of the humanities faded away very slowly, and then suddenly; the ability to believe in them and practice them seemed to evaporate for many. This makes sense given that all three almost demand a social reinforcement or communal practice component. Each of the three was something one believed in and was involved in so deeply that one couldn't imagine the world being conducted completely in that language, and then the language went away and a new language took its place, with a new community and new practices; one wondered where it all went. No amount of hand-wringing about the old language, old Christian country, old community, old center that used to hold will bring it back; no amount of quality improvement could either. Until there was, in the late 1940s and early 1950s, that brief moment—either a failure of nerve or turn to religion, depending on your perspective—a time when these departments of religion made sense to found at universities that were still desirous of maintaining something of the collegiate ideal.

40 I. A. Richards, "The Two Rings: A Communication," *Partisan Review* 10, no. 4 (1943): 381.

41 Richards, 381.

42 George F. Zook, "How the Colleges Went to War," *Annals of the American Academy of Political and Social Science* 231 (January 1944): 1–7; Raymond Walters, "Facts and Figures of Colleges at War," *Annals of the American Academy of Political and Social Science* 231 (January 1944): 8–13; Richard Altick, "The War of Nerves," *Journal of Higher Education* 14, no. 9 (December 1943): 477–82.

43 Clarence P. Shedd, "Education, but Not as Usual," *Intercollegian* (November 1942): 1.

44 Shedd, 1.

45 Shedd, 3.

46 Shedd, 3.

47 D. Elton Trueblood, "The Place of Theology in a University," *Religion in Life* 11, no. 4 (1944): 518.

48 Trueblood, 518.

49 Trueblood, 521.

50 "Religion Week" or "Religious Emphasis Week" was a common occurrence at colleges from the 1940s through the 1960s (and, in various

forms, from the 1920s to the present). Often sponsored by the religion department, campus ministries, the chaplain's office, and/or other interested parties, guest lecturers were invited to campus to give sermons, informative talks and spend time with faculty, students and classes to bolster religious community and knowledge. As the 1950s and '60s brought more campus diversity, if not radical plurality, the often-all-Protestant panels and activities were replaced with a format that could be described as a coming together of "Protestant, Catholic, and Jew" on campus to share in the new ecumenical and interfaith spirits of midcentury religious life on campus.

51 Trueblood, "Place of Theology," 522.

52 Trueblood, 519.

53 "Proceedings of the Stanford Conference on Religion in Higher Education," *School and Society* 55, no. 1432 (June 6, 1942): 647.

54 "Proceedings," 648.

55 "Proceedings," 510.

56 "Proceedings," 517.

57 "Proceedings," 516.

58 Theodore Greene, "The Seminaries and the Future of Liberal Education," *American Association of Theological Schools*, no. 16 (June 1944): 53.

59 Greene, 53.

60 Greene, 56.

Chapter Four

1 The most comprehensive discussion and analysis of the CSPR can be found in Frederick Beuttler, "Organizing an American Conscience: The Conference on Science, Philosophy and Religion 1940–1968" (PhD diss., University of Chicago, 1995). Beuttler argues that critics of the conference such as Sidney Hook, John Dewey, and other representatives of the new humanism misunderstood the intentions and promise of the conference meetings. They focused on Mortimer Adler and other extreme factions within the conference who were less active and less interested in dialogue. Such critics were also, he argues, predisposed to disagree with the conference's general project because they were not part of the organizing coterie, which was sympathetic to religious concerns. Beuttler focuses on several founders of religion departments whose voices were prominent in the conference debates: George Thomas, Edwin Aubrey, Theodore Green, and Erwin R. Goodenough.

2 Those academics and intellectuals opposed to the general framework and outlook of the CSPR established conferences of their own that

were meant to counteract the trend toward blaming a lack of religious and moral fortitude for the crisis of Western civilization. In turn, it was this critique by some of the leading scientists and philosophers of the day that founders of college religion departments used as a rationale for creating new departments, in order to counteract the ascendency of science over the humanities, and naturalistic philosophy over Christianity. These conferences never gained the notoriety of the CSPR, though they met several times during the mid-1940s under the name Scientific Spirit and Democratic Faith. The planning committee included *New York Times* science editor Waldemar Kaempffert, New School for Social Research professor Horace Kallen, New York University's Sidney Hook, Columbia University professor Robert Lynd, Yale University professor Harry Margenau, and *Time* magazine science editor Gerald Wendt.

3 Sidney Hook, "Theological Tom-Tom and Metaphysical Bagpipe," *Humanist* 2, no. 3 (Autumn 1942): 96.

4 Members included J. Douglas Brown (economics), Theodore M. Greene (philosophy), E. Harris Harbison (history), Whitney Oates (classics), Henry Norris Russell (astronomy), Hugh Taylor (chemistry), George Thomas (religious thought), and John Mackay (president of Princeton Seminary, an entirely separate institution, though geographical proximity did entail some cooperative efforts).

5 Princeton Group, "The Spiritual Basis of Democracy" (presentation, CSPR, Second Symposium, New York, 1942), 251.

6 Princeton Group, 251.

7 John Dewey, "Anti-naturalism in Extremis," *Partisan Review* 10, no. 1 (1943): 31.

8 Princeton Group, "Spiritual Basis of Democracy," 251.

9 Dewey, "Anti-naturalism in Extremis," 31.

10 Edwin Aubrey, "Pro and Con the Democratic Value of the Conference on Science, Philosophy and Religion," *Humanist* 3 (Spring 1943): 24–25.

11 Aubrey, 25.

12 Erwin Goodenough, "Needed: Scientific Study of Religion: How Long Will Free Inquiry Neglect This Basic Field?," *Commentary* 5 (1948): 272.

13 Sir Julian Huxley was a proponent of the idea that religion filled in the explanatory space that science could not. For Huxley, this meant that religion would over time come to occupy a smaller and smaller space. Goodenough did predict that science would also make the known world smaller by virtue of further scientific explanation, but he did not believe along with Huxley that humans would need less and less religion because of that.

14 Goodenough, "Needed," 273.

15 Goodenough, 273.

16 His frustration with the Society of Biblical Literature, though he served as its president for several years, and the National Association of Biblical Instructors (now the American Academy of Religion) prompted Goodenough to work with the American Council of Learned Societies' religion subcommittee in a well-funded attempt to create an organization—which, in 1959, became the American Society of the Study of Religion.

17 Erwin R. Goodenough, "Religionswissenschaft," *Numen* 6, no. 2 (1959): 77–95.

18 Robert Hutchins, "The Place of Theological Education in a University," p. 3, University of Chicago Special Collections, Robert Maynard Hutchins Presidential Papers, box 26, folder 3.

19 Robert Maynard Hutchins, notes for a speech, University of Chicago Special Collections, Robert Maynard Hutchins Presidential Papers, box 27, folder, 1, 10.

20 Editorial, *Christian Century*, November 17, 1943, 1327.

21 Editorial.

22 Hutchins, notes for a speech, 12.

23 Hutchins, 13.

24 Yale University's religious education professor Clarence Shedd kept unpublished notes in his personal files that focused on Hutchins's concern about the lack of respect accorded theology and ministers by society. Shedd's notes show he was delighted that Hutchins believed that metaphysics might unify the modern university and especially favored Hutchins's proclamation that "the decline of the church in this country [should be attributed to] the decline of the theological schools. . . . Why is it that the clergy do not command the respect that we should all like to feel for them? I think you will find the answer by looking at the catalogue of any divinity school. It is now made up of subjects which, it is assumed, will assist the pastor in coping with his first charge. . . . Theology, which deals with the intellectual problems of his profession, has almost disappeared from the curriculum." Hutchins, *Higher Learning in America*, 52–53.

25 Herbert Nobel, letter to Robert Maynard Hutchins, University of Chicago Special Collections, Robert Maynard Hutchins Presidential Papers, box 30, folder 7.

26 Lynn White Jr., letter to Herbert Nobel, University of Chicago Special Collections, Robert Maynard Hutchins Presidential Papers, box 30, folder 7.

27 George Rosser, letter to Robert M. Hutchins, University of Chicago Special Collections, Robert Maynard Hutchins Presidential Papers, box 30, folder 7.

28 In a letter to Dean Ernest Colwell of the divinity school, Hutchins explained why he would not be able to deliver the Federated Theological School inaugural address as it was originally scheduled:

> Let's be serious. On October 15, I speak twice to the Teachers of Minnesota. The University gets $400 out of this. On October 24, I am preaching in the Chapel. Nobody gets anything out of this. On October 29, I speak twice to the Teachers of Massachusetts. The University gets $300 for this. It will take me two weeks to prepare for each one of these engagements. I cannot speak on "The Place of Theological Education in the University" without at least two weeks to think about it. Get somebody else or change the date either of the Federation Celebration or of my Chapel sermon. (University of Chicago Special Collections, Robert Maynard Hutchins Presidential Papers, box 30, folder 7, correspondence, divinity school)

Hutchins placed the writing of the speech in the broader perspective of university finances but did want to spend time preparing for it. In order to keep his own faculty members on campus, Hutchins required professors to return honoraria for outside speaking engagements to the university.

29 Editorial, *Christian Century*.

30 Gideonse criticized what seemed to him a narrow view of the "disorderly" nature of higher education Hutchins had described. Gideonse argued that disorderliness was indeed what education in a democracy should look like. The neatness of Hutchins's general educational outlook was, to him, dangerous and unbecoming of a democracy. Harry D. Gideonse, *The Higher Learning in a Democracy: A Reply to President Hutchins' Critique of the American University* (New York: Farrar and Rinehart, 1937), 5–10. Whereas Gideonse took issue with what he thought to be Hutchins's too-radical educational philosophy, Brown wanted Hutchins to go one step further. Gideonse was himself closely aligned with the new religious humanism, most easily identified by those philosophers, ministers, and public figures who wrote for the journal the *Humanist*, many of whom signed the Humanist Manifesto in 1932, a document proclaiming the viability of a religious sentiment based not on supernatural religion but on the highest human aspirations.

31 Edward Blakeman, "Realistic View of Religion," *Religious Education* 7 (1944): 355.

32 Henry Nelson Wieman, "Wanted: A Structure of Religious Thought for Higher Education," *Religious Education* 35 (1940): 26–27.

33 Wieman, 26.

34 Wieman, 27.

35 George Thomas and Clarence Shedd did not publish their thoughts regarding Hutchins's proposals for education, but their personal papers each contain handwritten and typed thoughts about his critique of higher education's vocational focus and how such a focus undermined the foundational purposes of a college education. The Shedd papers are located at the Yale University Archives, and the Thomas Papers are located at the Princeton University Archives.

36 George Finger Thomas, "Religion in the American College," *Religious Education* 53 (1944): 102–7.

37 Thomas, 106.

38 Many educators during this period embraced the assumption that a common body of knowledge, language, and commitment was necessary for a coherent education. Thomas certainly fit well within this camp, though he rarely joined the chorus of those calling for a "general education" program. He wrote in his private notes, housed (but not fully organized at the time of this research) in the George F. Thomas Papers at Princeton University, that "secularism is abetted by the fragmentary nature of the curriculum." The general education movement was undoubtedly akin to the formation of religion departments in that it became another temporary location for the college ideal during the shift from the college to the university model in American higher education in the twentieth century. The general education movement did not always recognize "religion" as a positive contributor to its goals, yet it was very much related to the formation of religion departments and the college ideal.

39 Thomas, "Religion in the American College," 106.

40 Thomas, 107.

41 Thomas, 109.

42 Thomas, 107.

43 Thomas, 108.

44 Thomas, 108.

45 Thomas, 114.

46 Thomas, 114.

47 Thomas, 107.

48 John Dewey, "Commentary," *Humanist* (Autumn 1945): 105.

49 The label "humanist" was used by some humanities professors and literary intellectuals who understood their work as qualitatively distinct from the social and natural sciences in both style and content. It was used by new "religious humanists" to make clear their appreciation for all things human or humane (including actions and ideas that today would be considered "humanitarian" or "human rights" focused). *Humanist* was used as a derogatory term by some conservative or Fundamentalist writers and preachers to denote an individual whose worldview was centered on man, not God. The "humanities" in the college curriculum were from the first third of the twentieth century on, being defined and redefined in the process of finding their place in each institution (for example, history departments to this day may be found in either the department of social sciences or the department of humanities).

50 Iva Dolezalova, Luther H. Martin, and Dalibor Papousek, *The Academic Study of Religion during the Cold War: East and West* (New York: P. Lang, 2001).

51 W. Clark Gilpin, *A Preface to Theology* (Chicago: University of Chicago Press, 1996), 122.

52 Many Protestant educators argued that when the transcendent was removed from everyday life, political discourse, and university studies, the alternative was a secular mentality that espoused materialism and bred political doctrines contrary to democracy. Whether they were aware of it or not, these educators had come up against one of the basic conflicts of late modernity. Namely, if no divine authority (God) or divine representative authority (church) has power, then nothing would stop political ambitions and machinations from ruling the day. Just as one might assert that democracy is more a moral and social vision or goal (prescriptive) and not an objective assessment of reality (descriptive), these educators believed that one must rely on Western civilization's religious foundation to get to the prescription of democracy. The alternative was fascism or Nazism, and the so-called solution of communism was understood to be worse than the problem. Christianity offered, according to these Protestant elites, a mandate to infuse democracy with morality. This would provide a way out of the political, social, and cultural crisis.

Chapter Five

1 Benjamin Fine, "Yale Is Urged to Stress Religion as Curb on Intellectual Anarchy; Yale Urged to Put Stress on Religion," *New York Times*, August 5, 1945, 1, 17.

2 Fine, 1.

3 The other committee members were Arthur H. Bradford, a Yale Corporation Fellow and Union Seminary graduate; Richard C. Carroll, assistant dean of Yale College; Robert D. French, department chair of history; Sidney Lovett, chaplain, committee chair, and Woolsey Professor of Biblical Literature; Daniel Merriman, professor of oceanic biology; Richard B. Sewall, associate professor of English; and Luther Tucker, general secretary of the university YMCA.

4 *Yale University Report on the Strengthening of Religious Life and Instruction*, Yale University Archives, Charles Seymour Papers, box 135, folder 1143, 1–2, hereinafter cited as *Yale Report*.

5 *Yale Report*, 6.

6 Sloan, *Faith and Knowledge*.

7 *Yale Report*, 9.

8 *Yale Report*, 11.

9 *Yale Report*, 11.

10 Alfred Whitney Griswold, draft of "Religious Scholarship in a Modern University: The Need for Research in Religion," Yale University Archives, Alfred Whitney Griswold Papers, box 18, folder 36, 1.

11 *Yale Report*, 20.

12 *Yale Report*, 20.

13 *Yale Report*, 22.

14 *Yale Report*, 22, 26.

15 Protestant leaders from Reinhold Niebuhr to Henry P. Van Dusen considered this account of human existence and experience bankrupt because such a philosophy—along with its sisters, science and technology—had not delivered humanity from the horrors of modern totalitarianism. Both humanists and more orthodox Protestants alike claimed that their outlooks had not failed the twentieth century. Rather, they had not yet been properly implemented.

16 *Yale Report*, 28, 31.

17 A noteworthy feature of the Princeton report of 1935—that bears the closest resemblance to that of Yale's report in 1945—is the tone of the following sentence: "The various forces, religious, moral, and intellectual, of this powerful religion working in us, consciously and unconsciously, to this day make nonsense and confusion of our thinking and actions unless we are able to understand them and know what they are. We cannot really escape them." *Princeton Report*. Both reports give one the sense that the authors felt obligated to deal respectfully with religion, especially Christianity; that this subject somehow held the key to important cultural solutions heretofore undiscovered; and finally, that one could not remove oneself from the Western religious context, so learning about it was necessary.

Both reports also stated that divinity schools were doing something altogether different from what they wanted the new programs to accomplish. The Princeton report stated, "This whole phase of human experience has been, by the very nature of the foundation of those institutions, turned over to practical religious instruction, or to Divinity schools whose object was and is to produce a clergy for some sect or other. That is to say, it has not been a part of liberal humanistic training." *Princeton Report*. In other words, for the Princeton group, producing a clergy was a sectarian act, whereas humanistic training was by definition not a sectarian act. This distinction was a good example of the standard argument used by Protestant educators in the first third of the century to explain in part why the subject of religion had not been allowed an independent place in college curricula. Sectarianism was the culprit and, until some degree of unity among Christian scholars was achieved, such partisan Christian teachers had no right to spread their particular propaganda to students seeking a liberal or broad education.

18 Yale Corporation, minutes, February 9, 1946, Yale University Archives, Charles Seymour Papers, box 135, folder 166.

19 Erwin Goodenough, letter to President Charles Seymour, February 15, 1946, Yale University Archives, Charles Seymour Papers, box 135, folder 1143, 3.

20 Goodenough, 1.

21 President Seymour, letter to Hubert McDonnell (a potential donor in New York), April 30, 1946, Yale University Archives, Charles Seymour Papers, box 135, folder 1143.

22 Yale University, press release, May 5, 1946, Yale University Archives, Charles Seymour Papers, box 135, folder 1143.

23 Although Christianity and Protestantism were words less often used in public communications in this period, the mainline Protestant religious tradition was the understood "religion" that needed comprehending. Judaism and the Hebrew bible were being interpreted as an earlier stage of the Christian covenant rather than a living religion and religious text used by a modern religious community.

24 Erwin Goodenough, letter to President Seymour, February 15, 1946, Yale University Archives, Charles Seymour Papers, box 135, folder 1143, 3.

25 Clarence Shedd, letter to Luther Weigle (divinity school dean), June 19, 1947, Yale University Archives, Charles Seymour Papers, box 135, folder 1254.

26 John Schroeder (religion department chair), letter to President Seymour, Yale University Archives, Charles Seymour Papers, box 135, folder 1254.

27 Schroeder.

28 Schroeder, 1948–49 religion department report to President Seymour, June 16, 1949, Yale University Archives, Charles Seymour Papers, box 135, folder 1143.

29 Schroeder, 1952–53 religion department report to President A. Whitney Griswold, August 6, 1953, Yale University Archives, Charles Seymour Papers, box 135, folder 1143.

30 Professor Clarence P. Shedd, letter to President Seymour, Yale University Archives, Charles Seymour Papers, box 135, folder 1143, 1–2.

31 Shedd, 1–2.

32 Professor Erwin R. Goodenough, letter to President Seymour, February 15, 1945, Yale University Archives, Charles Seymour Papers, box 135, folder 1143.

33 President Charles Seymour, letter to Professor Erwin R. Goodenough, February 18, 1945, Yale University Archives, Charles Seymour Papers, box 135, folder 1143.

34 Professor Clarence P. Shedd, letter to President Seymour, April 12, 1945, Yale University Archives, Charles Seymour Papers, box 135, folder 1143, 3.

35 Apparently, the Princeton report was referred to by educators more often than it was read by them. Occasional letters from George Thomas to inquirers revealed that he himself did not know where to find a copy of the report, though he was asked for it regularly.

36 Robert Calhoun, "Comments on the Proposals for Strengthening Religious Life and Instruction in Yale University," Yale Divinity School Archives, Clarence P. Shedd Papers, box 13, file 6.

37 One of the strongest statements in favor of a religion department that held together both primarily academic and ostensible Christian values was Clarence Shedd's essay a "Proposal for Religion in Postwar Higher Education." This pamphlet was one of eleven such pieces produced by the Hazen Foundation, the source of many initiatives during the 1930s to 1950s supporting the renewal of Christianity in college classrooms. The Hazen Foundation's Series One Pamphlets included the following: "Religion in Higher Education" by Paul J. Braisted; "The Place of Religion in Higher Education" by Robert L. Calhoun; *The Resources of Religion and the Aims of Higher Education* by Julius Seelye Bixler; "Teaching Economics with a Sense of the Infinite and the Urgent" by Patrick M. Malin; "Relation of Religion to Education—with Special Reference to Citizenship" by Ordway Tead; and "Education and Religion" by George N. Shuster.

38 Shedd, "Proposal for Religion."

39 Shedd, 7.

40 In *That Noble Dream* (Cambridge: Cambridge University Press, 1988), Peter Novick writes about the numerous social science academics who moved away from their more "nihilistic" public proclamations when confronted with nihilism as a norm throughout the country and on the front lines of war. The monograph also addresses the quest for and then abandonment of objectivity in the history profession.

41 In his early career, he focused his research, writing, and teaching upon Justin Martyr and Philo of Alexandria; Hellenistic influences upon Judaism, from art and symbols to philosophy and myth, occupied the middle part of his career; and New Testament interpretation and

method in the history of religions took up the latter part of his career. Several of his students, including scholars such as Robert Eccles at Indiana and Jonathan Z. Smith at the University of Chicago, later held leadership positions within academe and the teaching of religion. Goodenough himself studied under formative and influential scholars at Harvard University, such as George Foot Moore. Goodenough's belief in the importance of religion as a subject of study and teaching was similar in tone to the scholarly piety expressed by Huston Smith of Washington University.

42 Goodenough wrote a spiritual autobiography, *Toward a Mature Faith* (New York: Prentice-Hall, 1955), and Robert S. Eccles wrote a brief biography of his adviser for the Society of Biblical Literature, entitled *Erwin Ramsdell Goodenough: A Personal Pilgrimage* (Chico, CA: Scholars Press, 1985), in which he traced Goodenough's life through themes.

43 Erwin Goodenough, "The Inspiration of New Testament Research" (presidential address, Society of Biblical Literature and Exegesis, 1951), *Journal of Biblical Literature* 71 (1952): 2.

44 "By scientific, I mean that we gather data not to prove that Jesus, Hosea, Mohammed, or Karl Marx is right—or wrong—but in order to find out what the religious experience of man has come from, where he gets his ideals, and which ideals have worked constructively and which not." Goodenough, 4.

45 Goodenough, 4.

46 Erwin Goodenough, "Scientific Living," *Humanist* 2 (1942): 9–10.

Chapter Six

1 It was not until much later that either university found it necessary to found undergraduate religion programs, and by that point in time, one might argue that the dual role was at most a dynamic among interested faculty members, not an institution-wide expectation.

2 Harvard University Committee, *General Education in a Free Society: Report of the Harvard Committee 1945* (Cambridge, MA: Harvard University Press, 1945), 4.

3 Harvard University Committee, 6.

4 Author and Harvard alumnus (1957) Alston Chase wrote about the implications of the general education program at Harvard:

> By 1950 the Harvard faculty was divided between those who, chastened by their experience in World War II and especially by the bombings of Hiroshima and Nagasaki, saw science and

technology as a threat to Western values and even human survival, and those—a majority—who saw science as a liberator from superstition and an avenue to progress. Both these views found their way into the Gen Ed curriculum. The dominant faction had little sympathy for the Redbook's [*General Education in a Free Society*] resolve to inculcate Judeo-Christian ethics. Because of the majority's resistance, many Redbook-committee recommendations were never fully implemented. These professors in fact emphasized the opposite of the lesson [President] Conant intended. Rather than inculcate traditional values, they sought to undermine them. Soon, 'Thou shalt not utter a value judgment' became the mantra for Harvard freshmen, in dorm bull sessions as well as in term papers. Positivism triumphed. . . . Gen Ed delivered to those of us who were undergraduates during this time a double whammy of pessimism. From the humanists we learned that science threatens civilization. From the scientists we learned that science cannot be stopped. Taken together, they implied that there was no hope. Gen Ed had created at Harvard a culture of despair. This culture of despair was not, of course, confined to Harvard—it was part of a more generalized phenomenon among intellectuals all over the Western world.

Alston Chase, "Harvard and the Making of the Unabomber," *Atlantic Monthly*, June 2000, 50. Chase's perceptions of the campus ethos were shared by leading Protestant educators at Harvard, inspiring them to ensure that the Redbook report was bolstered by a special report on the teaching of religion at Harvard in 1947.

5 Harvard University Committee, *General Education*, 30.

6 Harvard University Committee, 30.

7 The very fact that Harvard turned to well-known theologian and minister Reinhold Niebuhr—who was on the cover of *Time* magazine March 8, 1948, as a public intellectual for their twenty-fifth anniversary edition—and Colwell, who was the University of Chicago's president after World War II and a New Testament scholar, gives one the sense that the role of Protestant Christian public intellectuals in America was very different then compared to today.

8 *Report of the Commission to Study and Make Recommendations with Respect to the Harvard Divinity School*, July 15, 1947, Harvard University Archives, divinity school, dean's office files, 45, hereinafter cited as *Harvard Report*. It was made available for the general public and researchers to read no earlier than July 15, 1997.

9 *Harvard Report*, 45.

10 *Harvard Report*, 45.

11 *Harvard Report*, 45.

12 *Harvard Report*, 34–35.

13 The 1925 AAUP (American Association of University Professors) state-ment on academic freedom and its subsequent 1940 statement show another important development in the professionalization, if not secu-larization, of collegiate faculties. Each was also another important mile-stone for the formalization of academic standards that occurred just as the 1950s turn toward religion followed the formation of religion depart-ments, which made such statements fraught for many administrators and faculty as they executed the dual role of their departments (values incul-cation and academic legitimacy). Faculty, religion department professors included, in the early twentieth-century college model were less likely to see themselves as free to teach, write, research, and share publicly their observations as they wished, compared to how they would after the con-cept and practice of academic freedom as understood within the univer-sity ideal had become more common, documented, and protected.

14 *Harvard Report*, 47.

15 *Harvard Report*, 49.

16 Having served as a university, college, and also seminary vice president myself, it is clear to me the differences between the preparation of a report, commissioning the report as an administrator, serving on a com-mittee with internal faculty and external experts, drafting the report, finding funding to implement the report, implementing the report, shar-ing the report externally, having others follow recommendations from the report and our institution's implementation of such reports. In short, looking through the archives and public documents it seems fairly straightforward that reports are commissioned, released, followed, and contested; in practice, it is anything but straightforward. Many reports that are delivered and ostensibly implemented find no such life for their conclusions, recommendations, and assumptions. Varied motivations for any of those steps and the unintended consequences of them as well—to say nothing of wordsmithing by committee, implementation under funding pressures, and faculty members' prioritization of any set of courses in a curriculum—all ensure the story of any one committee cannot be accurately told. This certainly applies to most if not all the reports and committees that were part of this decades-long movement to bring religion back into colleges via religion departments. I have tried where possible to reveal the difference between commissioned reports and actual action within schools and across curricula. There are certainly additional stories that need to be excavated among these steps ranging from the formation of a committee to faculty members or alumni responses to the formation of said religion departments.

17 Henry Stimson, former US secretary of war and secretary of state and a Harvard alumnus, pressed for a "living Christian Spirit" at Harvard, not just a center for the study of religion, as noted in George Williams's unpublished study (when he shared it with me in draft form) of "Religion at Harvard," 976.

18 Divinity school Dean Willard Sperry noted the philosophy department's history of holding up religion before the undergraduates in a positive light, from Josiah Royce earlier in the century to William Ernest Hocking and Alfred North Whitehead toward midcentury.

19 Morton White, "Religion in the University," *Context* (1949): 402.

20 George Williams's unpublished "Religion at Harvard" manuscript, 986. Permission to quote given by the author.

21 White, "Religion in the University," 404.

22 *Harvard Report*, 36.

23 Paul Ramsey, "Religion at Princeton," *Religious Education* (March–April 1947): 67–69.

24 John F. Wilson (colleague of George Thomas at Princeton), interview with author, April 10, 1997.

25 It is difficult to imagine how it would have been possible to achieve the separation of the teaching and practice of religion in the ideal manner that is described in some Princeton documents. Religion professors had the knowledge and experience that was desired by Protestant groups on and off campus. So long as there was no formal connection, these professors continued to claim separation was both the ideal and the norm. Such a tension is still encountered by professors at present and likely will be in the future. Academic or pedagogical purity in advocacy or objectivity is difficult to obtain if not to proclaim.

26 Robert Root, "Princeton's New Curriculum," *Journal of Higher Education* 18, no. 1 (1947): 16.

27 Merrimon Cuninggim, *The College Seeks Religion* (New Haven, CT: Yale University Press, 1947), 190–91.

28 Cuninggim, 191.

29 M. Willard Lampe, Iowa School of Religion annual report, May 5, 1947, University of Iowa Archives, School of Religion Collection, Religion Department Files, 3.

30 Lampe.

31 Lampe, 7–8.

32 Robert S. Michaelson's career (Iowa and beyond) and life span (1919–2000) across this time period is similar in scope to Van Harvey's career a few decades earlier. Claude Welch, Ninian Smart, and William Clebsch's work just after the early department formation era was similar in scope and importance and would be important to document in a volume covering the 1960s to the 2000s.

33 M. Willard Lampe, Iowa School of Religion annual report, May 13, 1946, Iowa University Archives, School of Religion Collection, Religion Department Files, 3–9.

34 The University of Iowa's school of religion and program remained an important model in the twentieth century, one whose structure interestingly has found its way back into favor given that today, a religion department might have one professor with strong connections to Hinduism teaching Hinduism, one Catholic or former Evangelical teaching American religious history, one Buddhist teaching Buddhism, and so forth. In the early 1990s, my own alma mater came to blows over a faculty recommendation that a Jewish scholar teach New Testament. The resolution of and rationale for not choosing that candidate placed a chill on that department for years and called into question the nature of who can teach what to whom. The Iowa model recalls Martin Gardner's whimsical and often edited quote that the "University of Chicago is a Baptist school, where atheist professors teach Jewish students about St. Thomas Aquinas." Lampe, n.p.

35 Lampe, 5.

36 Arnold Nash, *The University and the Modern World* (New York: Macmillan, 1948).

37 Arnold Nash, "Totalitarian University and Christian Higher Education." *Theology Today* 6, no. 3 (October 1949): 336–347.

38 Nash, 338.

39 Nash, 338.

40 Nash, 342.

41 Nash, 345.

42 University of North Carolina president Frank Porter Graham asked Union Theological Seminary president Henry P. Van Dusen for an evaluation of Arnold Nash before Graham made the decision to hire Nash at North Carolina. Van Dusen wrote, "I have a high regard for Dr. Nash, and I would not wish to say a word which might discourage your favorable consideration of him. However, I must say with all frankness, that I was not initially enthusiastic about this nomination, mainly because of my conviction that you would be better served in this position, especially during the initial stages of the new department, by an American, preferably one who knows the South." Henry P. Van Dusen, letter to Frank P. Graham, July 31, 1947, University of North Carolina at Chapel Hill University Archives, President's Office Records, Frank Porter Graham Series, subgroup 2, series 2, subseries 2: "Academic Affairs," Department of Religion Files, box 19.

Chapter Seven

1 John W. Nason, "The Program of Faculty Consultations on Religion in Higher Education," *Educational Record*, October 1946, 3.
2 Nason, 5.
3 Nason, 5.
4 Nason, 7.
5 What exactly "the West" had come to mean is complex, but it certainly included the geographical boundaries of nonfascist western Europe and North America, the cultural boundaries of the Renaissance and Enlightenment (though the irony of fascist Germany and Italy as cradles of these two movements escaped many), the linguistic boundaries of the Romance languages and English, the religious boundaries of Judaism and Christianity, and the politico-philosophic ideals of Athenian democracy and Roman citizenship.
6 Beloit, Brown, Bryn Mawr, Carnegie Institute of Technology, Cornell, Dartmouth, Denison, Lawrence, Mills, Occidental, Pasadena Junior College, Pomona, Reed, Rockford, Scripps, Syracuse, University of Iowa, University of Oregon, Wesleyan.
7 Colby College president J. Seelye Bixler, Hazen program director Paul Braisted, Wesleyan University president Victor L. Butterfield, Florida State University president J. Hillis Miller, president of the American Council on Education George F. Zook, and president of Swarthmore College John W. Nason.
8 Nason, "Program of Faculty Consultations," 10.
9 Nason, 11.
10 Why was general education a concern for Harvard and for Hutchins? Because of the conflict between the specialist and the heritage of a common education. The new university was moving toward an expansion of knowledge via specialization, with its acknowledgment of the ever-growing complexity of society. General education involved two questions for the Harvard committee: What is implied in attempting universal free secondary education, and what were the complicating crosscurrents sweeping across schools and colleges from the broader society? The committee noted that as white steeples typified an earlier period, schools across the country typify the day at midcentury; society had moved from church to school as the dominant feature of the landscape. Hutchins believed that mere facts, departments, vocationalism, and specialists detracted from a real college education.
11 Robert Maynard Hutchins, *Morals, Religion and Higher Education* (Chicago: University of Chicago Press, 1950), 24.
12 *University of Chicago Bulletin* (1941), p. 32, University of Chicago Special Collections, university administration reports.

13   During his time at Swarthmore, in the early 1930s, George Thomas helped found the American Theological Society, a group of philosophers and theologians whose cooperative work was integral to the development of religion departments. The society met every spring at Union Theological Seminary. From 1933 to 1945, it boasted a membership that included many leaders in religious thought: Reinhold and H. Richard Niebuhr, Paul Tillich, Henry P. Van Dusen, John Bennett, Angus Dun, Georgia Harkness, John Knox, Benjamin Elijah Mays, Willhelm Pauck, Gregory Vlastos, Roland Bainton, Robert Calhoun, Theodore M. Greene, and Edwin Aubrey. Published in 1948, *The Christian Answer* contained the first public articles based on their discussions, including those by Tillich, Greene, Thomas, Aubrey, and Knox and an introduction by Van Dusen. This postwar jeremiad articulated reasons for choosing Christian faith as the answer to civilization's crisis. Thomas was given the task of presenting, critiquing, and arguing for the validity of "Central Christian Affirmations" in light of modern man's predicament, "which has resulted from his confident assertion of his autonomy: economic confusion, political tyranny, international anarchy, the disintegration of personality and community, the degradation of art and philosophy, and the weakening of religion by its association with a secular civilization." See Henry P. Van Dusen, ed., *The Christian Answer* (New York: Charles Scribner's Sons, 1948), 91.

14   John Dewey, untitled essay, in "Religion and the Intellectuals," *Partisan Review* 43 (1950): 129–30.

15   William Adams Brown's president at Union Theological Seminary—Henry P. Van Dusen, who did much of the heavy lifting for the Protestant argument for religion's place in college curricula and became one of the longest-serving Princeton trustees—went on the offensive against philosopher and educational theorist John Dewey. Van Dusen's attack on the philosophy of Dewey appeared less than three years after the publication of Dewey's *A Common Faith*. Van Dusen did not downplay the importance of Dewey's arguments, commenting that "the appearance of his book is an event of first importance in the religious world" and that Dewey was acknowledged as "the foremost among living American philosophers." And while he admitted that Dewey laid bare many of the contradictions and failings of supernatural religion, Van Dusen did not respond to Dewey's scathing critique of the most basic tenets of the liberal Protestant faith. Rather, he tied Dewey's proposal for a "common faith" to the "failed philosophies" of nineteenth-century naturalism and positivism. Dewey was wrong, he noted, primarily because his proposal for a common faith had already been tried and did not work. While Van Dusen led the way against the attacks on the part of Dewey, he was not alone in his call for the renewal of Christian belief because

it provided the answers to the crises of life. Henry P. Van Dusen, "The Faith of John Dewey," *Religion in Life* (Winter 1935): 123.

16 James A. Pike became one of the more controversial religious figures of the 1960s, eventually exploring séances to contact his son who died by suicide in 1967. In 1958, he became bishop of California after serving as the dean of the Cathedral of Saint John the Divine in New York City. Bishop Pike of Columbia University also joined the Center for the Study of Democratic Institutions, founded by Robert Maynard Hutchins. Later in his professional life, he had a very public breakdown and broke with the church of his ordination. He died in Jordan's desert in September 1969, having lost his way in the heat while researching a book on the life of Jesus. This was detailed in Anthony Towne and William Stringfellow's book *The Bishop Pike Affair* and covered on television by Leonard Nimoy in an episode of the documentary-style series *In Search Of . . .* , now available on YouTube, https://youtu.be/IeQBV _7E72w.

17 James A. Pike, "Annual Report of the Chaplain" (1950), pp. 19–20, Columbia University Archives, chaplain's office reports.

18 Pike, 20.

19 John Dillenberger remarked that Robert Henry Pfeiffer (Harvard) said you build tight fences between your personal belief and the religion courses you teach: "You can believe in the virgin birth but not through scholarship." Dillenberger, interview with author, May 1997.

20 Ursula Niebuhr was in contact with George Thomas at Princeton through letters in which they discussed her questions about his department as it related to her own at Barnard. Thomas was asked about and replied regarding the number of students in religion classes at Princeton (which was nearly a thousand that year), which classes were most useful, and the methods of teaching being used. George Thomas, letter to Ursula Niebuhr, June 7, 1955, Princeton University, George Finger Thomas Papers. Thomas corresponded with most of the major figures discussed here, including Paul Tillich, one time even confessing that he did not know why the president changed his title from professor of religious thought to professor of religion. He also revealed how much he was using the divinity school or seminary model even though he himself complained (along with others about him) that religion departments were too reliant upon it. Those graduate schools were where students had done the best graduate work, and that is why Thomas and others across the country in religion departments attempted to secure university permission for graduate programs as soon as they could.

21 John F. Wilson, interview with author, Princeton University, April 1997.

22   Pike, "Annual Report of the Chaplain."

23   Pike, 19.

24   Pike, 20.

25   Pike, 20.

26   Professor John Dillenberger, a Reformation historian, had studied at Princeton, taught at Columbia, and was hired at Harvard by President Nathan Pusey to revitalize theology at Harvard Divinity School in the late 1950s.

27   John Dillenberger, interview with author, May 1997.

28   John Dillenberger, "Teaching Religion: Problems and Requirements," *Review of Religion* (November 1956): 9.

29   Dillenberger, interview with author.

30   Horace Friess, "The Study of Religion at Columbia," *Review of Religion* 19 (1954): 36.

31   Friess, 36.

32   Associated faculty included Robert Gordis of Jewish Theological Seminary, teaching Jewish thought; Georges Florovsky of Columbia, teaching Eastern Orthodox thought; William R. O'Connor of St. Joseph's Seminary, Dunwoodie, teaching Roman Catholic thought; Paul Tillich of Union Theological Seminary, teaching Protestant thought; Virginia Harrington of Barnard, teaching American church history; and Horace L. Friess of Columbia's philosophy department, teaching "Oriental" religions. The New and Old Testaments were taught by regular department faculty, including Ursula Niebuhr of Barnard College.

33   Horace Friess, "Religion at Columbia," departmental report (1950), Columbia University Archives, series 1, Central Files 1890–1984, https://findingaids.library.columbia.edu/ead/nnc-ua/ldpd_4080177/dsc/1.

34   Pike, "Annual Report of the Chaplain," 22.

35   Morton White, "Religion, Politics, and the Higher Learning," *Confluence* 6 (Autumn 1950): 402.

36   White, 405.

37   White, 406.

38   White, 407–8.

39   White, 409.

40   White, 410.

41   White, 409.

42   White, 412.

Chapter Eight

1 Will Herberg, "The Religious Stirring on the Campus: A Student Generation 'Accessible to Good,'" *Commentary* 5 (1952): 242.
2 Herberg, 245.
3 Sidney Hook, "Religion and the Intellectuals," *Partisan Review* 42 (1950): 225.
4 Hannah Arendt, "Religion and the Intellectuals," *Partisan Review* 41 (1950): 115.
5 Arendt, 116.
6 Paul Tillich, "Religion and the Intellectuals," *Partisan Review* 43 (1950): 255.
7 Tillich, 225.
8 Tillich, 226.
9 Tillich, 226.
10 Tillich, 228.
11 Tillich, 230.
12 Buckley, *God and Man at Yale*, 7.
13 Buckley, 7.
14 On April 6, 1966, William F. Buckley Jr. interviewed James A. Pike regarding the teaching of religion.
15 Alexander Miller arrived at Stanford University in 1950 to launch the curriculum in religion. He was ordained by the Presbyterian Church of New Zealand in 1937 and held pastorates there. From 1943 to 1945, he was associated with Sir George Macleod in the Iona community in Scotland.
16 "Religious Studies at Stanford," Humanities-Special Programs 1962 (Religion), File Pre-4208, Stanford University Archives, SC 495, Alexander Miller Papers; Van A. Harvey's *Religious Studies at Stanford: An Historical Sketch* remains the finest description of Stanford's religion studies programs and is worthy of further study.
17 "The Teaching of Religion at Stanford" (1953), p. 2, Stanford University Archives, Donald T. Carlson Papers, box 1, folder 1.
18 "Teaching of Religion," 4.
19 "Teaching of Religion," 4.
20 Board of trustees, minutes, May 1947, University of Pennsylvania Archives, Central Administration Files, 2.
21 Hocking was Josiah Royce's student at Harvard and continued his school of interpretation understood as American idealism.
22 George Thomas met with the Penn faculty committee considering a religion department on May 6, 1948. Thomas made many such visits in the 1950s and remained in touch with faculty, deans, and presidents who were trying to create departments of their own. Thomas

also remained in correspondence with historian of religions Joachim Wach at Chicago and numerous additional professors who helped him fill his own department at Princeton with professors from primarily graduate divinity schools and seminaries such at Union Theological. Since Henry P. Van Dusen ("Pit") was a Princeton University trustee and president of Union Seminary, Thomas relied on him a great deal to "identify men who could teach here [at Penn]" and at other schools. Theologian and reverend Dr. Mary Lyman, dean at Sweet Briar College (1940–50) and author of a book about Jesus, was another who conspired with Thomas on such matters. Lyman was the first woman to hold a faculty position at Union Theological Seminary and likely one of the first women to hold such a position at any American seminary. She graduated from the University of Chicago Divinity School with a PhD.

23 Aubrey was born in Glasgow, Scotland, in 1896 and immigrated to the United States at age seventeen. He became a naturalized citizen in 1918 after having served in World War I with the US Ambulance Service in France and Italy. He taught at the University of Chicago as professor of theology and ethics. During his tenure as president of Crozer Theological Seminary in Pennsylvania, he addressed the issues of secularization, religion and higher education, specialization and professionalization, and the necessary decline of Protestant sectarianism.

24 Aubrey did not think that the "disinterested" study of religion as a phenomenon was as dangerous to the church as Stanford's Alexander Miller did, but Aubrey was also not as curious about the curricular contributions that such a study of religion would provide to the wider university or world.

25 Edwin Aubrey, *The Religious Element in Higher Education* (New Haven, CT: Ronald Press / Edward R. Hazen Foundation, 1952), 16.

26 Aubrey, 22–23.

27 Aubrey, 23.

28 Martin E. Marty, *Modern American Religion* (Chicago: University of Chicago Press, 1996), 3:90, 349.

29 Edwin Aubrey, *Secularism, a Myth* (New York: Harper, 1954), 27.

30 Aubrey, 50.

31 Aubrey, 51.

32 Aubrey, 71.

33 Lehigh professor, NABI (National Association of Biblical Instructors) president in the 1950s, and a founding voice of the AAR (American Academy of Religion) Roy Eckardt chronicled and analyzed the "turn toward religion," the surge of institutional religion, and the "revival of revivalism." Eckardt pointed to the ironic hazards of this "surge of piety." See his *Surge of Piety* (New York: Association Press, 1954). The

1950s brought a revival of church attendance, church building, and cultural renewal that inspired some Protestant educators to reclaim this role for departments. Aubrey himself criticized the 1950s' "rush to church." Aubrey was concerned with similar tensions in folk religion, what Eckardt called "the Graham version of the gospel" that attracted large numbers of people but also missed the point of the good news. Why, then, did people in the early 1950s turn to religion? The rapid development of mass communication, the social consequences of the aftermath of World War II, the atomic bomb scare, deeper understandings of the limits of European academia and arts (which had not halted fascism), and the powerful careers of Fulton J. Sheen, Norman Vincent Peale, and Billy Graham are aspects of the answer to that question.

34 Aubrey, *Secularism*, 170.
35 Aubrey, 176.
36 Aubrey, 183.
37 Wilder was the novelist Thornton Wilder's older brother.
38 Iowa School veteran Robert S. Michaelson remarked that while the Harvard report did not believe religion could play a unifying role in the curriculum or university, he believed the general education debate and impulse ultimately helped move forward the idea and creation of religion departments and teaching, minimally at Iowa and perhaps well beyond. Michaelson, interview with author, May 1998.
39 Will Herberg identified Paul Tillich, Martin Buber, Nicolas Berdyaev, and Jacques Maritain as the theologians who best exemplified this tradition in his book, *Four Existentialist Theologians* (Garden City, NJ: Doubleday, 1958).
40 See Amos Wilder, ed., *Liberal Learning and Religion* (New York: Harper, 1951), 37.
41 Wilder, 36.
42 Wilder, 43.
43 Wilder, 45.
44 Wilder, 53.
45 Edwin Aubrey, *Humanistic Teaching and the Place of Ethical and Religious Values in Higher Education* (Philadelphia: University of Pennsylvania Press, 1959); Aubrey, "Pro and Con," 24–25.
46 Wilder, *Liberal Learning and Religion*, 29.
47 Wilder, 31.
48 Wilder, 36.
49 Wilder, 45.
50 Wilder, 48–49.
51 Wilder, 50.
52 Aubrey, *Humanistic Teaching*, 54–55.

53 Randal Maurice Jelks, *Benjamin Elijah Mays* (Chapel Hill: University of North Carolina Press, 2012).

Chapter Nine

1 In a December 11, 1947, letter from Schroeder to Dean Edgar Furniss, the courses were listed as follows: John C. Schroeder, "The Meaning of God in Western Civilization"; Sidney Lovett, "The Old and New Testament"; Erwin R. Goodenough, "The Jewish and the Greek Backgrounds of Christianity" and "A Psychological Study of Religion"; Theodore Greene, "The Philosophy of Religion"; Kenneth Scott Latourette, "History of Christianity"; Archer, "Comparative Religion."

2 Religion department memo, December 17, 1945, Yale University Archives, Charles Seymour Papers, box 135, folder 1143. The initial staff of the department (undergraduate and graduate) included John C. Schroeder (director of undergraduate studies); Kenneth Scott Latourette (director of graduate studies); professors Roland Bainton, Millar Burrows, Robert Calhoun, Erwin R. Goodenough, Charles Hartshorne, Carl Kraeling, Sidney Lovett, and Richard Niebuhr; associate professors Albert Outler and Marvin Pope; and assistant professor Julian Hartt.

3 The divinity school was officially separated from the undergraduate and graduate departments of religion in 1962–63. This was cause for great concern on the part of many faculty members placed solely within the divinity school faculty. Some referred to it as a great surprise, an academic earthquake; to return to campus after an academic calendar break to find one's office either at the divinity school up the hill or down the hill on the main campus and thus more separated from teaching in the context of ministry at the divinity school.

4 This is a reference to William F. Buckley Jr.'s *God and Man at Yale* (emphasis in original).

5 John Schroeder, religion department report of 1952–53 to President Griswold, Religion Department Files, August 6, 1953.

6 J. Paul Williams, "The Present Status of Research in Religion (Presidential Address—National Association of Biblical Instructors)," *Journal of Bible and Religion* 15, no. 1 (January 1947): 3–9.

7 For a thorough analysis of these important gatherings, again see Beuttler's "Organizing an American Conscience."

8 Huston Smith taught at Syracuse University, whose religion department's history is important if not central to this history of leading religion departments. See "Religion Department History," Syracuse

University, accessed April 18, 2021, https://thecollege.syr.edu/religion/
official-history-syracuse-university-department-religion/.

9   A partial list of these schools would include the Virginia Polytechnic Institute (Virginia Tech), Tusculum College, Muhlenberg College, University
of Wisconsin, New York University, Bryn Mawr College, Dartmouth
College, University of Cincinnati, Rice University, Denison College,
Pennsylvania State University, Southern Methodist University, Dickin-
son College, University of Pittsburgh, Cornell University, University of
Michigan, Vanderbilt University, and Duke University.

10 Thomas, letter to Frank Reynolds (student at Yale Divinity School),
regarding Reynolds's paper on the subject of the department at Princeton, Princeton University Archives, George F. Thomas Papers, box 4,
file 11.

11 Other, more idiosyncratic issues surfaced as forms of these tensions
within the arguments and activities of George Thomas, Christian
Gauss, Theodore M. Greene, C. H. Dodd, and Paul Ramsey. These
more particular issues included (1) a Catholic presence on campus that
increased awareness of departmental homogeneity, (2) the appropria-
tion of the appreciation of religion as a primary pedagogical activity,
(3) the use of rhetorical devices that shielded criticism from various
constituencies, and (4) wartime or Cold War concerns as they entered
into the discourse. Princeton's importance in the reentrance of religion
during this period was palpable because of its growing reputation as
an academic institution, the outspokenness and influence of its religion
faculty upon other schools, and the force of the arguments made in
creating and expanding the department to ten faculty members in the
1950s.

12 Thomas did express concern that much of the philosophy department
was filled with followers of naturalism or materialism (in which transcendence is not necessary to explain anything that exists). He did,
however, have the support of Dean Christian Gauss and philosophy
professor Theodore M. Greene, before Greene left for Yale to join Robert Calhoun and others sympathetic to the reintegration of morality
into philosophical thinking. Teaching later alongside Thomas, a young
scholar, Van Harvey (later at the University of Pennsylvania, Southern
Methodist University, and Stanford University) describes Thomas's
Princeton ideal as having been the divinity school model, which was
problematic for many reasons, not least of which that Princeton was the
first to offer the PhD in religion without requiring entering students
received a BD (bachelor of divinity, later MDiv). Thus the curricular model was based on the divinity school, but students had no deep
years-long background upon which many divinity schools were rely-
ing in training their own PhDs. Also, Princeton University (Princeton

Seminary being a separate entity) was, under Thomas and later Paul Ramsey, training their students to be theologians or Christian ethicists in courses such as "Theology of the Holy Spirit" while they were trying to separate out their religion department as different from the mere practice of Christianity by the chaplain's office. The dual role of religion departments was on display alongside a department attempting to straddle the college and university models, all while training students to be in service to the nation. Harvey, interview with author, 2018.

13 One of President Woodrow Wilson's original preceptors, Gauss was a member of the National Committee of the American Civil Liberties Union and a critic of the House Committee on Un-American Activities.

14 Christian Gauss, ed., *The Teaching of Religion in American Higher Education* (New York: Ronald Press, 1951), 2.

15 Gauss, 10.

16 Gauss, 14–19.

17 Hoxie N. Fairchild, *Religious Perspectives in College Teaching* (New Haven, CT: Ronald Press / Edward W. Hazen Foundation, 1952).

18 More specifically Thomas cited the following as both the evidence and in part the cause of this change in attitude: (1) the growth of ecumenical movements and the decline of sectarianism had ensured that the teaching of religion was made less dogmatic or denominational and thus palatable; (2) the National Council on Religion in Higher Education was demanding quality and providing money and training for scholars in all fields; (3) general education was being emphasized in colleges, with curricula moving from free electives to coherent unity; (4) the underlying materialist and nihilist philosophy of secularism had begun to lose its appeal.

19 Still, Lawrence DeBoer, executive director of the Society for Religion in Higher Education at Yale (successor to the Kent Fellows program), noted, "The transition from college or university teaching to seminary teaching or vice versa, is made in many instances without an accompanying realization that a major change in vocation is involved. The lack of vocational clarity is seen in the autobiographical statements of graduate students in religion who applied for Kent Fellowships between 1958 and 1961. The vocational aim of these applicants was college, university, or seminary teaching, and many had no definite preference. . . . Many felt the change was strategic rather than substantial." DeBoer suggested that there were "several reasons for the absence of distinction between the vocation of the ordained minister and the university teacher-scholar. . . . Is it because the image of the religion scholar held by the undergraduate and perpetuated in graduate schools of theology precludes the decision to study religion outside the context of the

church and its mission?" Lawrence DeBoer, "Seminary and University: Two Approaches to Theology and Religion," *Journal of Bible and Religion* 32, no. 4 (October 1964): 343.

20 Quoted in George Elderkin, *The Roman Catholic Controversy* (Princeton, NJ: Princeton University Press, 1955), 32.

21 Quoted in Elderkin, 34.

22 Elderkin, 34.

23 For comparison, the University of Virginia, which currently has the largest university religion department in the United States, had that same year of 1959 two professors in its evolving department or school, depending on the year. By March of 1967, UVA had announced the retirement and release of those two professors (S. Vernon McCasland and David C. Yu, respectively), and it moved therefore from a department (nominally a school of religion) of no professors at all to the largest such department a few decades later. UVA added a master's degree and then a PhD degree in the 1970s and progressed as much programmatically each year as previously had taken decades. The religion program was originally created with the support of the Disciples of Christ Women's funds in the 1890s. Herbert Lockwood Willett, who later served the University of Chicago Divinity School, from where numerous Virginia professors came in the decades to come, was instrumental in the religion chair model.

24 Alexander Miller, "Teaching Religion and Teaching the Christian Faith," *Review of Religion* (January 1957): 9.

25 Miller felt that his decade at Stanford (the 1950s) was a time when Christianity had shown its worth and need not argue for its relevance or place at the university; it could be assumed. That time would come to an end at Stanford and other elite universities not many years after Miller's untimely death at the end of that decade.

26 Miller, "Teaching Religion," 13.

27 Miller, 13.

28 Miller, 15.

29 Alexander Miller, *The Renewal of Man* (Garden City, NJ: Doubleday, 1959).

30 Alexander Miller, *Faith and Learning* (New York: Association Press, 1960), 126.

31 Miller, 130.

32 Miller, 30.

33 Alexander Miller, "Religion in the Curriculum," *Stanford Review* 53 (July 1952): 8.

34 Huston Smith authored one of the two more commonly used textbooks in religion courses, *The Religions of Man*, the other being William Lessa and Evon Vogt's *Reader in Comparative Religions*; the latter is

an overview in line with a then growing, history of religions strain of teaching alongside Mircea Eliade, Rudolph Otto, and various anthropology researchers, who tended to religion as a human phenomenon.

35 Alexander Miller, "What Makes or Unmakes a Christian Student?," *Intercollegian* (December 1952): 5.

36 Miller, 5.

37 Miller, *Faith and Learning*, 130.

38 Miller, 130.

39 Miller, 130.

40 Miller, 133.

41 Miller, 133.

42 Huston Smith, *The Purposes of Higher Education* (New York: Harper, 1955), 128.

43 Smith, 129.

44 Smith, 130.

45 Smith, 133–34.

46 Smith, 131.

47 Smith, 135.

48 Smith, 135.

49 Smith, 137.

50 Smith, 137–39.

51 Smith expanded on the observation made by the founder of Penn's religion department, Edwin Aubrey, that *secularism* had become a "catch-all" for all things Christians wanted to criticize. *Religion* is no clearer when under attack from the secularists; the word is used variously as a synonym for dogmatism, ecclesiasticism, obscurantism, credulity, conservatism, absolutism, immaturity, and superstition. Smith's point was that *religion* as a term was as easily maligned as it was difficult to define and caused problems of understanding between camps who were in disagreement about the positive nature of religious life and belief.

52 Smith, *Purposes of Higher Education*, 141.

53 Among other curricular innovations, what Huston Smith added to the conversation was a studied appreciation of the fact that various individuals or groups were using the word *religion* to mean one thing in one context and something completely different in another context in order to further their own agenda, whatever that might be: "We judge persons more by the words they use than by the meanings they intend through them, and least of all by the way they live out these meanings in their lives." Smith, 137.

54 The response to Holbrook's book was mixed and could be considered a breaking point for those trying to hold on to some version of George Thomas, Clarence Shedd, Alexander Miller, and other department

founders' hopes that the college ideal could be accomplished while still seeking a more rigorous scholarship for religion as a field. Wilson believed Holbrook had not balanced this well. John F. Wilson, "Mr. Holbrook and the Humanities, or Mr. Schlatter's Dilemma," *Journal of Bible and Religion* 32, no. 3 (1964): 252–61.

55 Reinhold Niebuhr, "Higher Education in America," *Confluence* 6 (Spring 1957): 9.

56 Niebuhr, 10.

57 Morton White, "Religious Commitment and Higher Education," *Confluence* 9 (Summer 1957): 138.

58 White, 139.

59 White, 142.

60 In *The University Gets Religion* (Baltimore: Johns Hopkins University Press, 1999), D. G. Hart interprets the change in name of the National Association of Biblical Instructors, the *Abington v. Schempp* case, and the publication of Clyde Holbrook's *Religion, a Humanistic Field* as signs that confessional instruction was on its way out while affirming that Protestantism had indeed tried to win the day through religion departments. Hart attributes much meaning to the *Schempp* case, which is an excellent marker but did not in itself ensure any substantial changes were made in the teaching of college religion in state or private universities. Hart's interpretation is that religious studies failed, and he attributes many inadvertent and unintended consequences to scheming and strategy on the part of the maligned Protestant elites. Similarly but from an understandably skeptical perspective, Donald Wiebe in *The Politics of Religious Studies* makes sure to note the Christian piety among those religion department founders and NABI/AAR president, almost as if to suggest that such Christian professors would be able to have no particular slant, set of interests, or points of engagement in the field of religious studies. Such were the challenges resulting in the dual role of religion department founders.

Conclusion

1 A self-study committee of the National Association of Biblical Instructors recommended the name change to American Academy of Religion because of the shift away from the Bible as a central religious text for scholars of various religious traditions and an assumption that "instructor" indicated a lack of professional expertise in the academy. D. G. Hart's discussion of this change is the most recent and helpful analysis of this transition. Hart, *University Gets Religion*, 202.

2   Napier, founder of the University of Georgia's religion program, recalled that Julian Hartt was one of the two or three administrators responsible for implementing the decision. He was not pleased to learn he was to be located at the divinity school, as this was considered at the time to be a less prestigious or at least less academic position. Historian Jaroslav Pelikan also had concerns about this, as he came to Yale at that time.

3   Holbrook, *Religion*, 50.

4   Clyde Holbrook, "Why an Academy of Religion?," *Journal of Bible and Religion* 32, no. 2 (April 1964): 98.

5   Brown, *Case for Theology*, 3.

6   Several important attempts to teach undergraduate religion were underway at state schools, where faculty were working to develop departments based on similar rationale during this period: University of Iowa (W. Lampe), University of Florida (J. H. Miller), University of Virginia (V. McCasland), University of North Carolina (A. Nash), and later, Florida State University (R. Spivey). Various other private schools were in varying stages of developing their own departments, including Syracuse University, Oberlin College, Washington University, Howard University, University of Southern California, Cornell University, and Dartmouth College, among others. Under President J. Hillis Miller, the University of Florida created a Department of Religion in 1946.

7   Abington School District v. Schempp, 374 U.S. 213, 225 (1963).

8   DeBoer, "Seminary and University," 346.

9   Jonathan Z. Smith, "'Religion' and 'Religious Studies': No Difference at All," in "The Santa Barbara Colloquy: Religion within the Limits of Reason Alone," special issue, *Soundings* 71, nos. 2–3 (Summer/Fall 1988): 231–44.

10 Between 1946 and 1960, the number of religion departments in colleges and universities doubled.

11 The importance of examining midcentury arguments for religion instruction lies in understanding not just how religion came to be taught as a subject in colleges but how and why a particular kind of religion came to be taught. Teaching that resembled Sunday school sectarianism was on the decline in elite institutions, but such college courses also did not become a materialist social scientific interpretation of Christianity with little room for the transcendent. The debate continues today. That debate centers on not *whether* to create a religion department but *what kind* of religion(s) will be examined. Small liberal arts colleges with a Protestant church background and ties had religion department chairs who asked themselves, "Given our limited budget, what is better for our students, an introduction to Hinduism or Christian theology?" Priorities were determined, and the historical

and cultural deck was stacked in favor of Christian thought and literature at most institutions.

12 Present-day South African universities offer an interesting corollary to
North American colleges at midcentury. Language departments for
the study of Afrikaans are being shut down, and departments that can
help with racial reconciliation and economic development are being
created and bolstered. Religious studies departments there are already
trying to come to the rescue of the country by attempting pragmatically to negotiate contact points between the multitude of religious
communities in that country. If higher education does not exist to aid
the nation-state in part or its citizens as a whole, it surely fails in its
mission. If it exists to uphold the nation-state or its citizens against
its own better judgment (after research and academic discourse have
suggested a new direction), it has lost its mission, which is to serve
through critical investigation and discourse.

13 One could argue that on the larger stage of American higher education,
Harvard, Princeton, Chicago, Yale, Penn, Columbia, and Stanford were
able (sometimes barely) to bend the externalities—financial, social, cultural, religious—and push their influence outward, while most other
schools (though certainly not always, the University of Virginia and
Brown, among others, come to mind) at best were able to internally
resist some practical, philosophical, and financial externalities. These
other schools followed as best they could the developments of the Harvard Redbook, Robert Hutchins's Chicago dreams and failings, Princeton's very Protestant successes in creating the first undergraduate and
graduate PhD somewhat independent of denominational and seminary
or divinity school preparation, and Yale's decisive split of the divinity
school and undergraduate and graduate religion study in 1962. Because
of the systematic refusal of white Protestant and secular institutions
to welcome women and African Americans on to their faculties (a few
leading lights resisted or succeeded despite this little-acknowledged fact,
like Georgia Harkness, Virginia Corwin, and Ursula Niebuhr; Howard
Thurman, Benjamin E. Mays, and later, Charles Long, Nathan O. Scott;
and untold others), schools like Howard University, Fisk University,
Morehouse College, Spelman College, Wellesley College, Smith College, Mount Holyoke College, Barnard College, and so forth created
their own courses for the teaching of religion alongside other academic
developments. Virginia Corwin wrote forcefully about the importance
of teaching religion in the *Journal of Bible and Religion*. Corwin, "The
Teaching Situation and the Bible," *Journal of Bible and Religion* 19, no. 2
(1951): 57–62. She taught Diana Eck, who later became a major figure in
the teaching and study of religion at Harvard.

State universities were also part of the story, from the 1890s "Bible chairs" established by the Disciples of Christ denomination and various others, to the Iowa "zoo" model (wherein a professor from a particular denomination—e.g., a Catholic, Jewish or Black church scholar—would teach their own faith tradition), which in some ways came to be the dominant model in later decades, though with different expectations. In fact, after the period covered here, such universities took the edge of center stage thanks to the University of Florida and Florida State and, subsequently the University of Virginia, which in only the last few decades has come to have the largest religious studies department of any college or university. See Harry Y. Gamble, *God on the Grounds* (Charlottesville: University of Virginia Press, 2020).

14 Since the 1985 press conference in Stockholm, Sweden, during which he first shared his three rules, Stendahl's rules have been documented in many publications, most recently by Barbara Brown Taylor in *Holy Envy* (New York: Harper, 2019).

Index

Columbia University, New York City, New York, 17, 19, 24, 52, 126, 127; combining of religion program with Barnard, 146; creation of religion department at, xvi; master of arts in religion degree, 132; principles of religion courses, 129–30; religion department at, 108, 128–32, 137; tensions at, 166, 178

Colwell, Ernest, 105

Commentary, 68

Common Faith, A (Dewey), 24, 80

communism, 4, 5, 122, 162, 244n52; fear of, 52, 118; religion opposed to, 69; study of, 135

Conant, James, xvii, 52, 108

Conference on Science, Philosophy, and Religion (CSPR), 65–67, 68–70, 239–40nn1–2

Confluence, 180, 181

Cornell Daily Sun, 137

Cornell United Religious Work, 137

Cornell University, Ithaca, New York, 137–38

Council of Schools of Religion, 7–8, 12, 17, 222–23n1

Cox, Harvey, xv

credit system, 1, 32

CSPR. *See* Conference on Science, Philosophy, and Religion

Cuninggim, Merrimon: *The College Seeks Religion*, 112–13; "On the Status of Religion on the Yale Campus," 38–40

Daily Princetonian, 160, 167

Danforth Foundation, 119

Darrow, Clarence, 61

DeBoer, Lawrence P., 188–89, 262–63n19

democracy, 5, 51, 67, 68, 91, 99, 104, 162; Christian way of life and, 62; freedom and, 111; relationship to religion, 48

democratization, 2

denominationalism, 123

departmental system, 36

detachment, academic, 56

Dewey, John, 9, 22, 24–25, 45, 63, 65, 67, 82, 124, 136, 139; *A Common Faith*, 24, 80; criticism of, 78; on religion and intellectuals, 127; Van Dusen and, 254–55n15

Dillenberger, John, 128, 130, 136, 169, 179, 255n19, 256n26

Disciples Divinity House of the Disciples of Christ, 70

divinity schools, xvii, 29, 83, 101, 109, 110; as models for religion departments, 46; religious faculty educated at, 42

Dodds, Harold, 46, 47

dogmatism, 8, 14, 20–21, 37

Doniger, Wendy, 195

Drew University, Madison, New Jersey, 137

Eastern religions, 168, 170, 184

Eckardt, Roy, 258–59n33

economics, 74

ecumenism, 83

Edward W. Hazen Foundation, 18, 118–19, 121, 123, 160, 227n32, 247n37

elective system, 1, 8

Ellwood, Robert, 235n1

emotionalism, 56

Enlightenment, 32, 41, 50, 51

essential religion. *See* high religion

Europe: Jewish intellectuals from, 32; political crises in, 2, 4, 37, 45, 48

existentialism, 136, 147, 151

toward, 17, 39–40; implicit to explicit functions of, 44; indifference toward, 17; institutionalization of authoritarian forms, 141; as knowledge, 86–87; lack of seriousness about, 60; as nonconfessional category, 5; overintellectualization of, 20; as part of humanities, 29; perceived value of studying, 8; practice of vs. study of, xiii, 28–29, 31, 47, 61–62; as problem of education, 24; reason for neglect of, 78–79; as renewing force for colleges, 13; revival of, 40; role for, during World War II, 84; scientific study of, 70; as social science, 2, 4; special status for, 130; strengthening of, on campuses, 130; study of, as science, 33; study of, in other departments, 174–79; teaching about, not as practice, 3, 108–10, 113, 130, 132, 133, 135, 186; in teaching of other subjects, 14; turn toward, by intellectuals, 45, 127, 139–42; turn toward, by students, 138; in undergraduate life, 86; as undermining unity, 104–5; understandings of term, xix, 29, 33–34, 53–54, 122, 133–34, 136, 137–38, 147, 178, 228n41, 246, 264n53; understood to be Christianity, 5; as unifying fragmentary existence, 48, 51; unifying framework of, 55, 56, 57, 103; widening definitions of, 4; as worship, 86

Religion, a Humanistic Field (Holbrook), 183, 221n4

religion, teaching of: as academic subject, 2, 3, 5; basic argument for, 7; characteristics of, 122–23; church leaders and, 5; as countering secularism, 49; as divisive, 104;

importance of, 48, 106; legality of, 78–79; as moral inculcation, 3, 5, 9, 14, 28, 131; and practicing of that religion, 20; prescriptive vs. descriptive, 2, 3–4; purpose of, 162; rationale for, 100, 164; seen in practical terms, 69; as separate from chapel, 28; stages of, 43–44; at state institutions, 183; tensions in, 160–61

religion courses: at Columbia, 129–30, 131; confessional, 26, 131; dual role of, 4; enrollment in, 40; focus of, 40–41; goal of, 13; noncompulsory, 31; at Princeton, 28, 159; proposed, 40

Religion Department Advisory Board (Princeton), 146

religion departments: as bridging college and university ideals, 82–83; college ideal and, 17, 194; composition of, 86; criticism of, 51, 62; dual role of, 2, 5, 34, 62, 75–76, 85–86, 90, 99, 103, 107–10, 126, 130, 133, 166, 173, 177, 181–82, 188, 190–91, 194; fragmented identity of, 5; goals of, 161–62; in modern institutions, 196; needs of the nation and, xxi; overlapping roles with churches, 150; patterns in creation of, xix–xx; reasons for creation of, xv–xvii, 8–9, 12, 18–19, 32, 33, 64, 74–75, 92–93, 147, 149, 151, 197, 234–35n40; shift in philosophy of, 147–55; at state institutions, 74, 186–87, 266n6; university ideal and, 1

religion departments, founders of, 5, 17, 22, 23, 42, 53; crises of Western civilization and, 82; dual role of, 57, 83, 84; high religion and, 176; place of, 190; practical value of religious education and, 69; and turn toward religion, 142